The Art of Dying

The Art of Dying

A Journey to Elsewhere

PETER FENWICK

and

ELIZABETH FENWICK

continuum

Published by Continuum

The Tower Building, 11 York Road, London SE1 7NX

80 Maiden Lane, Suite 704, New York NY 10038

www.continuumbooks.com

First published 2008

British Library Cataloguing-in-Publication Data
A catalogue record for this book is available from the British Library.

ISBN 978-08264-9923-3

Typeset by Kenneth Burnley, Wirral, Cheshire
Printed and bound by Cromwell Press, Wiltshire

Contents

To

Gareth and Annabelle
Huw, Carwyn and Madoc

Jon and Natasha
Sebastian, Oliver, Benjamin and Juliette

Tris and Kako
Cameron and Ryan

We'll be there to meet you!

Acknowledgements

First, we would like to thank everyone who wrote to us and was prepared to share their very personal experiences with us. Their stories form the heart of this book and we owe them a great debt. It hasn't been possible to include every account, but they have all added a brushstroke to the picture we have tried to paint. We are also very grateful to the journalists who, by interviewing us, have brought the subject to the attention of people who might otherwise never have felt able to discuss these experiences openly and would certainly never have got in touch with us, in particular Danny Penman for his article in the *Daily Mail*, and Richard and Judy for their sympathetic handling of this subject on air.

We would like to thank Southampton University for their ethical approval for the research study, Professor Peveler of the Southampton University Department of Neuropsychiatry who hosted the project, and Shirley Firth and Tony Walter for their advice and suggestions. My research assistants Sue Brayne and Hilary Lovelace are responsible for the success of the study with the hospices, nursing home and palliative care teams, and brought a depth of practical experience to the research, without which we would never have gained the insights that we did. And a special thank you to Dr Sam Parnia who helped with and supported the study. Sam and I have been working together in this field for many years and the collaboration has always been a very happy and productive one.

To Allan Kellehear we owe a special debt, both for making us aware of the significance of the sociological context in which these experiences have occurred in different cultures and throughout recorded time, and also sitting in the cafes of San Marino between conference presentations, introducing us to the idea of 'Elsewhere' as a possible destination for the journey.

ACKNOWLEDGEMENTS

Our sincere thanks to the London Borough of Camden Palliative Care Team, who gave us our first opportunity to study these experiences in the field. Our thanks are also due to all the nurses, care assistants and chaplains who took part in the research and to the Phyllis Tuckwell Hospice, the Princess Alice Hospice and the Kingsley House Nursing Home, where we have been able to continue this research and to gain more insight into the impact these experiences have both on the carers and their patients.

Chapter 1

The Start of the Journey

Myths have always gathered around the deathbed and the dying. Every culture throughout history has had its chosen harbingers of death. The Norse warrior who saw the beautiful Valkyr on the battlefield knew he was doomed to die. For the Hapsburg family of the Austro-Hungarian Empire, ravens, and a White Lady who appeared before the death of family members, were the omens of impending doom. Black horses, black dogs such as the Gabriel Hounds who roamed the North of England, and even, in the Philippines, black butterflies, all traditionally presage a death. In Cornwall, blackbirds hovering over a house where someone is ill are said to be harbingers of death. Birds – ravens, owls, blackbirds, white cockatoos and, especially, crows – figure so widely in the folklore of death and dying that it is quite difficult to find a bird which hasn't been cited in some country or culture as an omen of impending death. Van Gogh's painting 'Wheatfield with Crows', with its sense of desolation and foreboding, has often been interpreted as the artist's own suicide note, partly because it was thought to be his final work and partly because of the flock of black crows which flies towards (or away from – the direction of flight is ambiguous) the viewer. A neat theory, but unsubstantiated, because 'Wheatfield with Crows' was not van Gogh's final painting and also because the evidence is that he was as appreciative of crows as he was of all things in nature and certainly didn't attach any symbolic meaning to them.

Travelling companions

Another body of tradition focuses on what happens after death – on the transition between this world and whatever happens next. These beliefs appear in some form or another in virtually every culture throughout recorded history, and there are indications that even in prehistory the dead may have been buried with some sense of expectation.[1] Indeed, so universal is the assumption that something *does* happen next that the reductionist scientific culture of the West is almost alone in its unshakeable belief in the finality of death.

Most of these stories focus on the journey that the dead must make to reach the next stage of their existence. In some cultures, the apparitions seen by the dying on their deathbed – the so-called deathbed visions – seem to have a dual role, as both the harbingers of death and as the guarantors of a safe passage to the afterlife.

In many native cultures it was the Shamans who acted as guides for the dying, journeying with them from the land of the living to the land of the dead. In some African and native American traditions the raven, because of its keen sight, appears at death and is the guide who leads the dead on their final journey. In Greek mythology it was, appropriately, the role of Hermes, the Greek god of travel, to guide the soul from this life to Hades and the realm of the dead. The phosphorescent lights, called 'corpse candles' in Wales, and 'fetch candles' in Ireland and Northern England, which are said to hover over the roofs of houses where a death is imminent, or appear over the body of a dying person, are said in some parts of the country to accompany the souls of the dead and to be extinguished when the souls leave the earth.

Certain religious traditions have elaborate rituals of instruction for the soul at the time of death. The Egyptian Book of the Dead and the coffin texts of ancient Egypt gave detailed instructions for the soul's journey to the next life. In the Tibetan Buddhist tradition it is the monks who guide the souls of the dying through death to their next incarnation. For Christians, guardian angels are the traditional escorts who guide the soul to paradise. The tomb of St Francis at Assisi depicts his arms outstretched at the moment of death to a host of angels who have come to greet him; and the ancient hymn, 'In Paradisum', which calls the angels to escort the soul to heaven, is still sung at Roman Catholic funerals.

Lavish funerals with complex rituals are still a necessity in some parts of Indonesia, as the belief is that the soul lingers around the living for some time during the primary burial, and only through the appropriate rites by the family can the deceased be guided to the land of the spirits. On the Indonesian island of East Sumba, when a noble dies a male cock and a horse are sacrificed – the cock to awaken the soul to get ready to start the journey, and the horse to accompany the soul during its trip to the land of the dead. The deceased is richly dressed and placed in a squatting position, with gold pieces and jewellery covering eyes, mouth and chest. The practice of burying treasure with the dead has meant that tombs – especially of the royal or the rich – have always been targets for grave robbers. The oldest known pieces of gold jewellery, from 3000 BC, were found in the tombs of Queen Zer and Queen Pu-abi of Ur in Sumeria, and the largest, and probably best-known, collection of gold and jewellery in the world was found in the second millennium BC tomb of Tutankhamen. However, as Christianity spread through the European continent, people ceased burying the dead with their jewellery, though it is rumoured that when Pope John Paul II died in 2005 he too was buried with a gold piece under his tongue.

Historically in the West deathbed visions are firmly rooted in the Christian belief in resurrection and the concept of a communion of saints – that is, the continued involvement of the dead with the spiritual welfare of the living. According to third-century Christian accounts of the life of the Virgin Mary, Christ appeared to her to tell her of the approaching hour of her death and to lead her into glory, and there are stories too of many early Christian martyrs and saints who were visited by Christ, Mary or another saint to warn them of their impending death and accompany them into heaven. One of the first written records of such a vision was by the eighth-century English historian Bede, who wrote of a dying nun who was visited on her deathbed by a recently deceased holy man. He told her that she would die at dawn, and indeed she did. Medieval texts such as the thirteenth-century *Dialogue of Miracles* by the German monk Caesarius of Heisterbach tell similar stories, but always within a theological framework.

Ghosts and apparitions

In the seventeenth century the phenomenon of apparitions and ghosts began to be studied seriously, and by the nineteenth century different types of apparition were being distinguished and described. It was suggested that when the apparition of a dead person – a ghost – was seen by someone alive and well, it was usually to give them some information. The ghost of Hamlet's father, for example, simply wanted his son to know that he had been foully murdered. But an apparition seen by a dying person had more specific intent, to tell them that their death was imminent, and usually to help them through to whatever lay beyond.

The first study of these apparitions was carried out in the late nineteenth century by the psychical researchers Gurney, Myers and Podmore. Their book *Phantasms of the Living*, first published in 1886, is a fascinating collection of unusual experiences including accounts of apparitions of dead people that had been seen by normal, sane people. I like the story of General Alfred Fytch who, on getting out of bed one morning in India saw an old friend, whom he assumed had decided to pay him an unexpected visit. He greeted his friend warmly and sent him to the verandah to order a cup of tea. When he went to join him, the old friend had vanished. Nobody in the house had seen anyone. Two weeks later, he received news that his friend had died 600 miles away at the time he had seen him.[2]

However, it was not until the 1920s that these odd apparitions aroused any serious scientific interest, and the first attempt at a systematic scientific study of them was made by Sir William Barrett, a physics professor at the Royal College of Science in Dublin. Sir William's interest in the topic was kindled by an experience of his wife, an obstetrician. Lady Barrett had been called into the operating room to deliver the child of a woman named Doris (her last name was withheld from the written report). Although the child was born healthy, Doris was dying from a haemorrhage. Lady Barrett described how, as the woman lay dying, she began to see visions:

Suddenly she looked eagerly towards part of the room, a radiant smile illuminating her whole countenance. 'Oh, lovely, lovely' she said. When asked what it was that she saw, she replied, 'Lovely brightness, wonderful beings.' A moment later she exclaimed: 'Why, it's Father! Oh, he's so glad I'm coming; he is so glad. It would be perfect if only W. [her husband] would come too.'

Lady Barrett then described how Doris spoke to her father again, saying, 'I am coming', and turning to Lady Barrett added, 'Oh, he is so near.' And then she added, looking rather puzzled, 'He has Vida with him, Vida is with him.'

It was this last remark that made Sir William take the story seriously. Vida was Doris's sister: they had been very close, and although Vida had indeed died three weeks earlier, Doris, because of her delicate condition, had not been told. The fact that Doris had seen her sister, who as far as Doris knew was alive and well, in this 'other place' and in the company of the father she knew to be dead, convinced Sir William that he could not simply dismiss the incident as insignificant.

In fact, it so impressed him that he began to collect similar experiences. His book, *Deathbed Visions*, published in 1926, concluded that these experiences were not merely a by-product of a dying brain, but could occur when the dying patient was lucid and rational. He also reported a number of cases in which medical personnel or relatives present shared the dying patient's vision.[3]

The first comprehensive and objective study of these visions was made by Karlis Osis and Erlendur Haraldsson.[4] In 1961 Osis conducted a questionnaire survey of 5,000 physicians and 5,000 nurses, asking about the hallucinations they had observed in terminally ill patients under their care. He analysed the 640 replies and categorized two types of hallucinations: non-human visions of nature or landscapes, and apparitions of people, usually dead relatives or friends who had come to help the dying in their transition to the next life.

Together with Professor Erlendur Haraldsson, Osis carried out two further surveys, one in the United States in 1961–4 and one in India in 1972–3. One of their most interesting findings was the apparent cultural bias in the travelling companions seen in these 'take-away' visions. In the United States survey the most common apparitions were of dead relatives and friends, while religious escorts were much less frequent. However, in the Indian experiences the reverse was true: it was religious figures such as the *yamdoot* – the messenger sent by the god of death – who were the most frequent take-away companions, while apparitions of dead relatives or friends appeared far less often.

It is evident, then, that whatever the meaning or purpose of these visions, they contain cultural components. There seems to have been a major change in visions in the West over the period of their recorded history from the early days of Christianity when Christ, or the Virgin Mary, or at the very least some holy man, might be expected to appear at your bedside as you died, to the nineteenth- and twentieth-century accounts where deathbed visitors are far more likely to be dead friends or family members. But whoever the visitor, these visions have always been reported as an enormously comforting experience for the dying person.

Exploring end-of-life experiences

My own interest in these end-of-life experiences (ELEs) was sparked off by an account Pauline Drew sent to me describing the day before her mother died:

Suddenly she looked up at the window and seemed to stare intently up at it . . . She suddenly turned to me and said, 'Please Pauline, don't ever be afraid of dying. I have seen a beautiful light and I was going towards it . . . it was so peaceful I really had to fight to come back.' The next day when it was time for me to go home I said, 'Bye Mum, see you tomorrow.' She looked straight at me and said, 'I'm not worried about tomorrow and you mustn't be, promise me.' Sadly she died the next morning . . . but I knew she had seen something that day which gave her comfort and peace when she knew she had only hours to live.

For some years I have been interested in the near-death experience, and Dr Sam Parnia and I have been studying near-death experiences which occur in coronary care units and which patients report after they have had a cardiac arrest.[5] We have found, as have other research workers,[6] that about 10 per cent of people who recover from a cardiac arrest say they have had a near-death experience during it. As these people were in fact clinically dead at the time, we felt it was more appropriate to call these not 'near-' death experiences, but 'actual death' experiences. These actual death experiences (ADEs) have the same features as near-death experiences (NDEs): that is, an entry into the light, a move to an area, typically an English country garden, and a meeting with dead relatives who welcome them and sometimes send them back; but the features which are most memorable and most significant for the person concerned are the peace and calmness and, in the deeper experiences, the intense compassion, love and light that are experienced. They are life-enhancing in that the person feels safe and cared for. They know that if they go with their dead relatives they will die and not come back.

The account which was sent to me intrigued me, first because it contained so many elements of the NDE – the experience of light, the feeling of peace, the feeling that Pauline's mother had been shown a glimpse of another reality from which she was reluctant to return and the abolition of any fear of death; and second because of the suggestion that after this experience Pauline's mother somehow knew she was going to die the following day. This made me think that we should perhaps not look at any of these experiences in isolation as something that occurs only as life is almost extinguished, but as part of a continuum – a single process, the process of dying – and that part of this process might be a preparation beginning in the hours or even days before death.

So I started to look at these experiences more seriously. A chance to gather more data about them came in response to an interview about end-of-life experiences which I gave to a Scottish newspaper. The public response to this confirmed that deathbed phenomena are both more common than I had imagined and more varied. Particularly convincing was the following experience, which happened many years ago, but made a deep and lasting impression on the man who told it to us.

Around 1950 a distant relative was in hospital in Inverness. It was a Sunday and my father went to visit John, to be told that he had died that morning at a certain time. The hospital authorities asked Dad if he would inform the next of kin, the deceased's sister Kate and her husband, who were sheep farmers living in a relatively remote part of Easter Ross and not on the telephone. Dad and I drove the 20 or so miles and up a hill track to the farmhouse, to be met by Kate who said, 'I know why you've come – I heard him calling me saying "Kate, Kate" as he passed over.' She was quite matter of fact about it and gave us the time of death, which was exactly the same as that recorded by the hospital. I found it an amazing experience and have never forgotten it, nor will I ever. I was about 17 at the time.

This was a lovely account of an entirely different phenomenon, the 'deathbed coincidence', very reminiscent of the story of General Alfred Fytch, mentioned on page 4. These coincidences are reports by someone emotionally close to a dying person of an awareness of that person's death, even though they may be at a distance from them and not even know they are ill. These experiences are short lasting and may take the form of a 'visit' by the dying person, who indicates that they have come to say goodbye, or may simply be a sudden strong conviction, with no rational basis, that the person has died, often again with the feeling that they have come to say goodbye. A common response is to feel that the dying person has been given permission to visit those they know well. When people do appear, they usually do so healed, and as if they were in the prime of life. They seldom speak, but simply indicate that they are dying, and that everything is all right.

It may be hard for those of us who have never experienced anything like this to accept, but these strong feelings that someone close to you has died are probably not rare, though people are often reluctant to talk about them openly, largely because they are afraid that they won't be believed. These experiences are part of the very wide range of phenomena associated with the dying process. Those that seem to occur, or at least to be reported, most often are these.

A wide range of phenomena is associated with the dying process, but those that seem to occur, or at least to be reported, most often are these.

Deathbed visions

These are perhaps the most commonly reported ELEs. Usually the visions seen are of dead relatives, frequently someone the dying person had a close emotional contact with, and their purpose seems to be to help the person through the dying process. They are almost always comforting and seem to provide a spiritual preparation for death. ELEs show a cultural influence. People with strong spiritual/religious beliefs may 'see' spiritual apparitions associated with their own religion. Christians occasionally see angels or a Christ-like figure, Hindus, Vishnu. The visions are usually seen in clear, or only moderately impaired, consciousness.[7]

Sometimes this process is taken even further, so that not only does the visitor appear in the room, but the dying person may journey with them to an intermediate reality that they perceive as being more real than the real world, and interpenetrated by light, love and compassion. Within this area they experience a widening of their spiritual vision. Both relatives and strangers may be seen, but nearly always they are experienced as a comforting presence, there to help with the dying process and holding out a promise of the possibility of a continuation of consciousness.

The mother of a 32-year-old woman dying of breast cancer described to me what happened in the last two to three days of her daughter's life:

She was conscious of a dark roof over her head and a bright light. She moved into a waiting place where beings, her grandfather among them, were there to help her and told her that everything would be OK. She moved into and out of this area, and was adamant that it was not a dream.

Something leaving the body

The perception of something leaving the body around the time of death is a little-discussed phenomenon, reported consistently by professional carers and, most importantly, relatives, but usually only when they are directly asked about it. The accounts are very varied, but central to this experience is a form or shape which someone present may see leaving the body, usually from the mouth, chest or through the head, though we have also had accounts of something leaving through the feet. Sometimes it will hover above the body before rising to disappear through the ceiling, and it is often associated with love, light, compassion, purity and sometimes with heavenly music. Not everyone who is in the room sees the vision, its appearance is transient and its perception is sensitive to interruption – people coming into the room or talking often make it disappear. Those who have had the experience, particularly if it is associated with love and light, feel enormously comforted, a feeling which may go on for many days after the death, and, more importantly, the experience remains a comfort over many years.

Suddenly there was the most brilliant light shining from my husband's chest, and as this light lifted upwards there was the most beautiful music and singing voices, my own chest seemed filled with infinite joy and my heart felt as if it was lifting to join this light and music. Suddenly there was a hand on my shoulder and a nurse said, 'I'm sorry love. He has just gone.' I lost sight of the light and music, I felt so bereft at being left behind.

The experience of light, sometimes shared by the carer, and usually described as bright and white and associated with strong feelings of love and compassion, is often reported. It usually lasts over the time of the death process.

Deathbed coincidences

There are many reports by someone emotionally close to a dying person of an awareness of that person's death, even

10

though they may be at a distance from them and not even know they are ill. These experiences are short lasting and may take the form of a 'visitation' by the person, or simply be a sudden strong conviction that the person has died, often with the feeling that they have come to say goodbye. A common response is to feel that the dying person has been given permission to visit those they know well. When people do appear, if they had had some injury in life they often look whole again, as if they were in the prime of life. They seldom speak, but simply indicate that they are dying, and that everything is all right.

When I retired to bed . . . I tossed this way and that until suddenly in the early hours my father stood by my bed. He had been ill for a long time, but there he was, standing in his prime of life. He didn't speak. My restlessness ceased and I fell asleep. In the morning I knew . . . my father had died late the evening before and had been permitted to visit me on his way into the next life. (Personal communication)

Other 'coincidences' associated with the time of death are clocks that are reported to stop – as in the old song about grandfather's clock. There are also reports of strange animal behaviour and of some animal or bird that has special significance for the dying person being seen from the sickroom.

In February 2007, in an attempt to see just how common these end-of-life experiences were, and as a foundation for this book, we discussed the study with a journalist, Danny Penman, who decided to run an article about them. This was almost immediately followed by an invitation to go on the Channel 4 *Richard and Judy* show to discuss end-of-life experiences. There was an overwhelming response to the programme, and within the next two or three weeks we received several hundred emails and letters from people who had had these experiences themselves, or been with dying relatives who had had them, or been told about them by members of their family. Many had never discussed them with anyone, and expressed enormous relief at discovering that others had had the same experience. And whenever we talked to our own friends and family yet more strange stories emerged – from the sudden intense feeling of disaster that struck our daughter's best friend at the moment her father was dying, 4,000 miles away, to the odd and inexplicable behaviour of a friend's cat after the death of the aunt on whose lap he liked to sit.

These stories were as varied as they were fascinating, but three points were made again and again in the accounts we received. The first was how comforting these experiences had been to both the dying person and those who witnessed the phenomena. The second was the conviction that what had happened was not a dream, or wishful thinking, or a figment of the imagination, or a drug-induced hallucination. And the third was the sense of relief our correspondents felt at being able, often for the first time, to talk freely about the experiences which had had such a powerful effect on them.

Sheena Harden's story was typical. It began in 1968 when Sheena's mother was very ill with double pneumonia and pleurisy. One night when her illness was at its height and she was in great pain she became aware of someone standing at the foot of her bed. An absolute feeling of calm came over her and she realized that it was her father who had recently died. He was smiling at her and holding out his hand to her. She wanted to go with him and began to leave her body to go with him but he shook his head and communicated to her that it wasn't her time and that her family needed her. She felt distraught as she longed to go with him and be out of her pain but he told her that when it was her time he would be there to take her with him. Sheena continues the story:

Ten years later, in January 1978, my mother was in hospital, seriously ill after an operation. When I visited her one afternoon she started to talk to me about what I should do after she had gone, how to look after the family, etc. I asked her where she was going and she said she was going to die – all her family had come to visit that afternoon (her mother, brother and sister had all died within the last eight years) and they were ready for her in heaven and it was her time to go. Her father had again promised to return 'very soon' to get her. She described them as standing in a semi-circle and all looking very happy. She was very excited about seeing

12

them. Obviously, I was a little upset but actually don't think I took much notice at the time. My father had just asked the doctors how she was and they said she was considered to be 'on the mend' and although her recovery would be slow, she was out of danger. My mother died very suddenly in the early hours of the next morning!

These experiences are something that I have often thought about over the last 30 years since she died, but they have not really been discussed within the family. I remember telling the family at the time what she had said but while my father seemed to believe me and I think took comfort from it, my brother and sister were very disapproving of it – obviously not believing it. I have told some close friends over the years but have learned by the reaction of some people that they consider me slightly unhinged for paying any regard to the experiences. Most people have suggested that my mother was drugged up to the eyeballs on both occasions, which would explain her 'lucid dreams'. As for me, I don't know what I think except to say that sometimes I truly believe that her family came for her and she was taken peacefully, and at other times I have wondered if these 'dreams' made my mother give up because she believed she was going to die.

In this book we are going to explore these experiences and see whether we can explain them or whether we should simply accept them and value them for what they so evidently are, a comfort to the dying and their families. But they also serve as an introduction to a much wider question – that of death itself, whether it is a process, what it means to us and whether we can prepare ourselves, and help those we love, to die a good death.

Chapter 2
Talking to Carers

A lot of people . . . might tell you half of something. They want to know whether you are OK with that. Then they might tell you a bit more. (An interviewee)

Whenever I gave a lecture about end-of-life experiences I found that there were always people in the audience who were eager to recount similar experiences in their own family. This happened so often that I wanted to see if they were also reported by the doctors and nurses in hospices and nursing homes, or whether for some strange reason only relatives noticed them. There is a medical index, PubMed (available on the internet), which lists articles in all the major medical journals, but at that time I could find only three which mentioned deathbed visions. Clearly this phenomenon had either not been researched, or simply was not classified this way by the medical profession. It seemed that it was one of the few areas in which you could become a world expert on the literature after reading two or three papers. There are plenty of papers about palliative care and pain control, but very few about the mental states during the dying process, or about the visions reported at this time by dying people. Perhaps this is because of the assumption that death is simply the shutting down of the brain, and this area is of little interest to the medical profession, who feel that at this point they cannot control the process and are no longer involved.

Although there is plenty of anecdotal evidence about the phenomena that are reported to occur at or around the time of death, medical practitioners have been slow to recognize them. There has been little research into the way carers respond when patients try to talk about these phenomena, or into how these end-of-life experiences influence the carers' work. Until recently, what scientific discussion there has been of end-of-life phenomena has largely focused on whether they provide evidence for the existence of life after death,[1] a debate which is likely to be ongoing, relying as it does on anecdotal and subjective evidence. Consequently, few satisfactory scientific studies have been carried out to look at the experiences in more detail, to find out how common they are, what explanation we can find for them, or the impact they have both on the dying person and on the family or professional carers with whom that person may want to discuss what is happening to them. However, quite apart from the question of life after death, it is now much more generally recognized and accepted that these experiences are indeed 'spiritual' in the sense that they have profound meaning and personal significance to the patient.[2]

It is always difficult to set up a research study in what are considered by one's colleagues to be areas of only marginal importance. First, the study has to be funded, and what funding body would look favourably on research into what it is like to die? Second, ethics approval has to be sought and the question of whether it is ethical to ask questions of the dying has to be considered. As there was so little work in this area, we felt the best plan was to question the carers of the dying rather than the dying themselves. After all, professional carers have sat with many dying people, and if these experiences did in fact occur, they should have either noticed them themselves or been told about them by the relatives of the dying. This also raised a subsidiary set of questions into whether professional carers were trained to recognize and to answer the deep spiritual questions of the dying and whether knowledge of end-of-life experiences was part of the routine training of professional carers.

While awaiting the result of several funding body applications, and after we had been given ethical approval to go ahead with a questionnaire study of professional carers of the dying, we decided to carry out a very simple pre-pilot survey. Sue Brayne, a colleague who is a bereavement counsellor and was also interested in this area of research, had a friend who was working with a palliative care team in a London teaching hospital and suggested that her team would be an ideal place to start and gain experience of the problems involved in this type of research.

Accordingly we approached the palliative care team and were asked to give a presentation of the research that we wanted to do. The team was very receptive, helpful and supportive and agreed that any of its members who wanted to take part in the study could do so. So we set up our pilot survey. Our interviewees were professionals, with considerable experience of caring for the dying, and we wanted to assess their professional observations on end-of-life experiences – for example whether these might simply be caused by medication, or whether they were something much more intrinsic to the dying process itself. But we also wanted to study the effect these experiences had on the interviewees themselves, personally and professionally, including the impact, if any, on their spiritual or religious beliefs.

Nine carers were interviewed, three of whom were doctors. The carers were initially sent a detailed questionnaire concerning the different types of ELEs and were asked to record those that they had experienced in the past five years. They then had a full one-hour, one-to-one interview. The data extracted from the typed transcripts of the interview, together with the questionnaires, were analysed.

We found that most members of the palliative care team we interviewed believed not only that ELEs occur, but that they occur relatively frequently, and are an intrinsic, transitional part of the dying process. Although they found ELEs hard to explain or to define clinically, all interviewees agreed that ELEs are an intensely personal and often a spiritual experience, helping the patient to become reconciled with events in their life, and therefore to come to terms with their death.

These positive results encouraged us to start further interviews in hospices and nursing homes, using the same format, and with the team augmented by a second interviewer, Hilary Lovelace, an SRN also with extensive experience of the dying and Macmillan nurse visiting. We recognized that palliative care workers were often not in day-to-day contact with the dying, but only visited the home. Thus their experience of deathbed phenomena might be more limited than those of hospice or nursing home carers who had ongoing day-to-day care of the dying.

We also planned to interview a number of hospice chaplains

from all the major faiths. We assessed the interviewees' professional observations on ELEs, including other possible causes of hallucination such as illness, brain pathology or medication. We also asked about the effect that ELEs may have had on the interviewees themselves, personally and professionally, including the impact on their spiritual or religious beliefs. To date we have interviewed over 40 carers, and the data referred to in this chapter are from both nursing home and hospice studies.

Our first studies were retrospective, which means that we were looking into the past and relying on the carers' memory, so we could not get exact figures for the frequency of ELEs. When the interviews in each hospice or nursing home were completed, we returned a year later to see how many ELEs had occurred during that year, but this time the situation was different, as the carers had all been trained about ELEs, had been given permission to discuss them and were encouraged to record them. Our prospective studies should enable us to get a much more accurate picture of the frequency of ELEs.

Several interviewees believed that ELEs were a prognostic indicator for nearing death, and that they needed to learn the 'language of the dying' to recognize what the patient was experiencing; when a patient started 'Granny visiting' talk, they knew the end was near, and this was the signal for them to pay more attention to the patient's spiritual needs. 'Once "Granny" has visited, or whatever, I know then they are almost certainly going to be peaceful as they let go of this physical world, and they've got this peace to look forward to what's next.'

But besides these archetypal 'take-away' visions, the carers we talked to were clear that they had experienced many other wider and more subtle phenomena associated with the death of people they had cared for. As one interviewee said, 'It's about letting go of this physical world and about preparing for what's going to happen next.' And in the words of another: 'I think there are deathbed spiritual changes that happen and sometimes it can just be a patient saying, "I felt very warm. Something came round me and I felt incredibly secure; I can't describe it to you, I just felt OK and I knew things were going to be OK".' Another interviewee talked about ELEs as an energetic change around the bed of the dying patient that produced a feeling of comfort. Four interviewees in the nursing home study spoke about experiencing a change in room temperature or atmosphere at the time of death, or shortly after. 'Sometimes the room is freezing. At other times it is really, really hot.' Opening a window often helps. 'You feel a calm going out of the window', said one interviewee. Another described feeling 'warm and nice' when she went into the room of a resident who had just died, and a colleague experienced the same warmth, but described it 'Like a feeling when you give love to someone, there's that kind of feeling of warmth and peace . . . I feel as though I am connected to it . . . Sometimes it's there when you're laying them out – there's a feeling that you are doing something for them.'

A few interviewees had more negative reactions. One said she sometimes felt the hairs on her forearm standing up shortly after walking into the room where a resident had died, 'I feel scared as if the person is still there with me,' she said.

Sighting apparitions was not so unusual for nursing-home residents either. Many reported seeing children just before they died. Three interviewees reported the same story concerning a resident who had died unexpectedly in hospital. 'After a few days his former room-mate, who was not on any medication, saw him sitting there in his usual chair. He saw him and he told the nurses: "You know that man came back! Yes I know he is dead. Why is he still there sitting in the wheelchair".'

The carers we talked to in all our studies felt confident that ELEs are not drug induced. Many, probably most, of the patients in their care were on some kind of medication, and the staff were well aware that some of these drugs induced hallucinations. But they insisted that drug-induced hallucinations were of a quite different quality from a true end-of-life vision, and had a quite different effect on their patients. We look at these differences in more detail in Chapter 6.

None of the interviewees reported that their personal religious or spiritual beliefs had been influenced or changed by witnessing ELEs, or by being told about them from relatives.

Talking about ELEs

The importance of encouraging patients to talk about these experiences was a frequent theme to emerge during the interviews, largely because the staff we talked to felt that ELEs were enormously helpful in enabling patients to die a peaceful death. It is perhaps not surprising that we found that patients preferred to talk to nurses rather than doctors about their experience. But we also found that many carers feel they are ill equipped to respond adequately to their patients' questions and concerns. In our palliative care team study the overall incidence we found was small in relation to the number of patients, but the first evidence is that carers in the hospices and the nursing homes we have interviewed reported many more cases, probably because they are in day-to-day contact with the dying and are therefore more likely see these phenomena when they occur.

Our interviewees felt that many ELEs may still go unreported, and suggested many possible reasons for this – embarrassment, the fear of distressing relatives or appearing mad, lack of public awareness of ELEs, language difficulties in a multicultural society, and the lack of privacy in a hospital setting. They also made the point that some patients may simply not want to talk about their experiences.

The frequency of ELEs that carers report may depend at least to some extent on the nature of the carer's contact with the patient. For example, one carer reported that while on night duty in a hospice almost all her dying patients told her of ELEs. When she changed to visiting the dying at home the frequency of ELEs reported to her was less, probably because of the change in her relationship with the patients, and the fact that she was not necessarily present shortly before the patient's death.

Openness and honesty, a willingness to listen, and normalizing ELEs were thought to be particularly important in encouraging patients to talk about these experiences. 'I deal with it by being open-minded, and saying to my patients that it's OK to talk about it', said one interviewee. 'Some of them [patients] are not sure and wonder if it's the morphine. It's about reassuring them that this is quite normal and it happens to quite a few people, and most people find it comforting.'

Another interviewee said that many patients wanted to ask him about his own beliefs. 'I'm happy to talk about my beliefs to patients if they ask. And sometimes this leads patients on to talk about the afterlife and things like that. So that's how they test the waters a bit.' A third interviewee echoed the need for patients to test the waters. 'A lot of people . . . might tell you half of something. They want to know whether you are OK with that. Then they might tell you a bit more.'

One interesting difference between the palliative care team and nursing-home studies was that none of the interviewees in the palliative care team mentioned a sense of afterlife presence, or reported odd paranormal incidents related to a death, whereas all of the nursing-home interviewees did so. They accepted without question occasional sightings of dead residents, a disturbing atmosphere in the room of someone who had just died, hearing voices or footsteps, or odd incidents such as bells ringing or lights inexplicably going on or off in the room of a recently deceased resident. This is probably because the palliative care team we interviewed, attached to a major London teaching hospital, was not involved in the day-to-day long-term care of the patients in the way that the nursing home staff were, who spent more time with the people in their care, had more of an ongoing, long-term relationship with them, and also were around more after the patient had actually died.

Helping carers respond to patients' needs

While some patients just want to share their experiences with someone who will understand, a few are distressed by what has happened and want answers. It isn't always easy for staff to give them what they need. As one observed, it is much easier to deal with the pain and the vomiting than to deal with the 'help'. One carer described herself as feeling as though she was expected to be the new 'priest at the bedside' but that her training had done nothing to help her when put in this position. Many of them said that they felt it was a taboo subject, and if they raised it they were not taken seriously. Carers felt they had been insufficiently trained in pastoral care and lacked both the therapeutic skills and the understanding of spirituality which would enable them to identify the basic characteristics and range of ELEs that occurred, and their significance to the patient.

When they were asked questions about these or about the spiritual aspects of death and dying, they did not know how to respond, and even though they could accept what they were told, their own reactions were often of unease and sometimes fear. Many felt they were floundering in the dark, and did not know what to say to avoid simply 'fobbing off' their patients' questions and concerns, or how to help those patients who were afraid of death or became angry or aggressive in their efforts to come to terms with it. Seravalli[3] has suggested that doctors and nurses are often adversely affected by death, either because they themselves fear death and identify with the dying person, or because they feel professionally impotent in the face of it. He maintains, however, that if we can better understand the particular world of the dying, these feelings might become bearable.[4] Carers themselves wanted advice on how to recognize the 'language of the dying' and to create a 'safe space' where patients could be open and honest in talking about their own approaching death. They suggested that a specialist hospital 'multi-faith' minister should be available for all community patients and medical staff.

At the simplest level, all our studies have suggested that most carers wanted a more general acknowledgement that these end-of-life experiences do indeed occur and are of great significance to their dying patients. They wanted to be able to discuss them more openly, and felt the need for further training to help them learn more about their nature and spiritual meaning. By encouraging patients to talk about these experiences, they believed they would be better able to help them through the dying process.

Chapter 3

Deathbed Visions

Versuchung im Glauben:
Temptation in the belief

I am glad you are doing this study, I think a lot of people probably have these experiences but are too embarrassed to tell anyone in case anyone thinks they are going mad! (An interviewee)

Deathbed visions have been largely ignored by the medical profession, though as we saw in the previous chapter, they are well known to, and often reported by, nurses and relatives who care for the dying.

The following fascinating and detailed account from Barbara Cane shows very clearly the parallel worlds the dying seem able simultaneously to inhabit. Barbara describes the last days of her 90-year-old mother, in hospital and dying of pneumonia at Christmas 2005. As the various members of her family visited her she was able to talk to them very calmly and clearly and was totally 'on the ball'. She talked to her grandson about his plans for the future, how proud she was of him, and how she wanted him to be

23

settled with a good partner as she had been. During all this time her heart and oxygen levels were being monitored and were steady.

During the hour or so he (her grandson) was with her she occasionally mentioned that she was aware that people were watching over her, and that they were in the gardens surrounding the hospital. She couldn't describe them, as they were behind the bushes, but she knew that they were there to help her 'if her head fell forward'. She said to my son that she also saw 'Dad' in the hospital room (as she used to call my father), and wasn't bothered by this. My son looked at her medical attachments and saw no fluctuation in the readings of the medical instrumentation. She would then continue talking normally to him.

When my daughter arrived, shortly afterwards, she too had a really good visit. Her medical responses were calm and steady, and when she referred to, and saw, 'these people' her heart and oxygen levels didn't move. At this time 'the people' were in the ward, but near the inside of the windows. She was very calm and explained that she knew my daughter couldn't see them – but would understand when 'her time comes'. She calmly waved and spoke to 'these people' and introduced them to my daughter – as if they were talking to her. She would then carry on discussing Christmas and other aspects of normal life. I joined my daughter, after an hour, at the hospital and we both sat chatting to my mother. She spoke to me about my life, remembering vividly situations and many memories. She spoke to me about my future – all interspersed with references to 'these people' who were now at the end of her bed. She told us that she wouldn't be there the next day as 'these people' would 'pick her up when she fell and take her on a journey'. We were slightly spooked at her comments, but she was totally at ease.

By about 5 p.m. that afternoon 'these people' were sitting on her bed next to her granddaughter, and she was having a three-way conversation with them. She then dismissed her granddaughter and told her to go out and enjoy herself as it was Christmas Eve. Her granddaughter left the ward, but in fact waited in the car park for her mother to join her.

It was about 45 minutes later that I arrived, and we walked into the ward together. The curtains were around the bed. We looked at the monitor and it showed really high blood pressure and oxygen levels of about 80 per cent. We went straight back to the nurses' station to find that they were in the process of phoning us, to tell us to return to the hospital as my mother had had a 'turn', probably a heart attack, and they were waiting for a doctor. We returned to her bedside and a nurse took her hand to try and wake her. She opened her eyes – but didn't really seem to see – and said, 'I've had a wonderful life' and closed her eyes. We telephoned my husband and my son to come back to the hospital, and we were all around her bed when she died peacefully at 9.55 p.m. on Christmas Eve.

We were comforted by her calmness – and her awareness of her forthcoming death – and the thought that she was totally at peace with it all. We think that there is probably a medical reason why the dying hallucinate – poison in the brain, medical drugs or lack of certain chemicals in the blood – but it was so strange that it was amidst totally normal conversation, and that she knew so much about her impending death – even down to the last detail of telling my daughter to go – so she wasn't there when she 'fell'.

It's interesting that 'these people' grew closer and closer to her as death approached, from being at first in the garden behind the bushes, until finally they were actually sitting on her bed. And that the 'real' world in which she was having totally rational conversations with her family was seamlessly interwoven with the other reality in which she communicated with 'these people'. It's also quite clear that she was perfectly able to distinguish between the two realities which existed side by side, and understood that only she could see the people but that others will understand when their time comes. Finally, she was apparently being given reliable information by her visitors, as she knew that by the next morning she would have left at last to go with them on her 'journey'.

Although these visions are the most commonly reported end-of-life experiences, there have been very few studies of the phenomenon. The most comprehensive is that already mentioned (p. 4) by Karlis Osis and Erlendur Haraldsson.[1] They carried out a pilot study in 1959–60, giving a questionnaire survey to 5,000 physicians and 5,000 nurses. Of these 640 (6.4 per cent) replied and 190 were followed up with a personal interview. They carried out two further surveys, one in the United States in 1961–4 and one in India in 1972–3.[2] These surveys showed that the majority of the experiences took place in clear consciousness, and that there was a marked cultural bias in the 'take-away' visions. In the United States survey it was apparitions of dead relatives and friends who most often appeared to take away the dying person (in 70 per cent of cases). Living people figured much less often (in 17 per cent of cases) and religious figures even less frequently (in 13 per cent). In the Indian experiences it was religious figures such as the *yamdoot* (messenger of the Hindu God of Death) who were the most frequent take-away companions – they were described in 50 per cent of cases. In only 29 per cent did apparitions of dead relatives or friends appear, and in 21 per cent apparitions of living people. Our own sample follows a very similar pattern to the US survey, though religious figures were seen even less often (religious figures, 2 per cent; relatives, 70 per cent; gestures of welcome or recognition, 28 per cent). In just over a quarter of our cases the appearance of a visitor was assumed by those watching, because the dying person behaved as though they could see someone, smiling in recognition, or holding out their arms as if in welcome. Nearly always the visitors mentioned were relatives or close friends. Strangers were rarely seen, and when they were, were often interpreted by the relatives at any rate as some long-dead or unrecognized relative.

We were given no reports of any apparitions of living people. Although people with a strong Christian belief may 'see' apparitions associated with their religion, this occurred relatively rarely. In the Christian tradition, for example, it has been guardian angels that have acted as the soul's guide to paradise, but angels made only a few appearances; in one case they were accompanied by pink light and in another someone heard angels singing just before they died. Chris Alcock's father was heard negotiating with angels to postpone his final departure. Chris was driving from Scotland to Gloucester to his dying father's bedside, but the car broke down and the journey was held up. His sister broke the news to their father that he had been delayed. Then:

My sister heard Dad talking very crossly to someone in his room. Fearing that one of her children had gone in and upset him, she went in to see what was going on. Only Dad was there in his bed. My sister asked him who he was talking to. He replied, 'I was telling the angels that I was not ready to go yet!' He knew I was coming and was determined to stay alive until I had seen him.

It is clear that deathbed visions are not dependent on religious belief – indeed, they seem to bewilder and amaze believers and non-believers alike. About the experience above, and another he describes on p. 36, Chris Alcock comments, 'All the people concerned (and myself) are and were practising Catholics, though this sort of phenomenon has nothing to do with our faith. We were all as surprised as anyone of any faith or no faith would be.'

Another of our correspondents told us about the death of his elderly aunt, a woman with a lifelong and deeply held conviction that death was the end of everything. They had had many discussions about this, as he himself had always doubted death's absolute finality. As she lay dying, she asked if she could speak to her nephew alone for a moment. 'Bert,' she told him, 'you were right after all.'

It is interesting how often these experiences do confound expectations. Judy Whitmore, who has been nursing for 33 years and is very familiar with deathbed visions, told us about the friend she nursed whose experience didn't conform at all to her previously held views about an afterlife.

I was nursing my friend who had definite views that there was no afterlife. In her last couple of hours she became very peaceful and arose from her unconsciousness periodically, saying clearly and happily such phrases as 'I will know soon', 'Come on, get on with it then, I am ready to go now', and 'It is so beautiful'. She would immediately lapse back into unconsciousness after uttering these phrases. She was very obviously content, happy and at peace. It was a wonderful experience for her partner and me.

Whether or not you regard these visions as nothing more than the product of a dying brain, their value to the person who has them is clear. A month or so before she died, Ivan Martin's wife would often tell him that she had seen her mother, appearing as a young woman, quite clearly at the foot of the bed:

I said, 'Are you sure you were not dreaming?', to which she replied, 'I know a dream from what I have been seeing.' She seemed very happy and would say little more, although I felt that the experience had a particularly calming effect upon her. I do not attach anything supernatural to all this as I am particularly cynical with regard to such occurrences. I am in fact an atheist. I do not think there is anything more than what goes on in a person's head, inside of which is all there is to our being. When we die there is nothing more.

Mr Martin also asks why so relatively few people have these experiences. Part of the answer is that we still don't really know how common they are, though the reports of palliative care and nursing staff (Chapter 2), as well as the responses from the general public, suggest they are probably much more common than anyone has previously thought. Often the presence of a vision is inferred by those watching because of the way the dying person behaves, rather than anything they say – and often of course by the time they die they are already beyond speech. It may be a change in expression – their face lights up as though they have seen someone they recognize and love – or they may reach out as if towards some invisible presence. And also of course we have no way of knowing what, if anything, someone who is unconscious just before they die experiences, though research on the near-death experience does suggest the possibility that they too may be experiencing something similar (see Chapter 12).

Absolute reality

What are the main characteristics of these visions? What all witnesses agree on is that they take place in real space. Often, at the moment of death, the nurse or relative who is with a dying patient notices that they look fixedly at a particular corner of the room or stretch out a hand as though someone is coming towards them, or their eyes may follow someone who is apparently moving around the room. The wife of a patient of mine who was dying of a cerebral tumour gave me this account of her husband's final moments.

He was going unconscious. When I looked at him, he was looking fixedly at something in front of him. A smile of recognition spread slowly over his face, as if he was greeting someone. Then he relaxed peacefully and died.

None of the accounts describe the dying person's eyes wandering randomly around the room. Always they seem to be looking at some specific point and their attention is absolutely fixed upon it. The following accounts are typical of the many we received.

I looked up and saw that my mother's eyes were wide open. My first thoughts were that she had woken up and I dashed to the side of the bed. She was staring straight ahead to a point roughly where the wall met the ceiling. I bent down over her so that her stare would meet my eyes, but she looked straight ahead. I just said, 'Who are you looking at Mother?', not really expecting an answer. It dawned on me that she was looking at someone who had come to meet her.

My brother was in hospital dying from emphysema. His breathing was very laboured, when all of a sudden he stopped and his breathing suddenly appeared normal. He looked at about 45 degrees upwards and smiled broadly, as if at something or someone: he turned to me and died suddenly in my arms. I am positive to this day that he wanted to tell me what he had seen. Those few seconds before he died will live with me for ever, it was so powerful.

Her eyes were wide open and she continued staring at the same place. This lasted for about 12 minutes. I called in the ward sister and she told me that I should contact the rest of my family. As my wife and I were looking down at my mother, her breathing got shallower. She closed her eyes, and seconds later she died.

There are also accounts of the dying getting out of bed as if to try to go with their vision. So absolutely real do these apparitions seem, that the dying person is often witnessed interacting with them, and expecting others to do so too. Hilary Froude, a practising nurse/midwife, was one of many nurses who told us about deathbed visions they had witnessed when caring for dying patients.

I was attending a patient with a fellow nurse – again around four in the morning. The male patient asked us to stand one on each side of him because he wanted to thank us for looking after him. He then looked over my shoulder towards the window and said, 'Hang on, I will be with you in a minute, I just want to thank these nurses for looking after me.' The patient repeated himself a couple of times, then died!

The following account also describes how someone who had been in a semi-conscious state for over two weeks following a severe stroke, seemed in his final days to be communicating on some level with something or someone. His right side was paralysed, he could not speak, and could not see. His only movement was his face and eyes, head, left arm, hand and leg.

Approximately four to five days before he died there was definitely some form of final meeting. At the end he very methodically shook each person's hand; there were at least three [perceived people]. He went to shake the last person's hand, which brought him very close to myself. I sat at the side of the bed, I interposed my hand in the space, he grasped my hand as if to shake it, then realized it was not right and very forcefully threw my hand away, shot me a look which said, 'How dare you?' and went back to shake whoever's hand he was meant to . . .

It was on [the following] day he said his very moving final farewell. Somehow he managed to pull my head down and place it between the side of his own head and shoulder and gave me the most wonderful hug and kiss. For a man so physically incapacitated and unable to 'see' or speak, I was dumbfounded as well as deeply moved.

Three days later he slipped into a coma . . . on his last exhalation he turned his head towards the window, slowly opened his eyes, the colour of which was the most piercing luminescent blue I have ever seen, after a few seconds the colour slowly faded back to normal and he slowly closed his eyes again.

Teresa Whichello's experience with her dying mother was similar:

When my mother was ill with cancer and my sister and I were nursing her at home, two days before she died she was talking quite clearly to us when suddenly she looked toward the wall at the bottom of the bed and said, 'Wave to your father, girls, he's waving goodbye to us.' (My father had died six weeks previously.) My sister and I, having heard of these sightings before, waved to my dad although not seeing him, and said 'Bye Dad'. She didn't say much more to us as she then slipped into unconsciousness before she died.

This is Barry Fletcher's account of the day his father died:

We were all around his bed holding his hands, stroking his arms, giving him our family love. I was at the end of his bed where the door was, he beckoned me to him with his hand, I went to him, he said something I didn't quite understand; he kept looking at the doorway at the foot of his bed and talking as if to someone there, then he beckoned again towards the door as if to invite someone in. By then he was completely calm, his breathing became shallower and slower, and finally he passed away: he was still looking and pointing to the doorway. We are all of the opinion that he was waiting to say goodbye to us and that either his mother, father, brother or all of them had come for him.

Rachel Scarott told a similar story. Her father had cancer and in his last few weeks he became too ill to be looked after at home and had to be taken into a home for the terminally ill.

The day before he died, I walked into his room and he asked me who the lady was that was with me. I started to tell him there was no one with me and then changed my story and told him she would be going soon as I could see he was convinced I wasn't alone. I initially put it down to the large amount of drugs he was infusing. The same afternoon, my brother was sat with me and suddenly Dad asked to be sat up. He hadn't said much for a few days but seemed at this point to know exactly what was happening. I asked if he was uncomfortable and he said 'No' but the lady needed to walk around him. I sat him up a bit but his head was trying to turn to see if this 'lady' was all right. I told him the lady had successfully passed and that all was well. His gaze followed around the bed for a few seconds and then he relaxed. It was the last words he spoke to me, as he died the next morning.

My brother and I didn't say anything about this for a few hours until I asked him if he thought it may have been our mother. My brother, known for his practicality said it was exactly what he had thought. Our mother had died nearly six years earlier with Alzheimer's and my father had been her carer for nearly seven years. It's something I would like to believe and to know that they are together again in good health.

'How nice of you to come'

How do the dying respond to their visitors? The apparitions are nearly always seen as welcoming, and the dying person responds with interest or joy.

Suddenly my Gran sat up in bed and smiled. She said, 'I'm going now and here's Dad and George come to meet me.' She then died still with this big smile on her face. My mother never forgot it.

A district nurse told us this very typical story of an 80-year-old lady she used to visit once a week, to help and supervise the family who were giving her care.

She eventually became weaker and was semi-conscious, only reacting to painful stimuli. She died, and I visited the next day to help.

Her daughter said that she was lying peacefully and suddenly sat bolt upright with a beaming smile on her face and said, 'Joe, how nice of you to come and see me.' [Joe was her deceased husband.] Then she lay back down again and died soon after. The daughter was very sensible and practical and really believed that her father had visited.

The third-party testimony of the nurse who told us this story indicates how compelling the daughter, in her opinion a thoroughly down-to-earth and credible witness, found the whole episode. It's also one of the many cases when a patient who has been comatosed or unconscious has a sudden lucid interval just before death. From being someone who only reacted to painful stimuli, this woman suddenly rallied, sat bolt upright, and recognized and welcomed her visitor.

By far the most common reaction is to feel the visitor as a comforting presence, there to help with the dying process and escort them over the borders of death. Quite often, too, they come as a surprise, though usually a pleasant one:

He would look at Mum so lovingly, then quickly turn to the window and when looking through the window he appeared to be disbelieving. This looking at her and then looking through the window lasted for a few minutes – loving look to disbelieving look – while all the time he held the oxygen mask to his face. Suddenly it was over. He looked at Mum one last time, then he just closed his eyes and relaxed, the colour draining from his lips, as though someone had pulled out a miniature plug. Dad was 50 years old. There was something or someone he saw through that window that he knew meant his death. Something or someone waiting. I don't know what or who it was, but I am absolutely certain that he saw what we could not.

'She seemed to come alive'

In many of the accounts we were given, this kind of description recurs again and again:

My mother's face lit up with joy.

She smiled the most marvellous smile. She seemed to come alive.

She suddenly sat up in bed, her arms out towards someone, with a great look of happiness and then after a pause sank back on the pillow and died not long after.

Osis and Haraldsson's survey[3] also found that a sudden rise in mood just before death was very common. Patients might become peaceful and serene, or cheerful and elated. A common observation by medical observers was: 'They light up.' In their US sample this elevation of mood shortly before the time of death (often within ten minutes) was independent of the patient's age and gender and they found no evidence that it could be attributed to medical factors or medication. They did suggest that although religious affiliation was of little importance as a causal factor, religious involvement might be. They also found that at the same time patients often seemed able to disengage from pain and other symptoms.

It is very tempting to attribute this sudden burst of euphoria to a deathbed visitor, especially when the person's gaze seems to be directed at something or someone, or they hold out their arms. But what we can also say with more confidence is that it provides more evidence that there seems to be nothing intrinsic in the process of dying which should make us fearful about our own death.

Lucidity

Another characteristic common to most of the visions is that they are usually seen in clear, or only moderately impaired, consciousness. Often the dying are heard talking to their visitors, and relatives who overhear the conversation nearly always describe it as rational and lucid. Marie Dowdall:

My uncle served in the First World War and experienced the horrors of the Somme, which lived with him for the rest of his life.

He had led a group of men, returned with only three survivors and was badly injured himself. He was awarded the Military Cross.

It was around 30 years ago, when he was dying of cancer, that the following event took place. During his illness my mother cared for him at home, and I remember one evening we were sitting with him talking quietly. He was too ill to contribute much to the conversation but liked to hear us chatting, when suddenly he leaned forward and stared across the room. He became very animated and looked very happy as he began to talk to people he could obviously see but we couldn't; he was calling them each by name and asking how they were and how wonderful it was to see them again. It became apparent from what he was saying they were some of the men who had served with him at the Somme and died there. There was a look of wonderment on his face and he forgot his pain.

I will never forget that night, and though I could not see his friends, I have no doubt whatsoever that they were there. I didn't see him conscious again, and he died a couple of days later.

Daphne Biliouri gives this interesting account of her mother's final days before she died from cancer. Daphne is from Greece and this is where her mother died. Although her mother was in excruciating pain for the last week of her life, and no longer aware of her surroundings or anyone around her, about three days before she died she started talking in *Macedonski*, a dialect used in the village where she grew up and the one she used only when she talked to her parents or visited the village.

She spent around four hours talking to two men (from what I could gather, listening to her and watching her shift her gaze between two different spots in the room). One of them was her brother who used to live in Australia and had died the previous year, and the other was somebody older, I think it might have been her grandfather. During this whole time she was very animated, happy and extremely lucid, unlike the rest of the time. The conversation ended with her waving goodbye to them, and although I tried to talk to her after that, thinking that she was lucid, she didn't recognize or acknowledge me. However, the positive thing is that the pain seemed not to exist any more for the remaining couple of days.

The following account describes a similar unexpected burst of lucidity just before death:

Suddenly a cool breeze came through the window, causing the long voile curtain to flutter upwards quite noticeably. Simultaneously, the look of my Dad's face changed – where it had been sunken, it was now full and the colour brighter, normal. Then Dad spoke, something that was so difficult for him, but his voice was strong and he spoke quite clearly and normally. He said, 'Yes, Mum, I understand. Yes, Mum, I'll do that Mum. All right, Mum.' He did not open his eyes at all.

We have been given many similar accounts of a dying person who has been confused or unconscious greeting their 'take-away' visitor in a sudden lucid window of consciousness just before death. Chris Alcock's mother died of cancer in 1974:

During her last week she said to my father that she could not be 'going yet' as nobody had 'come for her'. On the afternoon of her last day the doctor called and dosed her up with morphine and she sank into deep unconsciousness. My father was sitting with her when she suddenly woke up, sat up in bed and held her arms out towards someone, with an ecstatic look of happiness on her face. Dad wished he had asked her who was there, but instead he asked a much more mundane question: 'Do you want your potty?' Mum heard him and simply replied that she didn't. So she was all there mentally. She then sank back onto her pillow and relapsed into unconsciousness and remained there until her death.

Like many other people who wrote to us, the writer of the following letter stresses the way in which these visions seem to enable the dying process and facilitate a tranquil departure.

My father died in March 2006 after suffering a major heart attack. He had spent a few days in hospital but signed himself out and returned home. We did not know at the time his prognosis was so poor but as a family we knew that things were not good after a consultant visited us at home to explain he was lucky to have left hospital.

He deteriorated that day, was confused but we still did not realize he was dying and so didn't get him back to hospital. He went to bed at about 9 p.m., with my mother and I in the room, and he was very restless. He started to see wires hanging from the ceiling and insects on the bed, all very distressing.

At about midnight he started to fall asleep and became more restful. After about five minutes he sat up said, 'Hi Dave, what are you doing here, it's good to see you.' This was witnessed by my mother and I, and we couldn't believe it. He was calm, tranquil and quite lucid really. David was my mother's brother and good friend to Dad and he had died about 12 years before. Dad died shortly afterwards and in a quiet state, for which I am very grateful.

'Heaven is the most beautiful place'

Sometimes this process is taken even further, so that not only does the relative appear in the room, but the dying person apparently journeys with them to an intermediate reality that they perceive as being more real than the real world, and interpenetrated by light, love and compassion. They may drift in and out of this area in the days or hours preceding death, sometimes seeing spiritual beings who they don't know but whose purity is strongly evident.

Geoffrey Watson's father talked to him many times about the death of his own father, a deeply religious man who was dying of cancer of the throat:

My father was at his bedside, deeply distressed, but my grandfather quietly said to my father, 'Don't worry, Leslie, I am all right, I can see and hear the most beautiful things and you must not worry.' And he quietly died, lucid to the end.

Shortly before Paul Fleming's father died, he recognized a number of close family friends, all of whom had died, who he thought were in the room with him. He was quite specific about who he saw, though he could not understand why they should be there. The next night he informed Paul's brother, quite clearly, that 'heaven was a beautiful place', and started talking as if he had been there. Paul says that despite being on high levels of morphine, his father became far more alert and talkative at night, and adds, 'These comments are 100 per cent genuine and authentic. We believe something was happening close to his death that we did not fully understand.'

Preparatory visits

The visions are not always of people. The following account, sent to us by a woman whose mother was dying of cancer, describes what her mother told her the day before she died, and how comforting this vision was. It mentions the light that is a recurring element in the accounts sent to us, sometimes seen by the dying themselves and sometimes by their relatives – something that is discussed in more detail in Chapter 7. And it also illustrates what many of these stories suggest, that somehow in these visions the person is given an intimation of their own imminent death.

Suddenly she looked up at the window and seemed to stare intently up at it . . . this lasted only minutes but it seemed ages . . . She suddenly turned to me and said, 'Pease Pauline, don't ever be afraid of dying. I have seen a beautiful light and I was going towards it, I wanted to go into that light, it was so peaceful I really had to fight to come back.' The next day, when it was time for me to go home, I said, 'Bye Mum, see you tomorrow.' She looked straight at me and said, 'I'm not worried about tomorrow and you mustn't be, promise me.' Sadly she died the next morning . . . but I knew she had seen something that day which gave her comfort and peace when she knew she had only hours to live.

Although these preparatory visits occur most frequently in the few hours before death, there are many accounts of the 'visitors' making their first appearance in the days or weeks before death – occasionally even appearing as harbingers of death before anyone knows that death is imminent. Particularly interesting are the visions that sometimes appear to someone who is, or seems to be, perfectly well – or at any rate nowhere near death's door.

J. Tanner describes how one day her mother popped in to visit her grandmother who told her: 'I can't understand it! I just saw my mother standing in the doorway, as clearly as I can see you.' She goes on:

Her mother had been dead, of course, for probably 30 years. At that time my grandmother was no more ill than she had been for the past two or three years and perfectly lucid. My mother told me she instantly had a sense of foreboding – she had always heard that we see the 'ghosts' of dead relatives just before our own death. The next day, my grandmother suffered a massive stroke from which she never regained consciousness. After lying in a coma for four days, she died.

Susan Burman gives a similar account of the death of her grand-father many years ago:

He returned from church on a Sunday night, said he felt unwell and took himself off to bed. My grandmother went up with a cup of tea and he told her that he had seen 'our Mabel and our Doris', these were two of their children who died in infancy. Grandfather died that night.

These two accounts show very clearly that these visions have a validity of their own which can be independent of the dying process, independent of brain pathology, and, very significantly, independent of any expectation of death. They stand on their own and carry profound meaning for the individual. In terms of phenomenology, it is impossible to draw a distinction between these 'harbinger' visions and those which occur just before death, suggesting that they are all of the same quality and are not affected by the pathology of dying.

Sometimes the preparatory visit is made well in advance.

Pauline's 96-year-old grandmother had been one of five girls and had been particularly close to her sister Margaret whom they called Greta.

A couple of months before she died, my grandmother told me, on my return from work one day, that Greta had visited her that afternoon and that she had wanted to go with her but Greta had told her that she couldn't because 'it wasn't the right time'. On the night she died, my grandmother was struggling to breathe. All at once her eyes opened wide, she smiled (more than smiled really – her whole face lit up) and put her arms up as though greeting someone. From then onwards she was a lot calmer and died about 15 minutes later. I was sure at the time that Greta had come back and that the time was now right for my Grandmother to go off with her.

Delaying tactics

Occasionally, if their appearance is correctly interpreted as a pre-monition of death, the 'visitor' may be given short shrift at what the visionary sees as rather premature collection:

My mother told me shortly before she died that she saw my late father arrive on a white horse with the intention of 'collecting her', but she tripped up the horse and refused to get on the back of the horse with my father.

Several other people mentioned this kind of delaying tactic. Chris Alcock's father (p. 27 of this chapter) seems to have been able to negotiate a deal with the angels to let him stay alive until his son arrived to say goodbye to him. 'I was telling the angels that I was not ready to go yet!' Hilary Froude's patient (p. 30 of this chapter) was heard to tell his visitors to 'hang on, I will be with you in a minute, I just want to thank these nurses for looking after me'. There are many accounts of people who seem able to hang on until someone they love has had a chance to say goodbye – or even in some cases postpone their departure until their relatives have left, because they prefer to die alone.

The following account is interesting because it is one of the very few examples we have been given in which the 'messenger' was unwelcome, because the message was so profoundly distressing. It is perhaps surprising, given the common and natural human attitude that death is something to be dreaded, that so many people do seem to accept these portents of their own death with equanimity. Susan Grant:

Twelve years ago my husband, who had been ill for several years, had a fall and was taken into hospital. One day when I went to visit him he was distraught because he had seen his mother who had been dead for many years; he said she spoke to him. I asked what she had said, he replied, 'Just "Hello"', but somehow he knew that her coming meant he was going to die. I tried to comfort him, saying that she had come to help him get better, but I had heard of these apparitions before and I believe in life after death. He died a week later, and I believe she had come to help him 'cross over' but gave him a little extra time here with his family.

The experience of professional carers

Many of the accounts we have been given are from healthcare professionals who have wide experience in caring for the dying. Kate Dornan, a social worker who worked for 20 years in the field of palliative care in two hospices in Belfast, told us of the very many patients she had seen who seemed to be talking to, reaching out to, or simply smiling at something or someone no one else could see, and of families who had told her of a dying relative talking to or seeing people who are already dead. The following story is particularly interesting, because it illustrates so well what many other nurses and carers of the dying have told us, and what we found in our own interviews with carers (Chapter 2) about the conspiracy of silence that so often surrounds these experiences and makes it difficult for either staff or bereaved family members to discuss them openly.

One elderly lady, who was completely clear minded, told me of her mother standing at the foot of her bed. She said she could see a lot of others behind her mother, but they weren't clear. She presumed they were her siblings . . . all deceased. She was the last survivor of a family of 13. This experience had given her great comfort, as her mother had died suddenly when she was 15 years old. She was then in her 80s. When I conveyed this to the medical staff it was dismissed as being probably 'the result of the drugs on board'. I have to say I always found this patient totally lucid and there was no suggestion of confusion from the staff's observations. I had enough experience in this field to know when someone was adversely affected by medication. I am saddened that people are not prepared to be more open minded about this. It makes people reluctant to share their experiences as they fear they will be thought of as cranks etc. The elderly lady who shared hers with me was lucid enough to say . . . 'I can tell you this because I know you won't think I'm mad!'

When I started to work in palliative care I was at best agnostic but cannot dismiss the many experiences I witnessed and those that relatives chose to share with me. One mother spoke very movingly but with great clarity of the moment she perceived what she believed was her young adult daughter's spirit leaving her body . . . and she was a very intelligent and creditable woman.

A further account, which illustrates the uncanny accuracy of the estimated time of departure sometimes indicated by these visitors, was given to us by Mrs Judith Wilson, who used to work in an old people's home:

One lady was fading at the age of 97, just slipping away. She was talking to someone, we could see her doing it but no one was there. We asked her later who it was and she said it was her sister Alice who had died six months previously. She said Alice would come for her the next day at 2.30 p.m. I started work the next day at 2 p.m. and asked, 'Is she still here?' I was told she was dying, and as I was new to the job, someone would stay with me and see me through the death experience. Just before 2.30 p.m. she opened her eyes briefly, whispered 'Alice', held out her hand and passed away peacefully.

Mrs Wilson also witnessed a lady telling a relative not to visit the next day as 'she wouldn't be here' and she died in her sleep. Another carer in a residential home also commented that 'this sort of thing happens all the time'.

The latest one was a lady of 97 who was of sound mind when she died. During her life at the home she always lived in the present, never talked about the past or her relatives. Just before she died she said her mother was here to visit her, and that she had to go soon as her mother was waiting in the room, she didn't like to keep her waiting. Many of the residents who have died have said similar things; now we just expect it, we are not too surprised now. It's still kind of spooky though, isn't it?

Many carers feel that their training does nothing to prepare them for this aspect of the dying process, perhaps because their training is so soundly based in physical care that the tendency is to attribute everything to drugs or pathology, but also because these visions are not discussed in their training modules and if raised in class are dismissed as of little importance.[4] Even when staff members have witnessed one of these visions they are reluctant to discuss it among themselves for fear of ridicule. Julie Lewis told us:

I used to be very open minded, but during my nurse training I went through a stage of thinking that there had to be some scientifically measurable and demonstrable evidence for everything for it to be accepted. My thoughts then, about people seeing lights when they die, for example, were that they most probably could be explained by chemically induced hallucinatory experiences as the brain shuts down and cells die off. I didn't really explore beyond that to discover the variations and other experiences people have had that would suggest differently. A series of events took me away from that field, and now that I am removed from a research-based study area I've found I'm back to being much more open minded and accepting of things, whether I can explain them myself or not.

From all these accounts it is abundantly clear that deathbed visions are independent of pathology and drugs but are an intrinsic part of the dying process. Moreover, they occasionally occur as harbingers of death in healthy people who have no reason to think they are going to die, and in such cases one cannot possibly suggest a pathological interpretation of these visions. They seem to be clear, life-enhancing, motivating, and an intensely real part of the dying process.

It's also interesting to compare the features of deathbed visions with those near-death experiences which occur during cardiac arrest, which seem to occur during unconsciousness – indeed when the patient has to all intents and purposes temporarily died. In both, feelings of absolute peace, bliss or joy, and the experience of light, are common. And in both, the concept of a journey is central. The temporary death experiences (TDEs) are more narrative than deathbed visions and more detailed in terms of the world in which the vision is occurring. The TDE is a journey with a beginning, a middle and an end, which is the return. Sometimes the journey begins with an out-of-body experience, sometimes with a journey through a dark tunnel into a bright light. The area into which they move is usually well structured – usually culturally determined, and in Western experiences often a quintessential English garden. Here they may meet, and interact with, dead relatives or friends, or, less frequently, angelic beings, whose role is first to welcome and reassure them but then to indicate that the person must return because it is not yet their time to come and join them. It is always quite clear to the survivor that this is a point beyond which they cannot go – at any rate, not yet.

In both the deathbed vision and the TDE, the other world into which the person moves has a quality of absolute reality, but for the person experiencing a deathbed vision it is as if this world and the other reality overlap, dissolving into each other so that both can be experienced at once. The dying person can move freely from one to the other, and so too can the people who have come to collect them. The dying seldom seem confused by these two realities, and they are usually aware and accept that not everyone can see what they can see. They may retain their social awareness so that they conduct two separate conversations, and may even introduce the two sets of people to each other while still recognizing their difference.

Preparation for a journey

What is clear from all these stories is the message that these visions seem to offer to the dying. It is significant that although it is quite common for the person to tell their relatives that they won't be here tomorrow, they never say in so many words that this is because they will be dead. Always it is because they are going to be taken or collected, are going away, or will be on a journey. The purpose of the visions seems to be to prepare the dying person for this journey, sometimes giving a day or so's notice, and sometimes even an estimated time of departure, which often turns out to be surprisingly accurate.

Is this notion of a journey because the dying person can't conceive of their own death, which seems highly unlikely as everything in their situation points to it? What seems more credible is that something in the visions they have seen, the message conveyed by the visitors they have had, suggests continuity and not finality. It's an optimistic message – not simply heralding the end of a life, but the possibility of travelling hopefully onwards. It seems to be anticipation of this onward journey which convinces those who have these visions, just as it convinces people who have near-death experiences, that the prospect of death is nothing to be afraid of.

Chapter 4

Deathbed Coincidences

Ermutigung im Glauben:
Encouragement in the belief

I don't know what these things are – fantasies, dreams, wishes, delusions . . . I don't like them, they make my sense of reality wobble. (An interviewee)

Reported encounters with the dead still hold the same fascination for most people as they did when Gurney, Myers and Podmore published their survey over a century ago. And it seems that it is still remarkably common for a person to have a sudden realization that someone they are close to has died, and to discover later that this did indeed happen at the time they felt this strong intimation of the death. Often the people involved are living far apart, and the one who has the experience does not even know that the other is ill. In its most dramatic form they may see a vision of the dying person, usually either in a dream or on a sudden awakening from sleep, which seems to convey the

47

message that they have come to say goodbye and to give reassurance that all is well with them.

It is less common for these contacts with the dying to take place when the person is fully awake – in our own sample about two-thirds took place in dreams or on sudden awakenings, or in that drowsy state between sleeping and waking when it is hard to be quite certain whether you are in fact awake or asleep. In full wakefulness visions are seldom seen. More often a strong sense of presence of the person is felt, but they are not actually seen. Sometimes the waking person contacted is overwhelmed by a sudden realization that someone they love is ill or dying, or they may experience an uncharacteristic and inexplicable burst of grief or an intense feeling of unease, which they only later discover occurred at the time of the person's death.

Feelings of unease

Sarah Murray, a close friend of our daughter's, told us how she had been living in Florence for several months when one day, on her way back to her *pension* from an art class, she had a sudden, overwhelming feeling that something was wrong with her father – who, as far as she knew, was perfectly well and healthy at home in the USA. She had never experienced anything like this before, and the feeling was so powerful that she began to run, feeling that she must ring home immediately and find out if anything was wrong. When she reached the *pension* a phone message was waiting for her, telling her that her father had fallen down the cellar steps and broken his neck.

These experiences are usually brief, and while some, like Sarah's, give rise to a sudden strong conviction that someone they love is very ill or has died, other people simply have a feeling of uneasiness for no apparent reason. Katherine Knight was working in France at the time of her father's death in April 1986:

I had finished my work and was relaxing with work colleagues. I remember that I was in good humour and was laughing and joking. Out of the blue, I felt a shiver run down my spine and I momentarily became apprehensive. I remember that my first thought was about the money that I had in my room and hoping that it was safe. This feeling of apprehension was very out of character to how I had been previously feeling. I don't think it lasted for too long, but I can't be certain. I also can't remember the exact time, but it must have been mid to late afternoon.

I found out later that my father had died of a heart attack on a golf course in England. This took place about the same time as the shivering feeling occurred. Afterwards, when reminiscing about my father with family and friends, I used to joke that he was telling me to look after my money.

Kathie Guthrie's story is similar:

Sadly my brother was killed in a car crash some 20 years ago now. I had been at work intending to work till 5 o'clock. At 4.20 p.m. I was uneasy and began getting cross with myself, I just packed up and went home despite really needing to stay at work for one reason or another. I found out at 2.30 a.m. the next morning that my brother had been killed instantly by a drunk driver at 4.20 p.m.

These two accounts demonstrate how non-specific this feeling can often be. In the first case Katherine attributed her transient feeling of apprehension to her anxiety about the money in her room, and only in the light of subsequent events was another interpretation made. In the second case Kathie probably would not have given a second thought to her feeling of uneasiness had she not discovered the exact moment of her brother's death. It is ambiguous experiences like these two which reinforce the view that they can be dismissed as simply coincidences. And yet the feelings in each case were inexplicable and out of character, and the timing was approximately correct – indeed uncannily accurate in the second case.

However, in many of these accounts both the accuracy of the timing and the strength of the emotional response make it much harder to attribute them to 'just coincidence'. Here Wynn Bainbridge describes the day that her cousin died. Wynn was very close to her cousin, who had been suffering from cancer for about 13 months.

*On 1 January 2002 at about 12.45 p.m. I was working on my
computer when I started to feel really ill. I could not put my finger
on what was wrong – I had no pain or sickness, just an awful
feeling that everything was draining away from me: not like fainting, just a terrible weakness. This feeling lasted for about 20
minutes. Later in the day my cousin's son phoned me to let me
know that she had died. While she had decided not to have any
more treatment the doctors had expected her to live for another
couple of months, so it was very unexpected news. I asked him
what time she had died and he told me 12.55 p.m. I have always
found this to be extraordinary as this was the time when I felt so
ill.*

Janet Wright's story is equally convincing and, like Wynn
Bainbridge's account and many others, it emphasizes the close
emotional bond between the people involved:

*My husband died in 2005 and my son and daughter were with
me, at his hospice bedside, all through the night prior to his death.
My daughter, who was very close to her dad, is a professional
photographer; she had a wedding booked for the following day
and had no choice but to honour the arrangement, so, reluctantly,
she had to leave during the morning. At 1.30 p.m. my husband
passed away, without regaining consciousness from the previous
night (after we had all said our goodbyes). I couldn't immediately
phone my daughter [Jayne] as, obviously, I didn't want to inter-
rupt someone's wedding. She phoned me at about 2 p.m. and I
told her that her dad had passed away at 1.30. I heard her gasp,
but naturally thought she was upset at the sad news.*

*However, when she came to the hospice to see her dad she told
me that, although she had given her usual professional attention
to her work, trying to put her worries aside, she checked her watch
at 1.30, to ensure she was on schedule and then, inexplicably,
burst into tears – something she would not have allowed to happen
in the middle of someone's wedding. Given the exact timings, we
have always wondered if my husband 'visited' her at the moment
of his passing.*

The more detailed the accounts we get, the clearer it becomes that too often coincidence is an unsatisfactory explanation. This is Linda Denny's account of what happened on the day her husband's grandfather died. He had lived with them for three years, and had developed cancer of the oesophagus.

One night my husband – a musician – was working and another grandson was visiting him. I asked Granddad if he would like a cup of tea and he said, 'Yes please', so I went into the kitchen and put the kettle on. As I waited for it to boil, the phone rang and my husband said, 'Is Granddad all right?' so I said that yes, he was all right and I was just making him a cup of tea. He went on to say that he had been playing his guitar at work and a very strong feeling came over him that Granddad was there and he just had to get off the stage and phone me. I reassured him that Granddad was definitely OK and put the phone down. I made the tea, and just as I was about to take it in, my brother-in-law came out and said, 'He's gone.' He had just closed his eyes and died.

Although Linda's husband knew that his grandfather was term-inally ill, the fact that his feeling of unease was so intense that he was compelled to leave the stage and phone home, and the precise timing of his call at the moment his grandfather died, does suggest strongly that this was more than just coincidence. To maintain that both these factors are due simply to chance seems far more improbable than the alternative explanation – that this man had in fact somehow reached out to make contact with his grandson as he was dying.

Farewell visits

Sometimes these intimations of death are much more specific and take the form of a visit by the dying person, at the time of their death, to someone they are close to. Sometimes they are seen, occasionally they will speak, and often there is simply a strong and unmistakable sense of their presence. But always they seem to indicate that they are dying, have come to say goodbye, and that they are all right. There is no ambiguity about either the message or the messenger – the people who have this experience are never in any doubt about who it is who is contacting them, and what they are saying. This was Alex Cumming's farewell visit from his father:

I was a podiatrist and had just started my first patient. The time was 2.15 and while I worked I felt my father's presence with me in which he said that he had died and had just come to let me know. I acknowledged him and continued to work, knowing that he had passed on. There was nothing upsetting about it, it was quite reassuring. Half an hour later the phone rang and the receptionist answered it and I knew that it was my aunt (who was with my mother at that time) phoning me to tell me my father had died.

These visits, with their very specific farewell message from the dying person, are almost always described as comforting and reassuring – the relatives are left with the strong impression that all is well, and many say that they subsequently lose any fear of death. Jean Hallsworth contacted us after reading an article about approaching-death experiences, and her story is typical:

In 1979, my mother, 74 years old, had been taken in to hospital as an emergency due to feeling generally unwell on a Thursday. The following day she had perked up, and on Saturday it looked as if she would be coming home soon.

I did not visit her on Saturday night but went to see her on Sunday. She seemed to be recovering well. In the early hours of Monday morning, I awoke, half-asleep, and became aware of 'seeing' my mother in colour very clearly, standing in a spotlight in a very dark area, wearing her usual baggy everyday clothes. She was holding her hands together tightly and saying urgently and emphatically, 'Don't worry Jean, I'm all right.' This was repeated, then she faded. I turned to the bedside clock and it was 3.20 a.m.

I was told the following day by the nurse that she had died at 3.20 a.m. This was such an odd experience that I thought I had perhaps dreamed it or maybe I was a bit crackers, and I told no

*one at the time; but the article made me feel that perhaps I wasn't
as daft as I thought I was.*

Jane Herbert's mother died when she was 12, and after she
had died her father told her the following story.

*My mother had been suffering for two years from a medullary blas-
toma [brain tumour] only discovered post mortem. She obviously
had been deteriorating slowly but her death was not expected
imminently. She was in and out of St Thomas's Hospital and was
experiencing another stay there when she died. My father (a Cam-
bridge/St Thomas's doctor) is not a man given to flights of fancy,
nor is he particularly religious. He was lying in bed one night,
reading, when he heard or felt my mother's voice or presence. He
'understood' from her that she was 'going' and he put his book
down and just said, 'It's all right darling.' Ten minutes later, St
Thomas's phoned to say that she had died.*

Later in life Jane wished she had asked him for more details,
whether he physically heard her mother's voice for example, or
whether it was just an intense 'knowing'. Unfortunately, by that
time her father had a dementing illness and she could not discover anything further. But certainly the impression given is that,
like Alex Cumming, he took the visit very much in his stride.

Physical manifestations

Occasionally these contacts with the dying can take a very physical form. Anne Liddell awoke one night because someone was
gripping her hand very tightly. Next day she discovered that this
was the time her grandmother died. Jean Henfrey awoke at the
moment her grandmother died, with the comforting feeling of
her covers being tucked in around her. John Farr was woken by
the telephone at the time of his father's death, and heard no
voice, but music – his father had loved music and been a musician. The day of his mother's death, Jonathan Leiserach felt
someone tugging at his sleeve. The day his grandmother died,
John Grant was troubled by a strange smell which grew stronger

throughout the day. Mrs Collie describes how her father heard a child's footsteps at the time his child died in hospital.

My late father, Peter Kidd, was born in 1910 and was a farm servant in Banffshire. In 1939 his oldest son, then a toddler, was in hospital, having been burned in a fire. One evening as Dad sat at the fire he heard a child's footsteps pass by and disappear in the distance and he told my mother that the boy had died – which he had. My father was distraught and cycled to his parents' croft to speak to his mother, and on his way home he was still distraught, but he told me that as he cycled over a hillock he felt this burden being lifted from him.

Feeling the symptoms of the dying

Strangest of all these physical manifestations are several accounts from people who had inexplicable and often very distressing physical symptoms which lasted for several minutes and seemed, with hindsight, to mirror the feelings that the dying person may have been experiencing. Elizabeth Wood, Raymond Hunt, June Sullivan and Janice Ashton all describe such experiences.

Elizabeth's brother had terminal throat cancer but she did not know this. Although she had not seen him for several years, she feels she was closer to him than other members of the family, and feels it natural that this dying contact should have been with her.

It was during the night of Saturday 11 November 2006. I was woken up very suddenly by something incredibly violent. It made me sit bolt upright by the side of my bed saying repeatedly: 'I don't want to know, I absolutely don't want to know, it is too awful.' I walked to my bathroom to try and forget and think of something else but was seized by the overwhelming conviction that I was dying. I stood stooped in the middle of my bathroom floor, arms hanging down in front of me, panic-stricken by the knowledge I was dying, not knowing exactly why, except that all of my body 'felt wrong'. I tried to analyse what could be wrong but all I could feel was that nothing in my body felt right, my entire body was dying. I decided that since I was dying, I might as well lie on my bed. So I returned to bed and fell promptly asleep again. I would say it was by far the worst night of my life and I felt deeply affected and fragile the next day. I learned the following day, Monday, that my brother had died. He had had a massive haemorrhage . . . I believe that my extremely violent awakening was . . . the feeling of life leaving his body as his blood ran out.

The following two stories also suggest such a strong correlation between the physical symptoms felt by the dying person and the pain experienced by the person they are close to that it is hard to believe they are not linked in some way. In Chapters 12 and 13 we'll look a little further at some of the evidence which suggests that we may indeed be linked together in a way we don't yet fully understand. June Sullivan:

A dear friend of mine, considerably older than me, had been in poor health for some time. She had always professed a great deal of affection for me, having known me since childhood, and I had always visited her regularly in her home. On a certain Friday, a mutual friend telephoned me to say our friend had been taken to hospital, but was 'comfortable', so we arranged to meet the following afternoon to visit her. That night I awoke with severe pains in my chest which persisted for a couple of hours, although I never felt the need to call for any help. Suddenly, and quite miraculously, the pain went and I took myself to bed, glancing at the clock and putting my discomfort down to indigestion. At about 6.30 the following morning the phone rang and my husband answered it. Doris died at half-past two, exactly the time my pain had gone. I learned later that the surgeons had tried for two hours to save my friend's poor heart and their efforts had ceased at 2.20 and she died a few minutes later. I have always felt that for those two hours Doris was trying to get in touch with me.

Janice Ashton:

I was on the way to work. The time was around 8.15 in the morning and my husband had just stopped to drop me off at a point from where I used to walk the last 15 minutes or so to work.

As I shut the car door, I experienced a severe pain around my heart. I tried to wave my husband to stop the car but without success, and I therefore struggled to the back of the pavement and held on to the fence. At that time I then thought, 'I hope I'm not going to have heart trouble like Dad.' The pain then went away and I walked on to work.

I had only been at my desk for about ten minutes when I had a telephone call from my father's place of work – the manager rang to tell me that my father had had a heart attack and had been taken to the hospital. He had collapsed soon after arriving at work, which was 7.30 a.m. Around five minutes after this call I had another call saying that my father had been dead on arrival at the hospital.

In May 1966 Raymond Hunt was home on leave from the Merchant Navy to visit his father, who was seriously ill in hospital with lung cancer.

After visiting him on 26 May I had a few beers as normal at my local before retiring to bed, falling sound asleep . . . The next thing I remember was waking up with pains in my chest and trouble with my breathing. I tried to reach the light switch but could not because of the pains. I remember looking at the clock at the side of my bed and believe it was 4.15 a.m. The pains were now intense and I was fighting for my breath. I remember grabbing my mouth, forcing it open to help me to breathe. I was fighting for all I was worth but the pains were now unbearable. Then the pains subsided and I was overwhelmed with feelings of great peace and love. All the pain had gone. I cannot possibly describe the feelings of love and great peace I experienced. I did not want the feelings to end, and wherever I was or was going to I wanted that. I did not want to come back to my body or this world.

I awoke with a start with someone knocking on the door at about 7 a.m. It was a neighbour on his way to work who had kindly agreed to take any telephone messages from the hospital (we did not have a phone). I knew of course before I opened the door what he was going to say – that my father had passed away during the night . . .

The experience had not affected my body: I was just as fit and alive as before I went to bed. But I'm sure you can understand the enormous mental effect it had on me. I could not and still cannot deny what had happened to me . . . I realized that all living things are precious, from the smallest to the largest, including flowers, plants, trees . . . We must all strive for a better world, by helping each other, without hurting anybody in mind or body. I hope my experience can help others, which is maybe why it happened. I know there is nothing to fear in death, and my father was happy.

The fascinating thing about this experience is how very closely it mirrors the near-death experience. What Raymond describes – the intense pain which suddenly subsides, as though he had left his body, the reluctance to return to his body or this world, the very strong and lasting impression the experience made, and the total lack of fear at the prospect of death – are all described again and again by people who have had near-death experiences. It is as if Raymond was somehow sharing the experience with his father.

Two ghost stories

The majority of farewell visits from the dying occur either in dreams or on a sudden awakening from sleep, or in that drowsy half-awake, half-asleep state – the hypnagogic state – in which the person may not really know whether or not they were dreaming. They are experienced less often during the course of everyday life when the person is fully awake, and when they do occur the 'visitor' is seldom seen but only felt as a 'presence'. So the following two accounts, in which the dying person was seen in a very physical form during the course of a normal day, are unusual.

Gladys Asten's daughter wrote to us, at her mother's request, to tell us the following fascinating story.

This story dates back to a time during the Second World War. Mum had gone to visit her sister Irene who was a singer with a band working with the Entertainments National Service Associa-

tion away from home. During the day, around lunchtime, they had gone out for a walk along a towpath when Irene spotted a man in Fleet Air Arm pilot's uniform on the bridge looking towards them. She said to Mum, 'Oh, doesn't that man on the bridge look like Harold?' (Harold Shaw was Irene's boyfriend). They both agreed and made their way to the bridge to see if it really was him, or someone else who just looked like him and was wearing the same uniform that Harold wore. However, when they got to the bridge, the man had disappeared. There was no one around at all apart from the two of them, nowhere that anyone could have gone to without still being visible, and neither of them could work out how or when the man had disappeared from their sight. This left them both feeling puzzled, and they discussed it on and off for the rest of that day.

The following day, their plan was to return home together so that Irene could surprise her mother (my gran) with a visit on her birthday. When Gran returned home, the girls were both already there and Irene quickly hid behind the settee with the intent of jumping out to surprise her. However, when Gran came into the house, not knowing Irene was behind the settee, she immediately began to tell Mum of some terrible news – that Harold had been killed when his plane was brought down by enemy fire over the Orkneys. It had happened the previous day around lunchtime.

This story is especially interesting because both sisters saw the figure and both were equally convinced it was Harold, and also because the 'sighting' occurred when both were fully awake. The following account sent to us by Jenny Stiles is of a similar daytime sighting by someone who had no way of knowing that the person they saw had died, or was even ill.

My mother died just before Christmas, Sunday 17 December 2006 at 9.10 p.m. She had suffered a massive stroke six weeks earlier with no chance of recovery. I had been trying to contact my brother in the USA for several months to let him know she had been in a residential care home for 18 months and was rapidly declining. I knew he had moved from Nashville to Washington DC but I had no address or telephone number for him and the search was fruit-

less. Then, out of the blue, four days after our mother died, he called me one evening. He was not surprised to hear she had died, he told me he had seen her walking down the street in Washington the previous Sunday afternoon; the time difference between the UK and USA when he thought he saw her was the time she died, or was 'passing over'. He described what she had been wearing – it was a cream suit she owned – but my brother had not seen her for nearly ten years and would not have known she had bought that outfit.

It's very difficult to interpret these two experiences. Why, if they were truly farewell visits by the dying, did they not make a more personal contact with the person they had evidently come to see? And in the first account, why did both sisters see the figure of Harold when his emotional bond was only with Irene? Could it be that the emotional link between sisters allowed them both to view the apparition? Although it is fanciful, perhaps the reason that the airman did not come closer to say goodbye was just because both sisters seemed to be involved in the process. However, this does not explain the second account. It would be interesting to know what the son's emotions were when he 'saw' his mother, and whether she was indeed letting him know that she had died. The fact that he then rang his sister 'out of the blue' certainly suggests that it was his vision which prompted him to do so.

Dream visitors

By far the most common way for the dying to make their farewell visits was during a dream, or when the person suddenly awoke with an overwhelming realization that something was wrong, or that someone was trying to contact them. Of over 100 accounts, 66 per cent occurred either in dreams or on a sudden awakening from sleep.

In October 1987 Terry Woods was serving in the Royal Navy as a submariner on board HMS *Revenge* and had sailed for an eight-week patrol.

Two days after diving I was asleep in bed and had a very real dream that my grandfather had 'died'. The dream was very strange in that all of our family was waiting in the place where our grandparents had lived and that I was the last one to arrive. When I arrived and my grandfather saw that we were all there, he picked up my nephew's bike and said, 'That's it, I'm off' and pedalled off over a walkway and disappeared. I woke up the next morning and told my best friend that 'I had a really weird dream that my granddad had died'. My friend reassured me that it was only a dream and not to worry.

While on patrol, submariners are never told of any bad news. This was a problem for the Royal Navy as our next-of-kin were only allowed 40 words a week to inform us of any news (family-grams) – the Navy duly vetted such messages. My mother insisted that my wife put in the family-gram that she was 'sorry about Granddad'. On receipt of my wife's message, the Royal Navy withheld all family-grams for me for three weeks – so I knew something was wrong! The Captain then decided to tell me that the reason for my messages being withheld was because my paternal grandfather had passed away, at approximately 3 a.m. on 18 October 1987. I had no idea that he had been ill. At the time of his death I was fast asleep 200 feet under the Atlantic Ocean. Very spooky . . .

This again highlights the fact that space is no bar for these communications, and even being under water can't stop them. It is certainly not uncommon for people who are away from their families to have anxiety dreams about them, but Terry says the dream was very real, and strange, and this, combined with the precise timing, adds weight to the idea that it may have been communication rather than coincidence.

For Phillip Healey a premonition of his mother's death also came to him in a dream, a dream which he recognized as having some special quality. His mother, whom he was very close to, had dementia. He and his father and sister had looked after her for as long as they could, but finally had to put her in a nursing home.

On the morning of 26 July I had what I can only describe as a dream premonition. It was in colour and I have never had a dream like it before. Mum phoned me up and said, 'Hello Phillip.' I said, 'Mum, are you OK?' She said, 'Yes, I'm all right but I've got to go.' I woke up and knew it was real. The following morning she passed away.

Dream accounts are interesting because of the narrative quality of the experiences and the wrapping up of the information in dream imagery. Usually though the meaning of the dream is quite apparent to the dreamer. Here Laura Scales describes what happened the night her mother died:

I had a vivid dream. Mum walked into my dining room wearing shorts, walking shoes and a fleece jacket; she was perfectly well and looked younger than she had done for many years! She sat down in an old wicker chair in the dining room. I was in the kitchen and when I turned and saw her I ran across and shouted, 'What are you doing here? You're better!' As I looked along what should have been my hallway, I could see the Cottage Hospital corridor and one of the nurses walking towards me. I called out to the nurse, 'She's better – look!' Mum looked at me and said, 'I am ready to leave now.' I immediately knew that she meant that she was about to die and 'let go'. I looked at her and I said, 'But we haven't said goodbye' and I tried to kiss her, but my face passed through her face as if she wasn't really there. We both looked up and said quietly, 'Please God, just this once!' I was then able to kiss her properly and she disappeared from the dream.

I awoke with a start and looked at the clock in the bedroom – I knew that what I had dreamt was significant. It was 2.15 a.m. The next morning I got up at 5 a.m., anxious for news. The phone rang at 7 a.m. – it was the Cottage Hospital ringing to let us know that Mum had died at 2.50 a.m., just half an hour or so after my dream.

What makes the dream even more unusual is that Mum had not been able to visit my house for about nine months; she was unable to walk and was not well enough to make the journey. In that time I had made significant alterations to the dining room which Mum had never seen. In my dream the dining room was as Mum would have last seen it; it was as if I was seeing it through her eyes, not mine. Of course, you could say I wanted Mum to come and say goodbye and I needed that closure. Whatever the reason for the dream, it will always be a special moment in my life.

There is an interesting parallel here between this dream and those described earlier in this chapter in which people seem to experience the physical pain of the dying. Laura comments that it is as if she is seeing through her mother's eyes. This is again indicative, first of the strong emotional connection that is a common factor in all these coincidences, and second, that the experience is driven by the dying person, who seems to import their own world into the experience. It is worth remembering this, as in many of the accounts there are small hints that this is what is in fact happening.

Notice too the language in the three previous dreams. Terry's granddad: 'That's it, I'm off.' Phillip's mother: 'I'm all right but I've got to go.' And Laura Scales' mother tells her: 'I'm ready to leave now.' Valerie Feasby-Quigley's father (p. 82) also said 'I think I'll go now', language which is more suggestive of the beginning of a journey than the end of a life. This journeying language crops up time and again, and as we saw in the previous chapter, it's often mentioned by relatives who have witnessed the visions of the dying: 'He seemed to be talking to someone and just before he died he said, "Right, I am ready now, you can get my coat".' 'Death', it seems, is not a concept the dying recognize. It's interesting that the rather euphemistic phrase 'passing on' is so often used when describing death; perhaps we should not, after all, regard it as euphemistic but rather as a feeling which the dying may experience and which they try to convey to their survivors.

Richard Bufton is now a college lecturer and heading for retirement. But in the early 1970s he was a commercial diver out in the Gulf:

I was taking a diving vessel from Bahrain to Ras Tanurra in Saudi Arabia and I had just handed over control of the vessel to another diver. It was in the middle of the British postal strike and we had not received any post for some time. I was lying on the bunk in the forward cabin and in a sort of half-asleep state, when what I can only describe as a vision similar to seeing a teletype ribbon went past my eyes. The words – which I read in my mind – simply said, 'Your grandfather is dead.'

I jumped up and climbed the three or four steps into the main cabin, saying to my friend that I had to make a radio-telephone call. I put out a link call through Bahrain Radio to my mother in the UK, and when she answered the phone she said that she had some bad news. I interrupted my mother to tell her that the reason I had rung was because I knew my grandfather was dead.

In this accurately observed account, Richard describes his mental state at the time of the communication as half-awake and half-asleep. This is the mental state that was found to be effective for telepathy in the Ganzfeld experiment (see Chapter 6, p. 100), and it might perhaps facilitate a telepathic linking with the dying person.

The following account shows very clearly the intensity of emotion that these dreams can convey, and the absolute conviction that they are not just ordinary dreams. Jean Cheesman's husband was bipolar and committed suicide in February 1989. At the time, they were separated but remained good friends and very close. She had seen him the previous day and they had spent time together and he had seemed very positive.

I woke up crying at 3 o'clock the next morning out of a very 'real' dream where Vincent was sitting on the end of my bed and telling me not to cry any more and that it was all over and that he was finally at peace.

I got up, on 'automatic', did some work I needed to do, two clients phoned me around 8 o'clock and I freaked them out completely as I told them I would be taking some time out as my husband had just died. I went over to his flat with Merlin, our dog, and called the police. The Coroner's report was that Vin had indeed died around 3 a.m.

Jean's account demonstrates very well the special quality which these dreams have and which the dreamer recognizes. That she was convinced enough to tell her clients that her husband had just died before she had confirmation shows the quality of absolute reality that the dream carried.

All recipients of these dream visits have exactly the same reaction to them – they usually feel enormously comforted and reassured because so often the message their 'visitor' seems to convey is that they are all right. And because the person they love has come to say a final goodbye to them, there is a feeling of rounding off, of closure, which seems to make the mourning process easier.

Dilys Gannon's experience when her grandmother died conveyed just such a message, though she is clearly unsure whether she was truly awake or perhaps in some half-awake, half-asleep state at the time:

One night I was lying in bed when I was awakened, or at least I at first thought I had been awakened: afterwards I was not sure that I had experienced the 'happening' when I was truly awake in the accepted sense. There came into my vision a bright light and there I saw my grandmother looking at me through a mirror. The mirror had great significance for me and for my grandmother, as she had spent many hours with me, when I was a child, looking into this mirror. She used to ask me questions about things I could see through the mirror and what significance they had. As the light shone through and around this mirror, I saw the figure of my grandmother explaining to me that she had died, but I was not to be upset because she was extremely happy. There was an extreme moment of peace and quiet and I felt the light surrounding me like a blanket. When I woke up I telephoned my mother, who told me I must have been mistaken as we would have heard if my grandmother was ill. Later that day my aunt telephoned to say that my grandmother had died the previous night. She had not wanted to tell us about her illness, as she had hoped she would get better, and she also delayed telephoning us about the death because she was too upset to give us the news immediately.

Here again there are echoes of the near-death experience – the peace and quiet and light surrounding her 'like a blanket'. It is hard not to imagine that Dilys was somehow sharing her grand-mother's own experience.

Sudden awakenings

So many people have reported experiences which occurred during a sudden awakening from sleep, or in the 'half-awake, half-asleep' state that it does seem as if this is a state in which people are particularly receptive to farewell visits from the dying. In nearly every case the person is certain that they really did awake, and the whole thing was not a dream. Tina Myer, who has lived in Australia for the past 26 years, and has family living in London, told us what happened the night her brother died:

One night in 1991, while sleeping, I was suddenly awoken – but not in the normal way where one wakes up and is drowsy. From being fast asleep I was suddenly wide awake, and as my eyes opened in the total darkness of the room, there, coming towards me, quite fast, from the foot of the bed, was the face, in white, of my brother back in London. This was not a dream or my imagin-ation. I awoke my husband to tell him what had happened.

I subsequently learned that my dear brother, who had caught a cold which turned into bronchial pneumonia, had died. I can only assume that he was, at the time he was slipping away, think-ing of me and, I guess, that by his thinking of me his soul was instantly with me.

As in all these accounts, it is the dying person who seems to drive the experience, while the one they visit is simply a passive receiver. If we are to give credence to any of these experiences, we have to presuppose that 'mind' is not identical with 'brain', and that perhaps at death there is a loosening of the ties between them which provides a special facility at this time for this kind of communication.

Julie Salmon also experienced what she describes as a 'violent awakening' at the time of her mother's death:

My mother died at 2 a.m. on 10 December 1993. She had been suffering from breast cancer and was undergoing treatment. I had not been informed that she was terminally ill. However, she took a turn for the worse around 7 December and was admitted to Poole Hospital, Dorset and I visited her there on 8 December. I went to bed on that eve of 9 December and was fast asleep when I suddenly awoke, sat bolt upright in bed and called out 'Mum'. I actually physically reached for the phone to call the hospital, but on checking the time it was 2 a.m. I therefore told myself to 'get a grip' and that I was being hysterical and neurotic, and I eventually fell back to sleep a couple of hours later. I was awoken at 7.30 a.m. on 10 December by my aunt and stepfather to say that Mum had died – at 2 a.m. The experience was deeply upsetting and I shall never forget it. I am crying now while typing this – the whole experience of waking suddenly like that was what I can only describe as 'violent'. Maybe it was psychosomatic, who knows? But it was very real to me, and still is. I have no doubt that she reached out to me at that moment.

The intensity of emotion that these experiences so often generate is indicated very clearly by the fact that the memory of hers still has the power to reduce Julie to tears years later. Julie is one of the few people who described her experience as 'deeply upsetting' rather than comforting.

Kath McMahon:

My father was in hospital, and it was in the middle of the night. At the time of his death, around 3 a.m., he visited me and woke me from my sleep. He stood at the end of my bed, just smiling at me and looking down on me. It was the most wonderful and beautiful experience I have ever had; no words were exchanged. I can remember feeling incredibly content and happy, and I drifted back off to sleep in a state of euphoria. The next morning I got up and did my usual chores, forgetting all about the events of the previous night, and then the phone rang. I knew it was my mother, and before she could say anything I informed her that my father had died, last night. She was amazed at my experience.

A scientific explanation that could be offered for imagery seen on awakening is that it is a hypnopompic hallucination. Some people have very strong visual imagery when they awake, and it could be argued that Kath's account is simply a normal waking hallucination. However, some people regularly have these hypnopompic hallucinations and would recognize them for what they are. Kath makes it quite clear that it was just not like that. It was the most wonderful experience that she had ever had. Clearly there was nothing ordinary about the experience. But also note, as is usual in these cases, that no words were exchanged. It's the feeling and the knowledge that seem to be important.

Occasionally the visitor does speak, though usually simply to attract attention, usually by calling a name. It seems to be very rare that there is any sort of conversation between them. And in some of the accounts it is not always clear whether mind-to-mind communication was taking place without words being spoken, or whether spoken words were actually heard, as in the following account by Richard Geall:

While serving with the Royal Navy in Portsmouth I received a phone call from my mother in Brighton one Monday evening informing me that my father, whom I knew was very ill with cancer, had been admitted to a hospice and may not last out the week. My intention was to apply for compassionate leave the following day, but at about 3.30 a.m. I was suddenly awake and shot bolt upright in bed hearing my father calling my name. I did not 'see' him but I clearly heard his voice as though he were in the room. I did not go back to sleep but eventually went into work as normal, where I was informed that the duty officer had received a call saying that my father had died at about 3.30 a.m. But I already knew – my father had told me. My mother later said that he was calling for me as he died. I love him dearly and ever since that day I have had an overwhelming sense of his presence.

Malcolm McCallum and Carol Duncan were also both woken by someone calling their name. Malcolm's father had had open-heart surgery three months earlier, and although his life expectancy was not considered to be long, no one expected his death to be imminent.

On the night of his death he was at his own home in Darlington. I was with my own family at my home in a neighbouring village. At some time in the night I was woken up by my father calling my name. As he was calling, I could see what I can only assume to have been his spirit rising high into the night sky. Before picking up our telephone, which rang earlier than usual on the following morning, I was able to tell my wife that it was my mother ringing to tell me that my father had died.

Angie Baird's little girl was born in May 1979 but unfortunately was sick with a blood disorder and was kept in the intensive care baby unit. For 48 hours she hung on and the doctors were optimistic that the worst was over.

My bed was just opposite the nurses' station. I awoke suddenly at 3 a.m. on the third morning shaking and tearful and called the nurse and asked if I could be taken up to the next floor to see my baby. I am not a pushy person at all but had a really strong feeling that I needed to go right then and there. The nurse said it was a strange request at that time of the morning but would phone the ICU to see if they would mind. The nurse said that the phone in the ICU was engaged and she would ring again in a moment. Five or so minutes later the phone on the station desk rang. The reason why it was engaged when the nurse rang was that the sister in the ICU was trying to ring down to break the devastating news that my daughter had just passed away. At EXACTLY 3 a.m.!

That feeling I had at 3 a.m. was so strong. I just KNEW that something was wrong. It shows how deep a mother's bond goes, no matter how short the bonding time is.

In nearly all our experiences it has been very clear that it is the person dying who seems to be driving the contact. But in this example it is difficult to argue that a child only two days old is able to drive the experience in a way that one assumes an older child or adult might. It raises the question of the link between a newborn baby and its mother, and whether this link is somehow hard-wired between the two so that the mother senses at a distance the needs of a newborn infant.

Clairvoyant dreams

The following dream account, sent to us by Angelina Clements, is interesting and unusual because it seems to fall more into the category of clairvoyance than telepathy. It sounds very much as though she was in the drowsy state between sleeping and waking, though she herself is unsure about this and felt that she was wide awake.

At 6.11 a.m. on the morning her daughter was to die in a car accident, while she lay in bed, Angelina was watching what looked like a conservatory which started to rise up into the sky, and as it did so it changed from being a conservatory to a glass coffin. At the time it puzzled her and she could not explain it. She says:

I recall thinking, 'That was strange . . .' because I didn't feel like I had just woken up, it didn't feel like I had been dreaming . . . it felt like I was wide awake and had just returned from somewhere.

Later she discovered that the accident had happened exactly at the time she had this experience. She also saw a photo of her daughter's car, a new Mini Cooper with a glass roof on which was a white logo, and it seemed to her that she had somehow been there, at the time of the accident. She goes on:

If I was at the scene of the accident, watching down onto the roof of the spinning car, I believe my mind might well have thought I was looking at a conservatory as it tried to interpret what the glass and white lines actually were.

Preparatory visits

The following two reports are unusual in that a visit by a dead relative gives prior warning of a death to come. This is Margaret Catherine's unusual 'two-stage' experience.

Fifteen years ago, I was woken at 2 a.m. by a sharp push in the back. It woke me up suddenly, but I was not afraid, and just knew that my late mother-in-law was standing beside the bed. I knew exactly who it was, even though I could not see anything at all. I drifted back to sleep and had the most vivid dream, where my 22-year-old son was talking to me. He was telling me that he was dead but that I was not to worry or be upset because he was all right . . . When I woke I was very disturbed and tried to contact my son. I found out later that day that he had been drowned the previous night. I am convinced that he did contact me, as did his grandmother who loved him deeply. I have drawn great comfort from his visit to me over the years . . . I can assure you that I am not remotely unhinged and am a very down-to-earth lady, but I do know that my experiences are real, and I have talked to many people who have lost loved ones and had similar experiences.

The interesting twist in this story is that it combines a warning visit to the boy's mother from his grandmother before he himself appears in the dream. Was this a coincidence? It could be, of course. But this was a young boy whose death couldn't have been anticipated or expected. It does seem as though the only basis for disbelieving it is a strict adherence to the belief that it could not happen. Mike Askins described a similar premonitory visit before the death of his mother:

I had left England in early February 2002 to work on a copper project in northern Chile, having said goodbyes to my immediate family, including my mother who was 89 and in reasonable health. About three weeks later, on a Friday night I awoke around 12 midnight (5 a.m. British time) having experienced an unusual dream which involved me being a silent and unseen witness to an event where my grandmother and her son (my mother's mum and brother, both deceased) dressed in black entered a house stating that 'they had come to view the body'. It made me waken, and I thought then that my mother had died.

The next morning at the office at around 7 a.m. I rang home, with no response. It was a couple of hours later that my wife

*phoned me to tell me that my mother who had been taken into hos-
pital a few days earlier had died that morning in hospital. She
had died around 7.30 a.m. (2.30 a.m. Chile time) which was
about two and a half hours after my dream.*

A cool reception

Nearly all the people who have described their experiences to us
have said that they are comforting and reassuring. But very occasionally the visitors are unwelcome and their visits thoroughly
disconcerting, or even frightening.

Judy Gaskell describes how, on the night of her mother's
death, her mother was staying in Judy's sister's house with some
of her grandchildren and son-in-law.

*In the middle of the night, Alice, her favourite granddaughter,
was awakened by a figure standing at the end of her bed. It was
her grandmother, my mother, telling her she had died and to tell
her father as she did not want to shock her daughter, my sister, in
the morning. Alice felt frozen in her bed, but eventually awoke her
father who looked in on my mother to find her still warm but
dead. He called in the family doctor who lived nearby in the
village, and the doctor confirmed that my mother had only just
passed on and gave the approximate time of death as 2 a.m.
When Alice looked at her alarm clock in the morning it had
stopped at 2 a.m.*

Not only is the response unusual, but this seems to be a deathbed
coincidence by proxy, and it is interesting that Alice's grandmother told her in some detail the reason for the visit, and why
she was not contacting the next-of-kin directly, as it were. Her
comment about the clock stopping is also intriguing – several
people have told us about this particular phenomenon, and their
accounts are given in Chapter 8.

Aileen Wright was also too afraid to respond to her visitor.
Aileen had been with her husband to visit her father-in-law in
hospital:

As we left, I said to my father-in-law, 'See you again soon.' He shook his head and replied firmly, 'No'. Two days later and around 1.30 in the early hours of the night, I awoke in a sweat – my father-in-law was standing by our bed. He was asking me to wake John, because he wanted to say 'Goodbye'. But I let my father-in-law down, because I felt too afraid to do so and buried myself away from what seemed to be a very real person in our room! I replied that I was too afraid to do so. Kindly, he seemed to accept my let-down – I sensed he understood my fear – and conveyed 'Never mind' . . . Then my father-in-law faded away. A few minutes later – and due to my restlessness – John awoke and asked what was wrong. When I told him that I had just seen his dad, he replied, 'OK', as if I had dreamt it, and then returned to his slumbers. But I definitely did not have a dream! The next morning the telephone rang at around 8 a.m. It was John's mother to say that his father had died in the night. The time given – 1.30.

Here again, it is interesting to speculate about why it was Aileen who was awoken – or who awoke – and not her husband. We have found throughout this work that different people have different sensitivities. Some people see the deathbed visions of their dying relatives, others don't. Some people have farewell visits from the dying, others don't. It's not possible to say what this factor is, but everyone who does any kind of parapsychological research recognizes what is known as the 'sheep–goat' effect. With some people (the sheep), parapsychological experiments tend to work; with others (the goats) they never do. Maybe in this particular case we had a sheep and a goat in the same bed.

The following account by Derek Whitehead is one of the few cases we have been told about where the young recipient of a farewell visit not only failed to understand its significance but was scared stiff by it. Perhaps because of this he needed an additional hint given in a dream. Unfortunately he wouldn't have understood this either if his friend had not interpreted it for him.

When I was 18 I was in the Merchant Navy crossing the Pacific Ocean on the way to Australia. One night I was laid on my bunk reading a male magazine – Mayfair or Playboy I think. I looked up and my grandfather was stood next to me looking at me. Well, I shot off the bed, I did scream and he was still there looking at me – I ran for my life up to the bridge, shaking like a leaf. When I came back down he had gone – that night I dreamed that I was trying to visit a ship in dry dock but the crew would not let me on board – which was unheard of in real life. They told me that it was not for me. I awoke at about 4.30 and went onto the bridge and told the mate what had happened. He came from Buckie in Scotland and said that in fishing families, dreaming of a ship on dry land told of a death in the family. I put all this down in a letter to send to my parents. About three weeks later we got to Australia, and the pilot took the post ashore with him. Later that day the agent brought our post on board with a letter from Mum: the day and date were about the same time that Granddad had died.

Derek adds, 'I don't know what these things are – fantasies, dreams, wishes, delusions . . . I don't like them, they make my sense of reality wobble.'

The prime of life

An observation that several people have made about their visitors is that they are often described as looking as though they were in the prime of life, with any injuries healed. Laura Scales, for example, in her dream described on p. 61, described her mother as 'perfectly well and looked younger than she had done for many years'! This is interesting because it mirrors very closely what people report when they see dead relatives in the near-death experience. Brenda Barker describes a similar transformation in her father when he visited her on the night he died. Again, note that the implication is that the person is 'on his way' somewhere and has been given special 'permission' to make a detour.

When I retired to bed I was very restless. I tossed this way and that until suddenly in the early hours my father stood by my bed. He had been ill for a long time, but there he was standing in his prime of life. He didn't speak. My restlessness ceased and I fell asleep. In the morning I knew . . . my father had died late the evening before and had been permitted to visit me on his way into the next life.

Hilary Froude is an SRN who says she has been a practising nurse/midwife for many years, and during that time has had some unusual experiences.

The one that was the strangest but perhaps most comforting was when my father died last September. At 3 a.m. something woke me up, and after looking at my clock I noticed my father standing outside the bedroom door with his arms outstretched towards me – albeit a slightly younger version (40–50 rather than the 81 he actually was). I got up and went towards him with my arms outstretched, and he said, 'It's all right, I'm better now' before he disappeared through the wall. At that moment, my father was actually in a nursing home in the final stages of Alzheimer's and died at 6 a.m. that morning.

If we make the assumption that this experience is driven by the dying person, then we again have to conclude that mind and brain are to some extent different. In Alzheimer's disease the memory circuits are destroyed to the point where the sufferer has no memory of where or who he is or what his history has been, or even that he has a daughter. But here in the experience he is somehow linked to his daughter. In our nursing home study we again and again heard stories about people dying with advanced Alzheimer's disease, unable even to recognize members of their family. Sometimes in a brief, lucid interval shortly before death, they became alert, recognized their family and took their leave of them before dying. The mechanism for this is quite obscure, but the fact that it does occur is well reported.

Here Keith Scrivener describes the night his father-in-law died. He had been very ill from stomach cancer for a long time, and during his illness Keith and his wife had taken their infant son, the old man's only grandchild, to see him as often as possible, as his spirits were always lifted by the child's presence.

The doctors said my father-in-law only had a few more weeks of life, but his death was not thought to be imminent. He was, however, incapable of moving by himself and had wasted away to almost skeletal proportions.

At that time my wife and I shared a double bed, with our infant son in a cot beside us. We all went off to sleep, but later I awoke suddenly; I was wide awake, not sleepy or in a dreamlike state. There, bending over my son's cot, was my father-in-law, not skeletal but in his earlier healthy proportions. He turned to me and said, 'It's all right, I just want to say goodbye to the boy.' Although he was by then in his fifties, my father-in-law looked far younger, radiantly healthy and happy. I looked at the clock and noted the time, then lay back in my bed as nothing seemed strange about this nocturnal visit; in fact I was completely calm, as it seemed very peaceful and normal, and I was instantly asleep again. My wife [his daughter] had slept through this. When my wife and I awoke in the morning I told her about her dad's visit and what time it had occurred. Later, my mother-in-law contacted us to say he had died at the exact time I had seen him checking out his grandson. Neither I nor my mother-in-law had phones at the time, so there was no way I could have known he had died earlier.

As in so many other accounts, the visit is so calming and reassuring that the person simply falls straight back to sleep.

So what value, if any, do these experiences have? Are they imagination or wishful thinking on the part of the bereaved, who long to have the chance to say some sort of farewell to the person they love? Do they arise simply from a need for comfort? Are the dreams simply dreams, with no import and no meaning, or just inexplicable curiosities? Or are they giving us a very strong clue about what happens when we die? All of these questions we will look at in Chapter 6. The data are out there and freely available. It's important that we take it seriously, so that when our turn comes to die, as it surely will, we are fully prepared for what will happen.

Meanwhile Angelina Clements sums up very well what her

experience meant to her, and which reflects what many other people who have been lucky enough to have these experiences also feel:

Before this experience I didn't have any definite beliefs about death and the afterlife. I am now convinced that as my daughter became aware that she was going to die she managed to get in touch with me, and I was there to see that she was lifted peacefully from this earth and onto wherever the next life takes us. I don't know if I had ever feared dying – except that I know I had never wanted to die before my children had grown up and were able to manage without me – but now I don't mind how soon I die as I am convinced that my Sarah will be waiting for me whenever my time comes to leave this earth.

Chapter 5

Deathbed Visions:
Finding Explanations

Versuchung durch Verzweiflung:
Temptation through despair

Unless you experience something like this yourself, I can under-stand people not believing or feeling the significance of it. All I know is that I have no doubt. (An interviewee)

I don't know how to explain it, maybe it's best to leave it unex-plained and just be happy to know that someone you loved very much is still caring for you. (An interviewee)

The people who have witnessed a deathbed vision of a dying rela-tive, or who feel they have received a farewell visit when someone they love has died, have no doubt about the reality of what happened. But for the rest of us it is notoriously difficult to believe the evidence of other people's senses. We may have an entrenched belief that this sort of thing can't happen, and there-fore have to believe that it doesn't happen. And many of us feel a strong and intuitive resistance to the idea, because it shakes our view of reality; it makes us feel uncomfortable. Suddenly we are standing on a virtual quicksand, the earth not quite so solid beneath our feet as we had believed it to be. Derek Whitehead was one of the few people who were thoroughly unnerved rather than comforted by a farewell visit from a dying relative. He commented, 'I don't know what these things are – fantasies, dreams, wishes, delusions . . . I don't like them. They make my sense of reality wobble.'

Is there something wrong with us if we don't experience these phenomena? Or is there something wrong with us if we do? We constantly undervalue other people's subjective experience, believing that anything they experience and we do not, cannot be 'real'. We attribute the experiences to drugs, to wishful thinking, to an alteration in brain function due to dying pathology, to expectation, or to a need for comfort. In the last resort we fall back on 'coincidence'. And yet when we look at them closely, none of these explanations is really satisfactory.

Explaining deathbed visions

To say that deathbed visions are 'only' hallucinations is meaningless. A hallucination is defined as a sensory experience which is not based on a physical perception and which is not shared between people. And so by definition most deathbed visions *are* hallucinations.

The current scientific explanation of a hallucination is that it depends on abnormal activity in an area of cortex which leads to abnormal perception. Our current understanding of auditory hallucinations in schizophrenia is that it is the patient's own internal voice which is the basis of the hallucination.[1] Although we can correlate these hallucinations with activations in the auditory cortex, they are not based on any external sensations. In that sense they are 'real', but they are still private to the individual. If we looked at an image of the brain working in real time, as in a functional magnetic resonance image, (fMRI) we could certainly see a reflection of the experience, but this would not change our definition of it as a hallucination as we would not have access to the experience itself in the common shared reality of the outside world.

However, even hallucinations which we think we understand are ephemeral in the sense that they are subjective descriptions which are given to us. That the person is experiencing this we have to take on trust. A hallucination has no objective reality but is simply a subjective description of an experience by the experiencer.

The first thing we should look for is whether we can find a common factor which might account for these hallucinations. Houran and Lange[2] analysed 49 accounts of the cases quoted in Sir William Barrett's book *Deathbed Visions*[3] to see how far the experiences might have been shaped by a variety of factors. These included cultural or religious beliefs or expectations, such as angels or ghosts. They also looked for psychological factors such as fear, or physical or mental illness which might have played a part, and whether drugs had been given which might have facilitated hallucinations. Finally they looked at the whole context of the experience, whether possible 'embedded cues' within the environment or memory of the person might have been incorporated into a psychological experience – for example a vision of family members immediately following a visit by family members, or a smell of lilacs in a lilac-painted room – or whether some metaphorical or symbolic reference, for example a special religious day like the Sabbath or Easter, might have influenced the dying person's vision.

They found that medication was not involved, but that the psychophysical state of the person played a role in every experience. In 40 of the 49 there was at least one additional contextual variable, most frequently the presence of embedded cues. Cultural and religious beliefs, however, didn't play a significant role, and the researchers did not identify any symbolic or metaphorical references. They concluded that these contextual variables provided a perceptual structure for otherwise ambiguous dissociative or hallucinatory experiences. But they also acknowledged that their data did not provide conclusive evidence against a paranormal explanation for these experiences. On balance, however, they concluded that deathbed experiences were fundamentally hallucinations without further significance, albeit usually comforting ones.

The difficulty with this conclusion is that Houran and Lange were analysing data which are over 80 years old, and the main cultural bias at that time was different from that at the time of its analysis and may thus introduce errors of interpretation. The visions are of course hallucinations, as we have already said, but to conclude that they have no significance ignores the fact that their true significance is in their impact on, and the meaning they hold for, the dying themselves.

There is another puzzling aspect about the nature of these deathbed visions, which Houran and Lange did not consider. It is hard for most of us to understand why, if we ourselves were dying, our long-dead family members would be in the forefront of our minds. It is far more logical to feel that our thoughts at this time would automatically turn to the living, to the partners and lovers, the children and grandchildren we were leaving behind, rather than to relatives who are on the whole probably relegated to the back burner of memory. Why is this particular type of hallucination in these particular circumstances apparently so common? There seems to be no reason why we should be hard-wired for the experience – it has no survival value, and our genes, as Richard Dawkins has pointed out, are selfish and therefore unlikely to make spectacular efforts on our behalf when we are dying and in no position to propagate our species.

The role of drugs

Drugs are often cited as the most obvious cause of deathbed visions. Many dying patients are on some kind of pain controlling medication, and undoubtedly these drugs do cause hallucinations in a few people. In acute surgery wards, pain control is now excellent and the same drugs are used as those in hospices. However, there are no accounts in post-surgery patients of granny-visiting stories. We are clearly dealing with something that is different. The palliative care workers we talked to in our study[4] were all very clear that there is a real difference between deathbed visions and drug-induced hallucinations. Typical drug or fever-induced hallucinations described by hospice carers included patients seeing animals walking around on the floor, children running in and out of the room, devils or dragons dancing in the light, or insects moving in wall-paper or on the carpet. They also described patients 'plucking' at the air, and shivering. The patients themselves seem to be quite aware that the drug-induced hallucinations are not 'real'. 'You'll see them looking around the room rather quickly', one interviewee said. 'You ask them if they are seeing things around here that I can't see, and they will say, "Well, there's that little boy that keeps running in and out. Do you think he's really there?"'

Nursing home carers hold similar views about the difference between drug- or fever-induced and true deathbed hallucinations.[5] As one such carer said, 'You can tell from their eyes. When they have a high temperature they see things and it's an anxiety-based thing. You can see there's an underlying fear because they don't understand it . . . Whereas with the end of life experiences it's like a process, and once they have experienced it they move on to a different level. End of life experience is usually such a positive thing. It's like a journey.' Another carer said, 'You know it's a drug, and as soon as they change the drug it [the hallucination] stops. I can see that's different from when people have actually, truly felt they have seen or heard something.' And yet another carer in this study commented on the fact that when her patients had these end of life experiences she herself could get a sense of the real, inner peace they were experiencing. 'It feels more spiritual than hallucinations. It's a different thing altogether.'

The consensus seemed to be that although drug hallucinations are vivid, they are annoying rather than particularly frightening, and are never comforting or particularly significant to the patient. They are also to some extent reversible, because they can be controlled by changing the drug the patient is taking. We were told of one patient who experienced both drug-induced hallucinations, paranoid thoughts and deathbed visions at the same time. The patient reported seeing insects, and he thought the nurses were going to poison him. But he also experienced the comforting presence of his mother – who had died of lung cancer several years previously – sitting in the next bed. 'He knew everything was going to be all right because his mother was in the next bed, keeping an eye on him. Even though to me he was hallucinating, it felt very different when he spoke of his mother. It was a different language he used, very different.'

Valerie Feasby-Quigley nursed her father at home while he was dying of lung cancer. About two weeks before his death he started to tell her about the various dead family members who had been to visit him and whom he could see and talk to. She assumed that these 'visits' were due to the drugs he was on.

On a couple of occasions when I heard him talking, I thought he was calling me. When I went to his room to ask what he wanted, he would say, 'Nothing, I was talking to your mum.' On the day he died . . . he said, 'Look, there's your mum and David [her brother], they've come again. I think I'll go now.' I thought he meant he wanted to go to sleep, so I said 'OK Dad, just lie back and close your eyes – you can go to sleep now.' I held his hand; he lay back on his pillow, still looking at the wall opposite, and just sighed a deep breath and passed away. I put all this down to the medication he was on. When I cleaned his room after the funeral, I found the tablets that I had been giving him, and I thought he was taking, under the bed. He had not taken any of his medication. It then dawned on me that he was not hallucinating; he must have really seen my mother and brother, and they met him to help him on his journey.

Many of the people who have witnessed these visions have stressed that the person who had them was not confused, but was both sane and lucid at the time. Jan Mustoe, for example, told us what she noticed when her father, who was dying of cancer, was in the last stages of his illness:

On the two days before he passed away he was quite different. Although in a lot of pain and discomfort, he had softened, was content, and smiled and laughed a lot. He told me his father had been with him (he had never spoken about him before) and that my mother (who had passed away some 14 years earlier) was in the room and he spoke to her from time to time. He couldn't under-

82

stand why I was unable to see her. I should add that this state of
mind was not brought on by any drugs, as, apart from paracet-
amol, he had refused to take anything . . .

It does seem, then, that drugs cannot account for the visions, and
that there is a huge difference between drug-induced hallucinations and true end of life visions, which hold some kind of profound meaning for the patient.

Organic confusional states

Many patients who are dying have organic confusional states due
to organ failure, for example liver or kidney failure, respiratory
failure or cardiac failure. Any of these conditions may produce
organic psychosis with hallucinations, and as they progress may
finally lead to coma. These hallucinations have much the same
characteristics as drug-induced hallucinations. They are confusional, there is a marked impairment of consciousness, and they
have little meaning for the patient.

True deathbed hallucinations are quite different. They are not
confusional. Most occur in full consciousness; often, moreover,
an unconscious patient will regain consciousness and see the
vision in a brief lucid interval before they die. Relatives who
witness them say the patient is not only lucid, they are totally
rational, and indeed usually able to distinguish between the two
realities their consciousness is spanning.

Belief and expectation

One of the most frequently offered explanations for deathbed
hallucinations is that they are simply a comfort mechanism, con-
firming our beliefs and conjuring up the images we expect or
need to see. The truth is that very often these visions are against
both belief and expectation. Most of us have an entrenched
belief system of some sort, sometimes even entrenched *disbelief,*
but one indication of the power of the visions is the consummate
ease with which they seem able to overturn the most staunchly
held beliefs.

Bert Clatworthy told us this story:

My aunt and myself for many years had a discussion about whether there is life after death. She did not believe there is life after death, but I did. In the 1970s she was diagnosed with cancer of the bladder which quickly spread to other parts of her body, and she was taken in to the Royal Marsden Hospital. Just before we were going on holiday my father, mother, my uncle and aunt and myself visited her. We were talking quite casually when all of a sudden she said, 'I saw Mum last night and she said, "Why don't you come and join me and the rest of the family?"' I left the room while they all continued to talk. All of a sudden my uncle came into the room and told me that my aunt wanted to see me. When I came into the room she looked at me and said, 'Bert, you were right all along.' We all left, and the following day she died. Strange, don't you think?

Whatever it was that happened to Bert's aunt to change a lifelong conviction, it was certainly not fulfilling any expectation, and Bert has confirmed that his aunt was quite lucid at the time. Here's another example of a visit which confounded expectation rather than confirmed it.

Mum passed away in 2003. During the last few days before she died, she talked of her fears of being dead. She regretted having no real religious faith to help her to believe in some sort of existence after death. Much as people talk of being met by a loved one at death and wishing to be reunited, my mother said she had no faith in this. During the last hours of her life, Mum appeared to be asleep. Throughout this time my brother and I were by her side. She moved only once, turning her head and looking at us (clearly conscious of our presence and position within the room) and said, 'He's come.' She then closed her eyes, turned her head to face in front of her, and said, 'O my darling, I love you.' She never stirred again and passed away some six or seven hours later.

Time and again the predominant emotions the dying person expresses are surprise, delight and acceptance – they may not expect to see whoever it is that they see, but they are certainly pleased to see them.

It's natural to feel some fear of death as it approaches, but these experiences do suggest that the death process may contain elements which significantly reduce such fear. The visions of dead relatives are enormously comforting and reassuring, and the implied promise to the dying that they are going to be with people they know and love on this inevitable journey seems to lead to an immediate acceptance of death itself.

We do of course have to remember that people are usually more willing to report positive experiences than negative ones. In virtually all the accounts we have been given, the dying person showed no fear of their visitor, and the visions seemed to resolve any fear of death. What we do not know is whether there are other people who had experiences that did lead them to become fearful at the moment of death, or whose anxiety about death was not resolved by visions. The only way to check this out would be to carry out a stratified randomized controlled sample of the population with detailed interviews in which the interviewees would feel sufficiently secure and supported to be able to talk about the more negative aspect of the dying of those close to them.

Several people told us that witnessing or experiencing these phenomena have made them question their own lack of belief. John Burgess, who describes himself as an atheist, a man of science and an engineer by profession, had two experiences which made him question his disbelief. The first was the night his grandmother died. They were talking alone, and she told him that it was alright, because his grandfather (who was dead) had been to see her the previous night. The second experience was with his maternal grandmother, to whom he was very close:

The day she died, I was off work with a chest infection. At some point, I was standing in the bathroom washing my face, when all of a sudden I felt very faint and had to sit down. I looked at my watch at the same time. At the funeral a week or so later, my aunt, for no particular reason, just happened to mention that the nurses at the home had told her the exact time that Nan had died – it was exactly the same time as I had felt faint. I won't pretend that I still remember what the time was, but it shook me up quite a bit. Now I should add that I am an atheist, a man of science, an engineer by profession but both experiences made me question my lack of belief.

Ghosts at the bottom of the bed

Very hard to explain are those visits which precede the death of an apparently healthy person who has no expectation of death, let alone of any visit from a dead relative.

We had met at my son's house in August a few years ago because there was to be a small family gathering as it was my grand-daughter's birthday. My sister and I were talking (she was 17 years older than me) and she told me that our mother and father had visited her again. They had stood at the bottom of her bed and smiled at her. She was talking to them but they were not answering her – just smiling. My mother had died in 1953 and my father in 1998. I was quite upset at the time because I wondered why they had not come to see me! Her son confirmed this because he said he could hear her talking and thought she was dreaming. This had happened to her before. About a month later, she died. Now, if I'm not feeling too well and wake up in the middle of the night, I always check whether anybody is at the bottom of my bed.

Is there any other physiological or psychological mechanism that might account for all these end of life hallucinations? Can one argue that there is some psychotic process going on when the brain is shutting down, and that it always selects that particular memory store? There is certainly no psychotic process that we know of which routinely selects dead relatives.

Shared visions

One further intriguing aspect of these visions is that very occa-sionally they are apparently seen by someone else in the room. We have had only four such reports, and three of them involve children or adolescents. Perhaps children have an ability the rest of us have lost to share these visions. Gill Scrivener told us of a friend who, at the age of five, was taken to see her grandmother whom she had not been told was dying. She was sitting on her bed with her and couldn't understand why everyone was crying because she could see both her grandparents together and they seemed happy.

Another correspondent wrote:

My husband died in a hospice in August 2005, and although I was focused on him, my then 13-year-old saw a white figure of a woman at the end of the bed and we both thought that this was someone who had come to guide him on.

The following two accounts were both sent by people who were among the few adults who described seeing one of these deathbed visitors while they were at the bedside of a dying parent. Valerie Bowes:

It was the morning of 7 November 2006 when my beloved mother passed away. A care assistant was waiting at the door for us, and as we went into the room I saw a couple of female care assistants at the end of her bed and a man in a suit kneeling by the side of her bed. They all left the room and we just had time to kiss mother and tell her what a wonderful mother she had been, that we would be OK now and it was time for her to go. A couple of minutes later we noticed that her shallow breathing had completely stopped. The care assistants told us they had kept saying to my mum, 'Hold on Edith, your daughters are coming back', and they felt that she had hung on until we got there. I happened to say to my sister, 'Who was the man kneeling by the bedside when we came in, was that the vicar'? She said, 'What man?' I said, 'The older man in the suit.' She said there was no man in the room. She asked when had he left the room and I said I didn't really notice but assumed he had left the room when the female care assistants left, so we could say our goodbyes. I did not know the man but did not feel any creepiness about him – it just seemed natural he was there. I wish I could say it was my father who had come for her, or someone else we loved who had passed on, but it was definitely no one I knew.

My father died three weeks ago, and two days before he died (I had been told that there was nothing more that the doctors could do for him and he knew himself that he was dying) I was sitting in the small room in the hospital with him when I became aware of a figure standing behind me. I could see his (I think it was a man's) reflection in the glass window in front of me. I was so very aware of a presence and looked round to see who it was, but he was gone and I never saw him again. I then began to explore what it might be and spent some time looking at the window and trying out different movements, to look for reflections and to try to ascertain a more mundane explanation for what I saw. However, it became very clear that there was indeed someone in the room with us. I'm a minister of religion and thought that I might have seen Christ, but my more immediate reaction and thoughts at the time were that a relative of my dad's had come to accompany him on his last journey. I felt this very strongly.

We have no way of knowing whether these visions were truly 'shared', whether the dying person was also aware of what the person at their bedside was able to see, but certainly in each case the feeling was that the visitor's presence was natural and that they were there for a purpose. If they are indeed shared, then they are part of a shared reality between the two people concerned and can no longer, by definition, be classed as hallucinations. We have to assume that they are both seeing the same vision, and so their worlds are somehow linked.

The following account is interesting because here the dying man evidently did see people 'calling and beckoning for him to join them', while his granddaughter remembers 'many, many people', coming to see him. Geraldine English described to us how she nursed her father at home while he was dying of cancer:

He was perfectly lucid until the day before he died, and we had many conversations. During some of them he said 'they' were calling and beckoning for him to join them, he could see them as clearly as he saw me. He said he did want to go, but not quite yet. Only a couple of weeks ago, my youngest daughter (now 23) who was five when he died, started to talk about him and mentioned that many, many people came to see him as he was dying. I was puzzled, for there were only four adults and my two youngest children at any time. My daughter said the room had always been packed with people. I asked what they looked like. She said there were all sorts, men in 'suits', men who looked like farm labourers or workmen with dirty hands, ladies with full skirts and cardigans (not a fashion in vogue at the time), they all talked to my father. To Leonie's five-year-old eyes they looked as solid and real as we did. I asked her why she hadn't said anything before, and she said she thought I must have seen them too.

One interesting observation about these visions is that their imagery appears to have undergone a change. In many early written records, or medieval paintings depicting a death, it is almost always a religious figure who comes to collect the dying and see them on their way. The tomb of St Francis of Assisi for example, depicts St Francis with his arms outstretched towards a wonderful host of welcoming angels. Is this a reflection of the fact that the few written records we have of such visions during early Christian times, were both experienced and recorded by early Christians? The contemporary accounts we have been given overwhelmingly describe collection by relatives of the dying. In our sample, from a more secular society, only 2 per cent of the 'visitors' were religious figures, while 70 per cent were dead relatives or friends. In the remaining 28 per cent of cases, gestures of welcome or recognition were made by the dying person; but no words were spoken, so it is impossible to say exactly who or what they were actually seeing.

Although Houran and Lange[6] concluded that cultural and religious beliefs did not play a significant role in these experiences, analysis of contemporary data does suggest that cultural influences may be involved. Dr John Lerma is an American doctor specializing in hospice and palliative medicine at the Medical Center at Houston, Texas. He has interviewed more than 2,000 terminally ill patients and recorded more than 500 pre-death experiences, some of which are described in his book *Into the Light.* Although he does not give details of religious affiliation of his patients, these anecdotal accounts, in a society more fundamentally religious than our own, reflect a very strong Christian influence. 'Messages from angels' and visitations by Jesus are predominant; dead relatives apparently make far fewer appearances. The important point that Lerma makes is that these visitations are associated with strong spiritual experiences containing feelings of love and compassion, and perception of light.[7] Osis and Haraldsson's American sample also found a higher proportion (13 per cent) of religious 'take-away' visitors than our own, though the same proportion as in ours – 70 per cent – were dead relatives or friends. Osis and Haraldsson's Indian sample revealed much higher percentages of religious figures and lower of dead relatives – 50 per cent and 29 per cent respectively – which again reflects the nature of that society, in which there is a strong belief in collection by the Messenger of Death.[8]

But although the messenger may vary between cultures, the message seems to remain the same. Although the content of the visions probably depends to some extent on the worldview of the people involved, for nearly everyone they are intensely spiritual and meaningful. Certainly those with religious or spiritual beliefs can find support for their beliefs. But the experiences are also powerful enough to overturn a lifetime's disbelief. They seem to carry, for both the person who has them and the carers or relatives who witness them, a suggestion that there is something beyond death, that these 'visitors', whatever form they take, have come for the purpose of helping the dying through the death process and on a journey to elsewhere.

So, in summary, deathbed visions are comforting, unexpected, well formed and herald the imminent arrival of death. They are not due to drugs – carers and medical staff who are familiar with drug-induced hallucinations say that the visions of the deathbed are very different. An interesting parallel with the near death experience is that the visiting relatives usually appear whole and free from any previous physical defect or injury, such as the loss of an arm or an eye, and are usually seen in their prime of life. The dying respond to the apparitions usually with great energy, welcoming them with joy. These common features, so widely reported, do not suggest a confusional basis, a psychotic process, an expectation or a comforting pathology.

Using our current science, it is difficult to find any specific brain mechanism that would underpin and explain these wonderful experiences. Perhaps all we can logically do is to recognize first of all their validity for the dying person, and second their inestimable value both to them and to the families who grieve for them. If we are fortunate enough to witness or experience these events, we must acknowledge their spiritual significance, and never dismiss them as a meaningless by-product of the dying process. Dr Stafford Betty, Professor of Religious Studies at California State University, makes this point very strongly. 'If we don't make the mistake of assuming they are confused we are likely to feel some of the excitement they convey – for we are witnessing the momentary merging of two worlds that at all other times remain tightly compartmentalized and mutually inaccessible. The merging is what I mean by spirituality of death.'[10]

Finally, we also have to accept that these visions carry a message for us all, that a mechanistic view of brain function is inadequate to explain these transcendent experiences which suggest a wider and greater meaning to both life and death. Can we regard these experiences as a glimpse of the 'afterlife'? The difficulty here is that we have no precise definition of 'afterlife' – a question which David Fontana discusses more fully in his book *Is There an Afterlife?*[9] To suggest that it is a realm into which one can peek, rather like a glimpse through an open door, suggests that it has a material existence rather like our own. Perhaps it makes a little more sense to regard it as a continuation of consciousness after the physical death of the brain, something which we can only interpret using the tools and images available to us.

Chapter 6
Explaining Coincidences

Trist durch Zuversicht:
Comfort through confidence

Eventually there may occur one or more especially powerful synchronicities, unambiguous in their coincidental force and precision of pattern, that have a revelatory effect on the individual and mark a decisive threshold in his or her psychological or spiritual development. (Richard Tarnas)

It is even more difficult to find any rational explanation for coincidences than it is for deathbed visions, other than just that – coincidence, the chance, simultaneous occurrence of events. We have to remember how often people have these feelings before we assume a meaningful connection – how often, for example, you catch a glimpse of someone you think you know across the street, or dream of a disaster that does not happen, or how often a feeling of deep gloom and despondency settles on you for no apparent reason.

One of the first points that struck us was that these coincidences had a definite structure modified by the circumstances in which they occurred. In dreams, for example, or on the borders of sleep, the imagery of the experience was much richer and the acting out of the message more vivid – there was more likely to be sensation of physical contact, hugs and cuddles for example. Experiences during the day tended to be less specific and more ambiguous, and to involve strong feelings rather than visual images or physical contact. The response to the contact varied – although it was nearly always positive, the recipient was occasionally simply puzzled, sometimes distressed, and, rarely, scared stiff.

Usually there was a strong emotional bond between the two people involved, but sometimes there were other special factors which suggested that the experience seemed to be driven by the person who was dying rather than the one receiving the message. In one or two cases, for example, the recipient had been close to the dying person in the past but hadn't seen or even thought about them for years – though they were later told that the sender still retained strong feelings of affection for them. There were also examples of relationships in which the two people hadn't seemed particularly close or had been estranged, and the contact seemed to suggest that the dying person was trying to effect a reconciliation. And in a few cases the contact with the dying was experienced at the same time by more than one person, something which would stretch the limits of coincidence beyond credulity.

Often – and for the people concerned this is the most significant aspect of the experience – its emotional impact is so great that it remains a lasting source of comfort to the recipient and often has the power to alter their own perception of what death means. For them, whether what happened is dismissed by others as 'simply coincidence' is irrelevant: the fact that it happened is enough.

What is clear, then, is that these coincidences are very special for the experiencer. On this basis alone we can differentiate them from the ordinary coincidences of everyday life that we are all familiar with. If we want to make a more objective evaluation of the coincidences, then we need to look more closely at their structure, at whether there might be any correlation between the manner of death, the nature of the experience and its embedded context – the relationship of the two people involved, for example – and the circumstances in which the event occurred.

Summary of possible factors involved in deathbed coincidences

Sender	*Receiver*
Time of death	Timing of experience – before, at time of, or after the death.
	Whether they knew sender was ill
	Whether they knew sender was dying
Manner of death	*Nature of experience*
Expected	Comforting
Peaceful	Farewell
Painful	Physical symptoms
Difficult	Extreme emotion
Violent	
Accident	
Embedded context	*Embedded context*
Relationship:	Relationship:
close	close
past closeness	past closeness
no apparent relationship	no apparent relationship
Guilt	Guilt
Unfinished business	Unfinished business
Mental state at time of transfer	*Mental state at time of transfer*
Dying	Awake
	Sudden awakening
	Drowsy
	Asleep
	Dreaming
Belief system	*Belief system*
Practising faith	Whether the experience changed or reinforced an existing belief system
Agnostic	
Atheist	
Interpretation of message	*Interpretation of message*
	Intense comfort
	Joy
	Intense distress
	Fear

From the sender's point of view we want to know the time and manner of their death and their relationship with the recipient. Judging from what we have learned from the deathbed visions, the belief system seems to be irrelevant, and in none of the experiences we have been given has the respondent suggested that the person who contacted them had a strong belief in an afterlife. One thing we can't know is whether there was any intention on the part of the dying person to contact the recipient.

From the receiver's point of view the timing of the experience is crucial, and it is also important to know whether or not they knew the sender was ill or dying. We also need to know the nature of the experience and the effect it had upon the recipient, both at the time and afterwards. It is also interesting to note whether there was an element of surprise – whether, for example, they would have expected a contact from that person, and, very importantly, whether they have often had similar experiences, for example if the farewell visit was in a dream, and whether they often had anxiety dreams in which they thought someone close to them had died.

The following questionnaire will give some indication of the likelihood of an experience being a true deathbed coincidence, or just a random event. But always remember that you should never let other people judge or diminish your experience. If it held real significance for you, that is most important of all.

Coincidence scale

The following scale shows the likelihood of an experience being more than a simple coincidence.

1. Was the experience close (within 10–15 minutes) to the actual time of death? (Yes = 5, No = 0)
2. Did it have a strong emotional impact? (Yes = 5, No = 0)
3. Did this result in unusual or irrational behaviour? (Yes = 2, No = 0)
4. Was it clear at the time who the sender was? (Yes = 3, No = 0)
5. Did you only realize later who the sender was? (Yes = 1, No = 0)

6. Did you know the sender was ill or dying? (No = 3, Yes = 1)
7. Did it seem to give specific information that the sender was dying or had died? (Yes = 2, No = 0)
8. Did you feel physical symptoms which seemed to correlate with those the dying person may have experienced? (Yes = 1, No = 0)
9. Was there a clear message that the sender was OK? (Yes = 1, No = 0)
10. Have you ever had similar experiences which proved to be unfounded? (Yes = 0, No = 1)
11. Was the experience shared? (Yes = 1, No = 0)

Scoring:

15–24 points: Strong indication that this was a true deathbed coincidence and not just random chance.

10–15 points: This suggests that it is possible you may have had a farewell visit.

0–9 points: Your experience was more likely to have been due to chance.

Sometimes coincidence is a reasonable and rational explanation. But sometimes it seems much less reasonable or rational than the alternative explanation – that there is somehow a genuine connection between the people involved, and that the contact is 'driven' by the person who is ill or dying. Take this account, given to us by Julia Barnes:

When we were students at Bristol in the late 1960s my fiancé was estranged from his mother who was a doctor in Nigeria and he was living with his father. Around New Year we were both attending a dinner party at my parents' house when he suddenly began to cry uncontrollably and was consumed with grief. He went out to the kitchen to wash dishes, trying to give himself something to divert his mind, but nothing worked and eventually he gave up and drove back to his father's house where he was met by a policeman who told him that his mother had been killed that evening as she returned to London Airport for a plane back to Nigeria (though he didn't even realize that she was travelling that day in her car). He was not at all an emotional man, quite the opposite, and this strange episode has remained as one of the most inexplicable episodes of my life.

The strength of this overwhelming and inexplicable wave of grief was quite out of character for the man who experienced it. He had no reason to think his mother might be in danger, and indeed did not even associate the emotions he was feeling with her. All this, combined with the uncannily accurate timing, make this account so convincing that to maintain that 'coincidence' is an adequate explanation seems simply perverse. Whether one likes to regard this as telepathy, or as a visit by the soul as it leaves the body, it is very difficult to come to any conclusion other than that the minds of the two people involved were somehow linked at the moment of death.

This particular episode raises another question. Almost everyone who has these experiences says they have a strong, sometimes overwhelming, emotional impact. But why is it that although most people say the experience is hugely comforting, and describe accompanying feelings of peace and even happiness, others, like Julia Barnes' fiancé, are 'consumed with grief'? Even though death itself may be nothing to fear, no one has ever suggested that the actual experience of dying is always pleasant. Might it be that the feelings of dying are somehow being shared between the people involved? Wendy Lewis's account of her mother's twin sister's reaction to her death suggests that this might be so:

When my mother, Kathleen, died two years ago here in Hertfordshire, I rang my cousin, who is her twin sister Edie's son, and they live in Norfolk. He was very worried about breaking the news to his mother (my mother's twin) as they were 95 years old. He and his wife decided not to tell her that evening, as they were taking her to see her younger sister in hospital, and didn't want to upset her too much. They knocked on her door and she opened it and immediately said, 'Kath's died.' They were completely astounded, as there was no way she could have known. She then said, 'It's not very nice dying.' My mother had had a major stroke only the day before and had rather a harrowing time in hospital before she passed away. We are convinced that my mum visited her sister before passing on.

Does the comment here by the dead woman's sister that 'It's not very nice dying' suggest that she physically felt something of what her sister was feeling as she died, or simply that this was information somehow conveyed to her by her sister?

Telepathy

The feeling of knowing who it is who is phoning you just as the telephone starts to ring is a familiar one to many people, and has been investigated by Dr Rupert Sheldrake,[1] who found that when people were asked to guess who was phoning them, they were significantly more successful when the caller was someone with whom they had a close emotional bond (see Chapter 11, p. 194). The two people concerned in the following account had experienced this kind of 'telephone telepathy' in life, and it seems reasonable to suppose that this close 'connectedness' somehow facilitated the link between them as she was dying.

On 8 January 1999 one of my closest friends died, eight days after giving birth to her second son. I was in Wales at the time, but at exactly 1.57 p.m., the time she died, I felt her go, even though she was in London. She was one of those few people that, if the phone went I knew it was her, or she'd be speaking about me and I'd call her.

An interlinking of minds is also a feasible explanation for this experience, described by Donald Rayner:

On Easter Saturday 2001 I was working in my office when I was overcome by a feeling that my brother was in trouble. The feeling was overwhelming. I found myself agitated and saying out loud, 'Brian is in trouble, Brian is dying.' My immediate reaction was that I was overworking as I was reaching the climax of two important long-term projects I was involved with. By this time I was

99

pacing the room. I headed to the kitchen and made a cup of tea to try to calm down. At 11 o'clock I telephoned my brother Brian who lives in Australia – that is our usual contact time, 6 p.m. his time, but I had no reply. Over the Easter holiday I took my mobile phone in case there was a problem so that I could be contacted. Nothing happened, so I put it out of my mind and concentrated on the events that were programmed to climax at that period referred to.

Three weeks later, on 3 May at 11 a.m., Brian telephoned from the terminal cancer ward of the Hollywood Hospital in Perth. He said he was too ill to be treated, but the doctor was trying to build him up well enough to go home soon, and he would be arranging for me to fly out so he could show me around his special places. He went on to say that during Easter his legs had swollen up and his breathing became difficult. His local doctor told him that it looked like heart trouble . . . but he was advised to come back for a body scan on the following Tuesday. His lungs were filled with fluid and his kidneys had been all but destroyed with cancer.

Donald went out to Australia three days later and, sadly, on 13 May his brother died.

In our sample only about one-third of the experiences occurred during the normal waking state: about two-thirds occurred either in dreams, or on sudden awakening, or in the drowsy half-awake, half-asleep stage before the onset of sleep. This should not surprise us because this period between sleeping and waking is well known to be a prime mental state for both hallucinations (the hypnagogic and hypnopompic hallucinations which many people have just before falling asleep or just as they are waking) and also for parapsychological phenomena such as telepathy and precognition. But it also makes for difficulties in deciding whether such experiences are indeed due to the interaction of two minds at a distance, or whether they are hallucinations generated by one person only.

The Ganzfeld telepathy experiments

Human telepathy is at best a weak phenomenon, almost impossible to validate in laboratory experiments. It has been argued that if telepathic transmissions really do exist, they might best be picked up when the receiver's mind is open to the smallest sensory cues. The Ganzfeld telepathy experiments attempted to induce this particularly receptive mental state by sensorily depriving the subjects.

The 'receivers' in the experiments are made to lie down and relax in a warm cubicle, their hands and feet padded, their eyes covered with halves of ping-pong balls, their ears with headphones emitting white noise. After about a quarter of an hour in this state they begin to experience brilliant, dreamlike images. The 'sender', in another separated, insulated cubicle, is then shown still photos or film clips and tries to send these images to the receiver telepathically. These experiments have provided some of the most positive evidence for telepathy, but the verdict in wider scientific circles is that the jury is still out.

That telepathy has always been a 'hot potato' for scientists is inevitable. To accept its validity means acknowledging that consciousness is not limited to the brain – a concept that simply cannot be fitted into Western science as it stands. This dilemma is discussed in more detail when we consider the whole problem of consciousness in Chapters 11 and 12.

Dreams and telepathy

It's interesting that the premonition or knowledge of death is so often reported to occur in dreams, or on sudden awakenings from sleep. Dreams have always interested psi researchers because they too seem to be one of the main vehicles in which psi phenomena such as telepathy and precognition are expressed. Many of the people who have worked with dreams and dreamers for many years, notably Jung, believed that sleep created favourable conditions for telepathy, and collected many accounts of telepathic dreams. In the Maimonides dream experiments a randomly selected picture target was telepathically transmitted by an agent to a sleeper. The telepathic transmission would not begin until the sleeper had entered a period of dreaming (REM or rapid eye movement sleep). Towards the end of the period of REM the sleeper would be woken, asked to describe his dream imagery and then shown four pictures (one of which would be the target) and asked to match his dream imagery to one of them. Alternatively the dream images and the target pictures would be sent to an outside judge to determine how well the dream transcription matched the target. Although the experimenters claimed a high success rate, the experiments have been criticized on the grounds that ambiguous data could easily be retrofitted to support the telepathy hypothesis, although this seems unlikely as the judges were blind to the target chosen, as were the dreamers. A more substantial criticism is that replication has proved difficult.

We also have to remember that dreams are a notable vehicle for the expression of anxiety, and many people do have frequent anxiety dreams.

Driving home at night after a family holiday one year with our elder daughter, we were just behind a car which was involved in a horrific accident. The next day our younger daughter telephoned us in great distress. She'd had a terrible dream and had woken feeling certain that something awful had happened to us. We were all upset and distressed by the accident; if telepathic transmission of emotion is a possibility, this would have been a likely occasion for it to happen. On the other hand, our younger daughter's anxiety dreams are legendary within the family. When she first went to live in the United States we were regularly telephoned in the middle of her night to reassure her that her latest dream premonition of disaster had, so far at least, no basis in reality. Sooner or later, one might argue, she was almost bound to strike lucky.

So perhaps the first thing one needs to look at when assessing these dream coincidences is whether the person is a habitual dreamer of disasters, and whether there are particular factors which would give the dream a rational explanation; we have to attach less significance to a dream visit by a dying person if the dreamer knows that they are ill for example. But there are other factors too. The timing is obviously important, and so too is the question of whether the dream made a special emotional impact, and generated powerful feelings.

Denise Hamilton told us the following story about her mother-in-law's death. Denise was very close to her mother-in-law, Vera, who looked on her as the daughter she had never had, and who was diagnosed with a brain tumour shortly before Denise and her husband were married. She was too ill to attend the wedding, but they visited her immediately afterwards, and Denise's husband asked her not to die until they returned from their honeymoon, on the Hawaiian Island of Maui. Denise describes what she experienced one particular night:

I was awakened by a very vivid image in my dream, it was as if I was holding Vera's hand and I was loosing my grip of her and slowly her hand slipped out of mine and I then awoke immediately. I knew right away that she had left us. I made a note of the time and the day, but then I said nothing to my husband – there was nothing we could do in Maui, and it would only result in much sadness for both of us for the rest of our honeymoon. On returning to the UK, we were called over the airplane speaker system to make contact with a member of the crew – it was a message from my mother asking us to call her. I did, and the news was that indeed Vera had passed away on Monday 17 April 1989. The time and date tied up with my experience in Maui.

Denise knew that her mother-in-law was ill, so it is not too surprising that she should dream about her death, but again the timing, the vividness and significance of the dream imagery and the emotions it evoked suggest that it was more than this.

J. A. Kirton describes a dream she had the night her mother died. Although her mother had been taken into hospital with a suspected minor heart attack, there was no reason to think she was going to die.

The night after she was taken in, I was dreaming, for some reason, that I was visiting a garden centre with my sister. In the dream I became suddenly aware of a feeling that something was about to happen, that something I could in no way explain was rushing towards me. In the dream, I said to my sister, 'I have to go now, or I'm going to miss it.' Though I had no idea what the 'it' was. I awoke then to find that the feeling that something, some entity, was rushing, at the speed of light, to be with me. It was as though whatever it was that I was sensing came hurtling through the bedroom wall, and although I could see nothing, I was then aware that whatever this unknown phenomenon was, it was now hovering above me. I could not see anything, but the feeling of the presence, and the fact that it was my mother, was so strong, I remember it clearly today, eight years after the event. She then moved down towards me, and I distinctly felt her kiss the top of my head – something she had always done after visiting me as she said goodbye. Then she was gone. I knew without a doubt that the presence had been my mother, and that she had died. This seemed very odd, as I still had no expectation of her imminent death, and, feeling silly for having such thoughts, I said nothing to anyone in the morning. At 8 a.m. the telephone rang. It was my father. I said to him, 'You don't have to tell me. I know what you're ringing for.' She had died in the night of a sudden and massive stroke. To visit me in the way she did, to be able to say goodbye in her normal fashion, I feel the fact that the spirit does leave the body at the time of death to be the only explanation.

This is a particularly convincing experience – the timing, the fact that death was unexpected, the knowledge that the presence was indeed her mother, the explicit farewell message and goodbye kiss, all combine to make a visit by a departing essence – soul, spirit – seem a more reasonable possibility than sheer coincidence.

The following dream accounts are very unusual, because in none of them did the person who was visited feel a strong emotional connection with their dying visitor. There was certainly no reason for any of the dreamers even to be thinking about the person they were dreaming of, let alone feel anxious about them. It feels very much as if the 'visitor' was driving these experiences and the 'visitee' was simply the passive recipient of the visit.

Elizabeth Daniel:

Two years ago last September I was awakened by my ex-husband's voice at 4.15 a.m. He told me, 'Maggy, there is no need to talk about it any more.' I said, 'What don't I have to talk about?' But there was no reply. I put on the light and wrote it down, word for word. He and my parents were the only people ever to call me Maggy, and it was his voice with a Plymouth accent as clear as a bell. He could have been in the room, it was so clear. At breakfast I told my husband of 28 years that I thought my ex-husband had died. He thought I was mad as he lived in Scotland and we had been divorced for 29 years. I was nervous to phone his sister in Plymouth, so waited a couple of days. He had died that same day in the early hours.

Wendy Howard's mother's stepfather was an 85-year-old ex-coalminer who lived alone. Uncle Albert was an awkward person and did not get on with Wendy's mother. In the end they decided they wanted nothing more to do with one another. His own nephew was his carer and they saw very little of him in his later years. Wendy was the last one of her mother's family to visit him at Christmas 2004 with her husband. He was in poor health because of lung damage received when he was a coal miner, and found it difficult to breathe. They parted on reasonably good terms, but he made it clear he was happy with the way things were, with his nephew looking in on him, so Wendy didn't visit again even though she had heard he wasn't well and his lungs were getting worse. Then:

Last August 2006, during a very hot night I woke up around 3.30 a.m. to 4 a.m. I either dreamed, or actually did, get out of bed and walked towards the bedroom door, and there was Uncle Albert standing, looking quite young, probably middle aged. He looked happy and lively and said, 'It's over. I'm free. I can't believe I'm free at last. I can breathe' and we hugged one another as though in a final farewell. Then I got back into bed, or dreamed I did, and went back into a fitful sleep. However, around 4.30 I did wake up gasping for air. You have to remember it was a very hot night and the room was stifling. I threw off the bedclothes and this time staggered towards the door, gasping, unable to breathe. I got to the door and stood, propped up by the door frame, fighting for breath and having what can best be described as a panic attack. My husband stirred and I told him I was having a panic attack. In the 30 years I have lived in our house, and slept through many a stifling night,

I have never had this kind of reaction before. In the afternoon I called in to see my mother and she said she'd had bad news. The nephew had telephoned to say that Uncle Albert had died around 4.30 a.m. when I was busy gasping for air in my bedroom. The whole experience has baffled me. I am not a believer in the supernatural, but this has really set me wondering.

As well as the rather weak connection between the two people involved, there are other interesting features here. First, the fact that Uncle Albert appeared looking younger than his actual age (something often remarked on by people who see dead relatives in near-death experiences) and then his comment that he was free of his physical symptoms. All of this is typical of a visit at the time of death. But the writer's description of her own panic attack – which seems to have occurred at the time of his death – was half an hour or so later. It's as if the order of events was somehow reversed.

Mrs Edith Dickinson had been divorced from her husband for 23 years and had not seen him for 25 years, though she remained friendly with his family. This is her story.

On 14 April 1986 I was driving to the clinic where I worked as a health visitor, when I suddenly thought, 'There is somebody who is desperately ill and wanting me.' I immediately thought of my boyfriend of two years and my mother, an old lady of 85 years. When I arrived at the clinic I discussed this with the nurses, who were very concerned. We were helpless to do anything as we had to rush off to a lecture, which I attended but didn't hear a thing. All I could think about was who was ill and wanting me. After the lecture I contacted my boyfriend, who was fine, and explained the reason for my anxiety. I then went to Mother who was also well. Next I visited a few patients whom I had concerns about – nothing evolved. I was so upset and very frustrated – who was it? The message was very strong.

Between 4 p.m. and 4.30 p.m., I suddenly realized the 'message' had stopped. I knew that someone had died. It made me feel very sad, I made a note of it in my diary and described the strange experience I had undergone on 14 April.

Four or five days later I received a letter from the RAF to say that my ex-husband had died on that very day.

The interesting point here is that the experience made such a strong emotional impact, although the identity of the sender was unclear. It is as if the emotional component of the message (someone's dying) is more easily transmitted than the intellectual one (their identity). It is interesting to compare Mrs Dickinson's account with the following one. Again, the people involved were not close at the time of the incident, although they had been in the past.

I was born in London, and from the age of four to fifteen my best friend was a Spanish boy who lived opposite. We drifted apart as we became older, and I married and moved to Stevenage, but every time I returned to London to see my parents he would pop in and say hello. Some time later I was in Stevenage, asleep in bed with my husband, when I was woken by my friend coming into the bedroom. I was amazed to see him as he didn't even know where I lived. In a shocked voice I asked him what he was doing there and quickly glanced at my husband who was amazingly still asleep. I couldn't understand how he had not heard him come in. My friend said he had just come to see me, whereupon he gave me a cuddle and left. The following morning the 'dream' was still very vivid and I wondered what was wrong with me to suddenly be dreaming about someone who, although we were close, I had never dreamt of before, or even thought of very often. I had a busy life with two children.

Approximately two weeks later I went to see my parents in London and my dad gave me the awful news that my friend had been killed in a car accident in the early hours of the morning some two weeks previously. He was only about 22. I wish I had put the dream on the calendar as I cannot be sure if it was the same night that he died. But the coincidence is amazing.

She goes on to add: 'I have since had a relationship with a man who died of cancer and I willed something of a similar nature to happen, but it did not.'

And this of course is another question to which there is no easy answer. There are people who are desperate for a sign that the person they love has somehow survived death and is in contact with them, and yet they receive no signs, no visions, nothing. And yet for others these experiences occur out of the blue, unexpected and unsought. There seems little evidence to support the view that hope or expectation can account for them. If it did, many more of us would report them.

Most of the 'rational' explanations for these deathbed 'visits' are based on the premise that they are the product of either wishful thinking or a fertile imagination. But it is worth remembering how many similar stories are also recounted by professionals who work with the dying and who are able to make more objective observations than the people directly involved. In 1970, Gordon Thomas, a founder producer of BBC TV's *Tomorrow's World*, was making a documentary film about the work of Dr Josef Issels, the German cancer specialist, at the Ringberg Klinic in Bavaria. Dr Issels and his staff specialized only in the treatment of terminal patients and had treated some 5,000 such patients over a 20-year period. He told Gordon of many deathbed events he had experienced, among them the account of a patient who asked for his bedroom slippers to be placed on his bed, at his feet, facing the door. He had told the night nurse that he expected to 'go for a walk soon'. Given that he was totally bedridden, the nurse had smiled. Next morning she found the patient dead. A relative of another patient rushed to the Klinic in the middle of the night soon after she had awakened to hear the patient's voice telling her he 'had no more pain as he was in a wonderful place'. When the relative arrived at the Klinic, a journey of several hours, and the time of death was checked, it turned out to be within moments of her being awakened.

Taken overall, the hypothesis of extended mind manifesting at the time of death is a much more persuasive explanation for most of these experiences than coincidence or expectation. And the more the details of the accounts are studied, the more apparent it becomes that they have a very specific structure, which again mitigates against a simplistic notion of straight coincidence.

Getting in touch with the Emergency Services

The near-death literature abounds with reports of individuals who have been involved in an accident having a near-death experience in which they observe the accident scene as if hovering above it.[2] In some accounts the person describes how they tried, but failed, to make contact with the Emergency Services personnel working at the scene below them. Levine cites an account of a friend who reported watching police and fire personnel during a NDE in the aftermath of a car crash and trying to decide whether or not to get in the ambulance with his body.

Dr Richard Kelly is a retired Detective Lieutenant in the Massachusetts State Police who decided to investigate this further from a different point of view – that of the Emergency Services personnel themselves. Dr Kelly served for 13 years with the State Police Psychological Services Unit, was Chief of the Health and Safety Branch for the United States Marshals Service for seven years, and is a professional clinical counsellor.

In a preliminary study[3] Dr Kelly had found six Emergency Services workers (four police officers and two paramedic firefighters) who reported feelings of contact by deceased victims at the scenes of fatal injury in the form of sensing a presence, attachment, or plea for help. In two of these cases two of the workers felt the same thing – in one case that the dead person was somehow 'clinging' to them, in the second that they were being watched. In the third case the Emergency Services worker felt a bonding to the deceased immediately after eye contact, and later as if 'he was on your back'. In the fourth case eye contact was part of a continuing, personal and strong connection to a victim, along with a nagging sense of unfinished business. The workers involved were all at first reluctant to describe their feelings, and in neither of the two instances where both partners working at the scene had had this feeing of communication, had they discussed this between themselves, although in every case each partner corroborated the other's description of both the feelings and the perceived location of the deceased, as hovering above them and watching. In all cases the feelings lingered, and in all cases the Emergency Services workers were clear that their perceptions were connected specifically to the victim, rather than to the event in general.

By the time he had collected the fourth account, Dr Kelly concluded that these stories could not simply be dismissed as anomalies, and decided to initiate a larger study to try to determine their frequency.[4]

Using questionnaires and interviews, he asked a group of 90 Emergency Services workers (68 police officers and 22 firefighter/emergency medical service personnel) if they had ever experienced a sense or feeling of 'communication, presence, or attachment' from victims of fatal injury whom they had attended at death. Of the 90 subjects, 15 respondents (17 per cent) reported having experienced feelings of presence, communication or attachment by deceased victims. These 15 respondents described 23 specific events. One subject described three experiences; three subjects reported feelings of presence at *all* death scenes; one subject identified 17 events; and two other respondents, due to their lengthy careers, estimated 100 experiences each. These responses combined equal 229 reports of presence.

None of these 15 subjects showed any evidence of fabrication or mental illness, and all were clear that the source of their feelings was not imagination or 'internal voices'. They described the experiences not as apparitions, visions or heard voices, but rather as thoughts, ideas, images or feelings. They were quite aware of the unusual character of these experiences, but were equally clear that they were real. None were extremely religious, and all accepted a spiritual explanation of the presence as plausible. None had discussed their experiences with others.

The major difference between these accounts and others we have discussed is the apparent lack of emotional connection between the people involved. None of the personnel involved had any personal knowledge of or relationship with the dying victim. But the reverse is also true – why contact a firefighter rather than make a last lightning farewell visit to a parent or lover or friend? Stephen Levine has suggested that in the particular circumstances of a traumatic unexpected accident, one can postulate that the dead or dying individual might be confused, vulnerable or frightened during the transition from physical life.

Someone who is popped out of their body without much prepara-tion, like a teenager in the fullness of life who has a fatal accident, may after the smoke clears wonder, 'What the hell was that all about? What happened to my body? I can't be dead because this is still happening around me.'

It may be, he suggests, that for those spirits wrapped in con-fusion, the Emergency Services worker is available, at least subliminally willing, and capable of sensing an attempt for communication from a 'troubled soul'.

However, what does emerge very clearly from Dr Kelly's study is that these contacts between victim and rescuer occur rarely and to only a few people who seem to have the facility to recognize them. The figure of 17 per cent is in the same region as the percentage of people who have near-death experiences after a cardiac arrest – between 10 per cent and 25 per cent (see Chapter 12).[5] It seems that this is the proportion of the general population who are open to such experiences. It could be argued that those who report frequent contacts do so because they have come to expect them. Or equally, one can argue that having had one such experience may simply make the receiver more open, or more sensitive, to subsequent contacts. But most likely, about this percentage of the population have a special facility for sensing experiences of this type (see this chapter, p. 114).

Stepping outside the scientific framework

As we have seen, many of these coincidences, though not all, seem to fall into the category of telepathic experiences. They do at the very least suggest a 'connectedness' between the people concerned. Take, for example, the following account. One of our correspondents, Mary, is now over 90 but says that personal ex-periences she has had throughout her life have aroused and sustained an interest in NDEs and parapsychology. The first such experience happened when she was 11, in 1918:

I was sitting on a stool in front of a fire writing a letter to my Uncle George, who was with the army in France – I had paused and was looking into the coal fire, thinking of anything more to write to him, and a thought came into my mind, 'Uncle George will not get this letter.' I was a bit startled but very curious. A few moments later my mother came into the room to tell my father that she had just heard from her sister that Uncle George had been killed. I did not tell anyone, but that was the beginning of my interest in what happened.

As a schoolgirl she often had what she called 'future dreams' when at times (sometimes but not always in dreams) a picture would come into her mind of an event which would follow a day or two later. Although she did sometimes write them down so that she could check back later when the event happened, again she did not tell anyone, because 'in those days if you were weird or unusual you were thought ready for a lunatic asylum!'

Her next experience was after her marriage. Her husband, Francis, had driven from Cambridge, where they were living, up to London with some friends and she was expecting him home around 3.30.

At 3.15 I was writing some letters when I saw in my mind a car with a wheel rolling along the road. I said, 'Oh, Francis, slow down, be careful.' He arrived home about 6 p.m. saying, 'Sorry we're late, a wheel came off.' I told him what I had seen and he told me that he heard me say to him, 'Slow down', and he thought, 'That's silly, there's no traffic, but Mary says slow down, how can I explain it to the others?' But he slowed and then he saw a front wheel ahead of him and was able to steer to the bank and stop.

Mary and her husband were both committed Christians, and regarded these experiences, which continued when Francis was with the airborne forces as a paratrooper during the Second World War, as God-given guidance. On his last leave they both had a strong feeling that Francis was not going to survive.

On 9 June 1944 I was walking to collect our son from kindergarten and walked 50–60 yards at one point without knowing it, because my mind had gone over to France and I saw a series of pictures like present-day slides of a field with a brick wall, seven or eight feet high with holes in it at intervals for people to walk through. Francis was walking across the field and then dashing for a slit trench and falling – I naturally hoped he was only wounded but felt he had been killed. As I became conscious of walking again his voice said, 'Look up, Mary.' I did and saw his head and shoulders above a white cloud and he gave a character-istic wave of his hand, saying, 'You're right my dear, goodbye.' I was quite calm, and because of all that was going on did not receive the telegram till 26 June. I checked with the War Office and he had been killed on 8 June (interesting the gap from 8th to 9th?). Later another officer who knew us well asked me when we met after the war if I would like to know what had happened. I asked him to let me tell him and described the mental slides. He said nothing till I had finished and then said, 'You might have been there.'

After the war, Mary and her son visited the village where Francis had died and she saw for herself the field, with the wall and the slit trenches as she had seen them in her mental picture.

While working in Japan we were told about a Japanese civil servant who had made a study of Japanese women who were widowed in the Second World War and had collected a number of stories very similar to Mary's, in which the widows described the battlefield and circumstances in which their husband died. I tried to go and see him so that he could tell me about his unusual collection, but unfortunately by that time he was too old and I was never able to do so. It is sad that the accounts were never pub-lished. They would have contributed to the evidence that experi-ences like these are not confined to one cultural group but are spread widely across the globe.

For a number of years parapsychological scientists have been experimenting with a technique known as remote viewing. The subject records details of a distant remote target and then through various statistical measures it is decided whether or not they had truly seen the target which had been chosen or whether they had simply guessed. At the time of the Cold War it was clearly important for the USA to obtain classified information about strategic sites in Russia. In 1974 the US Intelligence Service set up a Remote Viewing Unit, headed by Dr Puthoff and Dr Targ at the Stanford Research Institute. Part of this Unit was declassified in 1995 and information about it can be obtained online from a paper by Dr Puthoff.[6] A paper published in 1996 by Jessica Utts and Brian Josephson, the Nobel Laureate concluded:

> For the past decade the US Government experiments were overseen by a very high level scientific committee consisting of respected academics from a variety of disciplines, all of whom were required to critique and approve the protocols in advance. There have been no explanations forthcoming that allow an honest observer to dismiss the growing collection of consistent results.[7]

As is always the case with parapsychological experiments, there is a divided view within the scientific community about remote viewing. But Mary's experience described above would certainly fall neatly into this framework. We have quoted her letter at length because it shows that throughout her life she has been sensitive to receiving telepathic and clairvoyant (remote viewing) impressions. It is well recognized in parapsychological research that there is a 'sheep–goat' effect – some people (the sheep) have the facility to receive such communications while others (the goats) don't. Mary clearly fits into the 'sheep' category. This sensitivity to receive these impressions may be a reason why some people report deathbed visits, while others – who may long to have some contact with people they love at their death – do not.

Shared coincidences

Particularly interesting are the handful of accounts we were given in which two people had apparently identical experiences independently but at the same time. Carole McEntee-Taylor's mother had just recovered from a very debilitating stroke, was diabetic and had high blood pressure and lived in fear of having another stroke.

On 15 July 1998 I woke up at just after 4 a.m. for no obvious reason. I did not need a drink or to go to the toilet or anything. I felt incredibly happy, at peace and joyful. I felt so good that I got out of bed, went downstairs and just looked out at the sky for a while. I then went back to bed. At just after 6 a.m. my father rang me to say that he had gone to wake my mother for her hospital appointment and she was dead.

My daughter at the time was living with her boyfriend and I did not see her or speak to her until later that day. When I did, one of the first things she said was that she had woken up at about 4 a.m. that morning for no particular reason but that she had felt incredibly happy and at peace. We both knew that it was my mother saying goodbye and letting us know that she was happy and at peace.

The similarity of the quality of emotion felt by Carole and her daughter is striking, although it was only after they knew that her mother had died that they made the link with her death. Even so, the strength of the emotion, the simultaneous timing of the experiences and the probability that they coincided with the time of death (though this isn't known exactly) make this a very convincing account.

A very similar experience occurred to Jean Wareham and her sister at the time that Jean's mother was slowly dying of cancer. Jean and her sister sat by her bed for many hours, not knowing when she would die. Then:

One night I had a very strong experience that she had come to me in the night and said she had just come to say goodbye. The next day when I was told she had died, I already 'knew' because she had told me. When I met my sister I was very surprised to find that she had had exactly the same experience at the same time.

Chris Alcock described how in the early 1950s one of his school friends, Kit, was a young army officer on active service in Korea. One night Kit's mother, a girlfriend of his, and Chris's sister, who was also sweet on him, all had independent similar dreams in which they saw Kit, who appeared looking worried and said 'I'm lost' and then faded away. All three woke up and the experience was so vivid that they all feared the worst. Later they found out that the experience coincided with his death in Korea. When writing to us, Chris asked his sister to describe her own dream:

She said she dreamt that herself, myself and Kit's younger brother Peter were all sitting on a hearth-rug in front of a big fire in a large room of an old house. She said that the door across the room opened and Kit came in. He was very white and cold. My sister then said, 'Come in Kit and join us and get warm.' Kit replied, 'I can't, I don't know where I am.' He then went out, closing the door behind him.

All the people concerned (and myself) are and were practising Catholics, though this sort of phenomenon has nothing to do with our faith. We were all as surprised as anyone of any faith or no faith would be.

To keep on citing 'coincidence' for all the very convincing accounts we have been given becomes first a weak and then a frankly implausible explanation. But to find any other feasible explanations, we have to step outside the current reductionist, mechanical, scientific framework.

Telepathy, if we accept the concept, would be a reasonable explanation for many deathbed coincidences, especially those in which a person is engulfed by overwhelming and inexplicable physical or emotional feelings as someone they are close to is dying. But even telepathy does not seem an adequate explanation for the experiences described on pp. 104–7, in which the person who received the farewell visit felt they had no real emotional bond with their visitor, or for those experiences which two people share. Neither can it explain the large number of experiences which apparently occur at the moment of death, or even just after it, when the brain may no longer be functioning and consciousness is lost.

Another explanation – equally unsatisfactory from the point of view of reductionist science – might be that there is a state at death or just after death in which the person has some kind of existence in which their personal consciousness somehow persists independently of their brain. There is some support for this concept in the actual death experiences which we refer to in Chapter 12, when during cardiac arrest brain function is so severely disrupted that consciousness is not possible, and yet the experiencer reports leaving his body and witnessing his own resuscitation from the ceiling. This points to mind being able to separate from brain in this situation. If these findings are confirmed, then it is not unreasonable to argue that mind in this state has the capacity to travel and interact with other minds to which it is closely linked. This explanation is attractive as it has explanatory power for most of the phenomena that have been described to us.

Next, should we consider these experiences not as paranormal, but as transcendental, spiritual ones? We should then look at the area of depth psychology in which Jung, one of its founding fathers, described synchronistic events in which he noted a deep transcendent personal component, with an external, apparently independent event in the real world. These events he called synchronistic, which stressed their relationship to time. The word is derived from the Greek '*syn*' (together) and '*chronos*' (time). Jung had been working on this concept from as early as 1909 when he was influenced by conversations about relativity with Einstein and, many years later, with his friend and patient, the quantum mechanical physicist Wolfgang Pauli. Jung's central concept was that nothing happens by chance and that events happening at the same time do so for a reason and have a profound underlying linkage.

Jung experimented with, among other things, the I Ching, in which the falling of the bars and the trigrams which they produce are not random, but suggest a relationship between the present moment and the deep underlying issues of the person who throws the sticks. His last papers on the subject were published in the 1930s. The most well-known example is a patient of Jung's who was highly defensive and resistant to allowing Jung to explore her sexual feelings. One day she was reporting a dream to Jung about a golden scarab beetle that was central to her dream imagery. At that moment there was a tapping on the window by an insect that seemed to want to get in. Jung opened the window and found that it was a common beetle whose wing cases reflected a gold sheen. He is reported to have said to the patient, 'And here is your scarab beetle.' This was the break-through moment in their analysis, as the woman was able to see the relationship of the here-and-now, real beetle to the scarab of her sexual dream imagery. For Jung, synchronistic events were not chance happenings. The here-and-now event pointed the way to a deep, often archetypal complex within the person. Jung pointed to many classical archetypes which exist in mythology throughout the world, such as birth, rebirth, the hero, the great mother, the child, the trickster or joker, and death the Great Reaper. If one is to apply the concept of synchronicity to the events of deathbed coincidences, then one is arguing that the very profound archetype of death is activated at that moment, allowing real-world synchronicities to occur.

Richard Tarnas is a philosopher and educator whose first book, *The Passion of the Western Mind*,[8] illustrated a depth of understanding of the way the Western ego has developed since the time of the Greeks. In his new book, *Cosmos and the Psyche*,[9] he looks at factors within the universe which have a psychological influence on the here and now of ordinary people. Discussing Jung and synchronicity, and the relationship between the conscious and unconscious, he states (p. 55):

Eventually there may occur one or more especially powerful synchronicities, unambiguous in their coincidental force and precision of pattern, that have a revelatory effect on the individual and mark a decisive threshold in his or her psychological or spiritual development. Not infrequently, synchronicities of this category occur in association with births, deaths, crises and other major turning points in life.

In our present state of scientific knowledge, Jung's formulation of synchronicity seems to be the closest we can get to explaining the amazingly rich phenomenon of deathbed coincidences.

Chapter 7

Bereavement and Hallucinations

Versuchung durch Ungeduld:
Temptation through impatience

*I know that when you're bereaved, it's very easy to see or hear
things, because you do go a bit mad, in the nicest sense of the
word. (An interviewee)*

The intention of this book was to look only at those coincidences
in which contact between the dying and those close to them
occurred more or less at the moment of death. But very many of
the letters and emails we received were from people who
described having some kind of contact with the person in the
weeks and months following the death.

Many of the explanations which might be feasible when
looking at a communication between two people, one of whom is
alive and one who is dying, are no longer appropriate when one
member of the pair is dead.

Here we enter an entirely different field in which there is
already a large scientific and anecdotal literature – the area of

119

after-death communication. To review this area fully is way beyond the scope of this book, but in view of the large number of these experiences we were sent, it would be interesting to see whether these fall into any kind of pattern and whether they are helpful in extending our understanding of the dying process.

Contact with the dead

It has been acknowledged for many years that it is very common for bereaved people to have hallucinations of their dead partner. A National Opinion Poll of 1,467 Americans in 1973 found that 27 per cent said they had been in touch with someone who had died,[1] and an Icelandic survey of 1,132 people by Erlendur Haraldsson found that 31 per cent claimed to have some sort of contact with the dead.[2] A more recent interview survey of over 3,000 people in North America suggested that about one in five bereaved Americans have experienced this kind of after-death communication.[3]

In the UK the first important survey was that of Dewi Rees, a General Practitioner working in Wales.[4] Of 227 widows and 66 widowers he found that almost half had had hallucinations of their dead spouse. The hallucinations often lasted many years, but were most common in the first ten years of bereavement. Men and women were equally likely to experience them, but young people were less likely to do so than those bereaved after the age of 40. The incidence of hallucination increased with length of marriage and was particularly associated with a happy marriage and parenthood.

Dewi Rees concluded that these are 'hallucinations which comfort', and are probably psychological in origin, quite benign, and indeed providing considerable comfort in bereavement. He found that the most common phenomenon was to sense the presence of the dead partner. Visual or auditory hallucinations were less common. Least common was the feeling of being touched.

	Males	Females	Total
Sense presence	43.9 %	37.9 %	39.2 %
Sees deceased	16.7 %	13.2 %	14.0 %
Hears deceased	10.6 %	14.1 %	13.3 %
Speaks to deceased	19.7 %	9.3 %	11.6 %
Touched by deceased	1.5 %	3.1 %	2.7 %

Haraldsson found that visual hallucinations were the most frequent, the sense of an invisible presence the second most common experience. Less common were the feeling of being touched, and sensations of smell that had been characteristic of someone when they were alive.

Like coincidences at the time of death, these apparitions tend to occur more often when the person is resting or drowsy. One-third of Haraldsson's sample were physically active, going about their daily work, while one-third were resting, and another third on the point of going to sleep or just awakening.

Grief was a factor in only a few of Haraldsson's cases – which suggests that it is not simply, or always, a 'comfort mechanism'. None of the medical or physiological factors which are known sometimes to cause hallucinations were present. Nearly all those surveyed were in a normal healthy state; only six were bedridden, none were feverish, only one was taking medication. Most interesting though are the 13 cases in which the percipient did not know at the time of his experience that the person he hallucinated had in fact died, thus ruling out the factors of grief, comfort or expectation as an explanation.

The field of after-death communication is now a thriving area of parapsychological investigation. From being largely the province of mediumistic communication, this has expanded in the past decade or so to include ITC – Instrumental Trans-Communication. These are reported communications from the dead via television, tape recorders, radio or telephone.[5]

Who is contacted?

In our own sample it was not only bereaved spouses who experienced this contact, it was also commonly reported by people who had had other close relationships – parents and children, grandparents and grandchildren particularly. The nature of the contacts reported by our own sample was much the same as that described by Dewi Rees and other workers, and also much the same as those people who had told us about visits they had received from the dying at the time of death – a sense of the presence of the person was the most common, hearing or seeing them rather less so. Several people described a sensation of comforting physical contact.

I felt him come and sit on the end of the bed at night, and one night while I was reading the paper I felt him flick my fringe as he used to do sometimes as a token of affection.

Since his death I have felt his presence around the house and on occasions seen his face on the pillow of his bed next to mine.

Since my mother died I have experienced the phenomenon of someone lying down next to me when I'm in bed on my own, i.e. before my husband comes to bed. I can be reading or if I'm tired just lying there and I feel the weight of someone lying down on the bed. Once or twice I've fallen asleep, felt the weight of someone lying down, turned to kiss my husband goodnight and realized he hasn't come up to bed yet. This doesn't happen every night, but if I've been upset or ill I've felt it more strongly. Also I've experienced the feeling of someone tucking me into bed which is what my mother used to do when she came to say goodnight when I was a child.

My Father died on 30 April 1989 in the United States, where he lived. I could not go to the funeral because I was nine months pregnant. My son was born on 17 May 1989. Three days later . . . I was in my private room in hospital and my son was in his clear cot near my bedside; around 3 a.m. my Father actually came into my room – I saw him fully. I even remember sitting up in bed, because I did not think he was real, but he was there in my room. I did not think at the time, 'Oh, he is dead.' He walked over to the cot and looked at my son and smiled. Then we smiled at one another and he nodded his head in approval and left. The next morning I remember his visit vividly. It was a wonderful experience.

A few accounts suggested that these 'visits' were experienced by other family members too – as in the following three accounts.

Evie's husband died of lung cancer in October 1998.

As the weeks went by, I dreamed a great deal about my husband, which I guess is completely normal. I was awake one night for a while and I guess I fell asleep again – that's my explanation. But I could feel my husband in bed with me, with his arms around me, and I remember thinking, 'This must be real, because I'm awake.' But I guess I had dozed off again and it was another dream.

I've experienced the smell of cigar smoke (he smoked cigars) several times in the house, and once had the very, very strong feeling that someone was stood at the foot of the bed when I was awake in the night. This, I'm sure, is all quite normal.

The strangest thing happened in the August after he'd died. I was out early one morning with Bertie (my dog) across the fields. It was a very calm, quiet day, with no traffic noise and no one else around. Totally peaceful. And all of a sudden I heard Ron's voice shout, 'Evie!' It sounded like a warning. I whirled round and of course could see nothing. I decided I was going mad, and walked home saying to myself, 'I'm going mad. But I know what I heard. It was Ron's voice. But that's not possible, I'm going mad.'

Anyway, I thought no more of it, except that madness was obviously setting in, and a few days later I called my sister-in-law, Mandy. We had a chat and I told her what I've just told you. She went very quiet and asked when this had happened. I explained a bit more. Then she said that the week before, when she was alone in the house, she had taken a cup of tea out into the garden to sit and relax. The doors and windows were open as it was a lovely day, when she suddenly heard a man's voice call (again, as if a warning), 'Mandy!' She jumped up, thinking her husband had returned home early from work – but there was no one there. Now I knew nothing of this when I had my experience, so I guess auto-suggestion can be ruled out. But very strange, that two women can experience exactly the same thing.

I know that when you're bereaved, it's very easy to see or hear things, because you do go a bit mad, in the nicest sense of the word. I've not experienced anything else for several years now, so I'm not really sure whether there is life after death. If there is, I just hope my husband is having a good time, although as a cricketer, he would not have been impressed by our Ashes performance!

A hallucination is, by definition, a subjective experience that is not shared. That these two women evidently experienced the same kind of contact by the same person at what seems to have been more or less the same time means that, in this particular case at any rate, hallucination simply will not do as an explanation. It's interesting that each woman heard her own name, as if a common stimulus was interpreted subjectively and personalized by each of them.

The following account is interesting, not just because of the particular dream that allowed the dreamer to 'let her father go', but because her sister had the same dream, possibly even at the same time (though this isn't certain).

My father suddenly died in August 1998 . . . I found it very hard to come to terms with his death because everything happened so rapidly. I kept dreaming that we buried him alive, and I was very afraid to wake up in the middle of the night after these dreams. This had been going on for a few nights until one night I had a completely different dream. My father appeared, looked alive and well and told me that he was fine and happy and staying with his uncle. Since that night I stopped having bad dreams about him and was able to 'let him go'. But the most surprising experience came after that. I went to see my sister at Christmas whom I had not seen since our father's funeral in August. She started telling me about her bad dreams about our father's death that stopped when one night our father appeared in her dream and said that 'he was fine and happy and staying with his uncle'. She was telling me exactly the same things that happened to me, and possibly it happened with us at the same night.

Dreams are a way of coming to terms with a death, and this is clearly a possibility here. But is it likely that both would have had the same dream with the same dream imagery – or is after-death communication more probable?

Martin Howard's son Matthew died in 1998. He drowned in a neighbour's garden pond when he was two years old. Here Martin described what happened three days after his death:

In the early hours of Tuesday morning I woke up. We have a window above our bedroom window. I could see a shadow of a baby's face looking through the window, I couldn't make out any features but I knew it was Matthew. I think I dozed off. Later I heard a rustling noise (like the noise of a baby walking and his nappy rustling). The noise started near the door and moved across the foot of the bed and up towards my wife. I was reluctant to open my eyes (I was scared, to be honest) but when I did there was nobody there. When I got up in the morning the house alarm had reset itself during the night.

I didn't mention this to my wife at first as I didn't want to upset her: I told her a couple of days later. She said she had heard exactly the same thing as me, which freaked us both out a bit. Both of us heard the same thing but did not want to mention it in case it upset the other.

Now, Matthew had been doing this for quite a while before he died. He would wake up in the early hours, come into our room past the foot of the bed and up Janette's side, and we would hear his nappy rustling. She would then either take him back to his room or pick him up and put him in between us for a while. One of us would take him back to his own bed later and tuck him in.

I was always a bit sceptical of these stories . . . It's only my own experiences that have made me question what happens when we pass on. I don't know if these experiences happen to other people, it can be a bit daunting mentioning it for fear that they will think you're crackers.

The fact that both Martin and his wife heard the same thing rules out hallucination as a possibility – by definition, hallucinations are not shared experiences.

Ann Gerry also told us of an experience she had as a child when her grandfather died, which, like many others, is an indication of the strong link that is often forged between grandparents and grandchildren.

When I was ten years old (I am now 39) my maternal grandfather, whom we called Papa, died suddenly from cancer . . . My parents decided not to tell either myself or my 14-year-old sister that he was ill. At that age I had no understanding or experience of death. At the end of the October half-term holiday we suddenly found ourselves . . . driving with our parents to our grandparents' home in Paignton, Devon. We had no idea of the real reason why . . . It was just wonderful that we were going to Nanna and Papa's and that we would be having extra days off school . . .

When we arrived at Nanna and Papa's house our parents were whisked off to the kitchen. Dad emerged a little while later and told us that Papa had gone. I must admit I did not understand that 'gone' meant for ever. The next morning I walked downstairs to the sound of someone cleaning the hearth of the open fire in the lounge . . . There was no hallway and the staircase led straight into the lounge. The sound was something I found painful and confusing as the job to clear the hearth had always been Papa's. I remember looking through the banister rails to see who had had the audacity to do Papa's job, only to find that it was him. I could hear Mum, Dad and Nanna talking in the kitchen and I tried to work out why they had lied to me. When the kitchen door opened and Nanna came into the lounge he stood up and just smiled. It was not a broad grin, but the gentle kind of smile that says it's all OK. By the time I reached the bottom of the stairs he had gone. I only ever told my sister until many years later, and for most of those years I kept wondering if I had seen him because I had wanted to.

It is undoubtedly easy to make a case for a psychological cause for many, perhaps most, of these 'hallucinations that comfort'.

There are many cues in everyday experience associated with a particular person, and even after death those cues might evoke a memory or arouse the feeling that the dead person is still somehow present – the smell of a particular scent or cigarette smoke, for example. We know that the human brain is adept at creating a whole new synthetic world – the out-of-body experience, for example, can be generated by extreme stress, from shock, pain or sheer terror. And of course – and this is the most significant difference between these experiences and deathbed coincidences – the person who has the hallucination knows that they have lost someone they dearly love, they are in need of comfort. Is it so surprising they should dream about them, sense their presence, even feel their touch? An infinite number of times during the day and night they will find themselves in situations where they would expect to see or feel or hear the person they have lost. Is it so surprising that they should do so?

But if we accept that the deathbed coincidences discussed here may suggest that there is some kind of link between the living and the dying, then is it entirely logical to dismiss all the hallucinations of the bereaved, which are in many ways so similar, simply as a psychological comfort mechanism, to maintain that they are an entirely different phenomenon? Having opened this Pandora's box of speculation, where does one stop? Hallucinations of the bereaved map onto a whole new area of human anecdote and legend – of ghosts, of mediumship – which is way beyond the scope of this book to either explore or explain. This is tiger country for scientists, but intriguing nonetheless.

Chapter 8

Grandfather's Clock and Other Odd Incidents

Trost durch Geduld:
Comfort through impatience

My grandfather's clock was too large for the shelf,
so it stood ninety years on the floor.
It was taller by half than the old man himself,
though it weighed not a pennyweight more.
It was bought on the morn of the day that he was born,
and was always his treasure and pride.
But, it stopped, short, never to go again,
when the old man died.

(Henry Clay Work, 1876)

Odd events at the time of death don't always take the form of a vision, or even a presence. Often they are much more prosaic. We have been told of unexplained knocks or rappings, doors banging, photographs which drop off the wall or fall face downwards. Telephones have been reported to ring at the moment of death, though in only one account does the phone ring to order, as in the following story told to us by Mary G.

Before my husband died, a friend had told me that she had seen the ghost of her sister at the time of her sister's death. That scared me a bit. My husband was very close to death, and as much as I loved him I didn't know how I would react if I saw his ghost, so I telepathically sent him a message saying I didn't want to see him, but please could he ring me. He died in the early hours of the morning, and that morning as I was just waking up, I dreamed that I heard the phone ring, and I answered it and his voice said 'Hi'. He sounded very well and very cheerful. A little while later the hospice where he was staying rang me to say he had passed away. All of this has convinced me that there has to be something more after this life.

Many of the carers interviewed in our nursing home study also talked of inexplicable incidents such as lights going on and off in the room of a resident who had recently died, clocks stopping, pictures dropping off the wall. Others mentioned a bell in the room of a resident, which mysteriously continued to ring on the day of his funeral even though no one else was in the room, 'As if', one interviewee commented, 'the spirit of the dead person was still with us.' Several others described sensing the presence of a resident who had just died, hearing footsteps or seeing apparitions, as if the residents seemed to 'hang around' for a while after death. One interviewee described a feeling as if she were being pushed on the shoulder after she had entered the room of a resident who had died.

Smells associated with the deceased are quite often experienced – Keith Wilson smelled the 'overpowering smell' of his father's tobacco smoke in his car on the way home after his father died. Occasionally music is heard, and Katherine Knight told us of this unusual experience of her sister's, around the time of their uncle's death.

He died in the early hours of the morning in a French hospital in July a couple of years ago. My sister was suddenly awakened around the same time in her London flat by an animal howling. She thought it was a wolf. She said that it felt as if it was a recording of an animal, and that someone had pressed the 'Play' button on a tape recorder as it was instantaneous. The howling lasted two or three seconds and suddenly stopped as if someone had pressed the 'Stop' button. She was overcome by a sense of extreme fear and had to keep putting her bedside light on. She also huddled underneath the bedcovers because she was so frightened. While she was feeling scared, she also remembered that the atmosphere was uncannily still. This whole experience lasted approximately 15–20 minutes. We didn't find out until lunchtime the next day that our uncle had died.

Mechanical malfunctions

We normally think of the mechanical world as being independent of us and quite indifferent to us. But if we look at our behaviour, there are many mechanical objects that we have a very close relationship with. Our cars, for example, are not just cars – some people even give them names and have very tender feelings towards them. A number of parapsychological experiments have shown small effects of mind on mechanical systems.[1] In the 1980s Uri Geller carried out demonstrations of spoon bending by an act of mind, and countrywide drawers of snarled-up cutlery bore witness to the numbers of children who tried to copy him. However, a few parents were convinced that their children were truly able to bend spoons. Professor Hasted, who was working at Kings College London, investigated some of these children and has some convincing data on them, though this remains a controversial area.

There is also evidence that people who do very fine work need to have a still mind, not only because this produces a steady hand, but because it seems that their relationship with the object is also of prime importance. Deathbed coincidences show that mind can affect mind and so it is perhaps not such a great leap of faith to suppose that mechanisms may also be affected by minds, and so by minds that are dying. The following story, in which both a TV and an alarm system failed, illustrates this very well, as does the nurse's comment.

Lucie Green and her uncle were sitting beside her father as he lay in a coma in his hospital bed.

The TV screen went totally blank, the sound went totally and then a nurse came rushing into the room and asked why we had pressed the alarm. At that very moment my father, 58, took his last breath. Nobody had rung the alarm, yet it was ringing in the nurse's office and nobody can explain why the television started malfunctioning. A short while after my father's passing, the TV returned to normal. I later spoke to the nurse about the alarm going off and she said it happened all the time at the point of somebody passing. I am neither a believer or non-believer in an afterlife, but this has certainly opened my eyes to something out there that nobody can understand.

Mechanical malfunction on a flamboyant scale is described by Ron Baker, who sent us the following account. Ron says that it has been the only odd experience of his life, and has intrigued him ever since.

In 1954 I was serving in the RAF at a radar establishment at RAF Fairlight, near Hastings in Sussex. On a Bank Holiday weekend, when most of the camp was on a 72-hour pass, I was duty driver for the whole weekend, when only a skeleton staff was on the base. Late in the evening . . . I was sitting in the PBX having a late cup of coffee with the duty operator. At exactly 11 p.m. the switchboard shut down and even the green light which indicated that the board was on mains power went out. What should have happened then was that a red light should have lit, indicating that the emergency power supply had cut in. However, no red light showed and the switchboard was absolutely dead. The teleprinter which, like the PBX board, operated from a dedicated GPO landline, was also out of action. This meant that the station, one of the Chain Home radar watch units which protected our coastline during the then very worrying Cold War, was out of contact with all other units and therefore causing a break in the radar network, an extremely serious situation. While the PBX operator carried out every possible check on the equipment, I went to the guardroom to report the problem and to arrange for someone to travel into Hastings to report the problem to the GPO emergency service.

This all took half an hour, then at exactly 11.30 the switchboard came back to life. This allowed us to call in the GPO engineer, who carried out a complete check without finding any fault at all. So, beyond making a report of the happening to our parent unit Duty Officer, no more could be done. But at 9 a.m. the following morning a telegram arrived for the Station Commander from the family of an airman named Brown, one of the PBX operators who had gone home on leave, saying that he had been taken suddenly ill and had died the previous night at 11 p.m.!

Further checks by the GPO and by our own technical staff failed to find any fault with the landline or the switchboard or teleprinter, and the problem never occurred again.

Here again there is the relationship of the operator to the equipment, and the appearance of a sort of sympathetic dysfunction of it when he died. This odd interaction between man and machine also often crops up in the parapsychology literature, when poltergeist activity associated with adolescents seems to cause interference with electrical and telephonic equipment.[2]

But perhaps the most intriguing of these odd phenomena associated with the time of death, both because of the frequency with which it seems to occur and the way it has entered our folk memory, are the clocks that are reported to stop – as in the old song about grandfather's clock. Now clocks do, in most people's experience, sometimes stop and even start again for no apparent reason, and if they happen to do so at the time of a death, coincidence often seems as reasonable an explanation as any other. But in the following account, the extraordinary coincidence in time, the close connection between the dying man and his clock, and the fact that he pointed to it at the crucial moment of his death, make this a particularly persuasive story.

In the early 1970s my great-uncle (my grandmother's brother) died at home. He lived with my grandparents. On the wall at the foot of his bed was an old casement clock. It was about 100 years old and had been 'passed down' to him. To my knowledge, it had never worked. My grandfather said that as my great-uncle was dying, he suddenly pointed to the clock. It struck 4 p.m., about the right time, and then my great-uncle died.

In this account coincidence is piled on coincidence like Pelion upon Ossa. It struck – for the first time in living memory – at the moment her great-uncle pointed at it. It struck approximately the right time. And it struck at the moment of its owner's death.

Margaret Catherine and David Eccleshall described very similar experiences. Margaret:

When my mother was terminally ill with motor neurone disease, although speaking was very difficult for her she made me understand that someone had come and stood beside her bed and reassured her that she should not be frightened, and they would be with her when she died. I could not understand who it was that visited her, but she was greatly reassured and peaceful and accepting after that visit. That was just a few days before her eventual death. On the morning of her death, I went in to the garage to get my car and I saw her clock, of which she was very fond, and which had just been packed in the garage with all her possessions when we had cleared her flat. The thought came to me that it was a shame to keep it in the garage, and I took it into the house and put it to the right time, left it on the table and went to work. While at work a nurse phoned to tell me that my mother had died at ten minutes to eleven that morning. She had not been expected to die that day, and I was very upset that I had not been with her. I drove straight home, and the first thing I saw on entering the house was that the clock had stopped at ten minutes to eleven exactly. I had only wound it that morning, there was no explanation for it stopping, and 21 years later it is still going strong on my mantelpiece.

Jennie Stiles described how, when her aunt died suddenly and in tragic circumstances, she had the task of clearing her apartment in London, which she knew well. 'The first time I entered her apartment following her death I noticed that every single clock had stopped at the same time. The exact time of her death.'

It is certainly reasonable to argue that people have a close relationship with mechanical clocks. They have to wind them each week, and because mechanical systems are seldom totally accurate they have to reset the time every now and then. You could argue that we are involved with our mechanical clocks. But it is difficult to make the same argument for electric clocks. After all, these are simply plugged in and then they go, and they don't need to be tended at regular intervals. One might even hypothesize that mechanical clocks and watches would stop at the time of death, but electrical ones would not. However, a moment's thought would probably negate this view. Clocks are an intimate part of our lives. We regulate our behaviour by them, we are always glancing at them, they tell us when to get up and when to go to bed. So perhaps we should not draw a hard and fast distinction between mechanical and electric clocks. The following story is not the only one to show that the mechanical-only hypothesis does not hold.

David:

My father died at 3.15 a.m. At about 8.30 a.m. I went to see my Uncle Archie, who'd been close to Dad, rather than phone him, to tell him about losing dad and bring him back to the house if he wished. As Uncle Archie opened the door it was clear he was distressed, and as I began to tell him of Dad's passing away he interrupted me and said he already knew . . . he said no one had telephoned him but told me to look at the clock on the mantelpiece – it was stopped at 3.15, as was indeed his own wristwatch, his bedside clock and all other clocks in the house. There was even an LED display, I think on a radio, flashing 3.15. I was completely taken aback, but Archie seemed comfortable with the phenomenon and was just concerned at losing someone close.

Perhaps it is more logical to accept that nothing in nature occurs singly, so if bells ring and electrical systems fail to work, then there is no reason why clocks, with which we have an even more intimate relationship, should not be influenced by someone's death in the same way.

Julie Lewis's grandfather had a clock he had won as a prize for running, which stopped when he died. She adds: 'My granddad told my grandma that he was leaving her just shortly before he died; I'm not sure how he knew, only that he did know that his time had come.' And Janice Aston also told us of an interesting 'clock coincidence'.

For several weeks (before he died) my dad had been messing with an old clock which had been lying around the house for some time and which did not work. Every time I visited at weekends he seemed to be playing with it and eventually he got it to work.

On the day of his funeral this clock was on the mantelpiece and keeping good time – I noticed this before going to the funeral. However, following the funeral, on looking at this clock I observed that it had stopped, never to go again, and it was in fact thrown out.

Peter Turnbull described how a small battery-operated clock of his father's stopped at the time of his father's twin brother's death. It was restarted easily without a change of battery and then ran perfectly until his father began to develop dementia, when the clock started to speed up, until towards the end of his father's life it was going about twice as fast as normal and was useless as a timepiece.

I knew that it would stop when he died, and I got into the habit of putting my ear to the clock, and if I heard its soft but rapid tick I would say, 'Still with us then, Johnny boy?'

In fact when his father did die, Mr Turnbull forgot to look at the clock for two or three days, but then found it had indeed stopped – at 4.37 a.m., eight minutes before the officially given time of death at 4.45 a.m.

I will never know whether the clock stopped in anticipation as if having some prior knowledge of the moment of his death or whether by chance it was showing the right time at the moment he died. Anyway I opened the clock, withdrew the battery, superglued

136

the thing shut and put it back on the shelf with my father's flat cap on top of it. It sits there still, showing the time of my dad's death. A bit morbid for some, but my dad was a good egg.

Just as strange are the accounts we were given of clocks that, after years of inactivity, mysteriously started again at the time of death, as in the following two accounts.

Janice Lane:

My father died 18 months ago. On the morning of his funeral I decided I wanted to wear a watch that he bought me for my eighteenth birthday. I hadn't worn this watch for approximately 18 years. When I took the watch from a box that I had packed away it was ticking and it was exactly the correct time. My watch is a wind-up watch that doesn't run on batteries. The experience of my watch helped me get through the day of the funeral and I felt as though my dad was with me. Before this experience I didn't believe (although I wanted to) in life after death.

Eileen Chamberlain:

My neighbour Mary Holmes, here in Yorkshire, brought her mother over from Lancashire to live with her. Her mother brought a few of her things with her, among which was an old granddaughter clock. After a couple of weeks my neighbour was forced to let the clock run down as its chiming was very loud, especially at night.

Three years after that, Mary went on holiday and her mother went back to Burnley for a short break. During her stay there she became ill and was taken into hospital in Burnley. One day the hospital rang me (Mary was not on the phone then). I fetched Mary, and the hospital told her that her mother had died. I went back to Mary's house with her and made her a cup of tea. As we sat down, the old granddaughter clock on the wall struck twice. For three years it had never made as much as a tick, and in the following months that they kept it after her death it didn't. At the time the clock struck we were sitting about six yards away from the clock and had not walked by it. I have never been convinced when I have read similar stories, but to this day I cannot work out any

137

explanation as to how the old lady's clock could have chimed after her death after having been left run down for at least a couple of years

I don't have any opinions on these kinds of things, but it was something I could never explain. When I told a friend that I was going to write to you, she told me a strange story about her mother-in-law's clock. When her mother-in-law died, her husband brought back an old Westminster chime clock from his mother's house. It wasn't working but he put it in a cupboard, intending one day to have it repaired. Again, a few years later, they were sitting talking about the mother-in-law and the things she did. Suddenly they heard the sound of the clock in the cupboard chiming.

OK, maybe there was an explanation – but she says, like my experience, that there was no one moving around the house, and they were a few yards away from the cupboard.

Take care when clocks are around!

After we had received more than a dozen clock-related reports we began to realize that these stories were more than just the stuff of legend, and decided, out of interest, to discover the origin of the grandfather clock song. The story is this.

In the early years of the nineteenth century the floor clock, or long-case or coffin clock (as they were then called) of the song stood in the lobby of the George Hotel in Piercebridge, North Yorkshire, which was run by two bachelor brothers named Jenkins. The clock had been there for many years, and had one characteristic unusual in an old clock – it kept very good time.

One day one of the brothers died and suddenly the old clock started losing time. By the time several clocksmiths had tried, and failed, to mend it, it was losing more than an hour each day. When, some time later, the surviving brother died at the age of 90, the clock, though fully wound, stopped altogether. The new manager of the hotel never attempted to have it repaired, but left it standing in a sunlit corner of the lobby, its hands indicating the moment the last Jenkins brother died.

About 1875, an American songwriter named Henry Clay Work happened to be staying at the George Hotel during a trip to England. He was told the story of the old clock and decided to compose a song about it. Henry returned to America and pub-lished the lyrics that not only sold over a million copies of sheet music, but gave that particular type of clock the name it still has today.

These very physical or mechanical happenings are interesting because they suggest the possibility of connectedness between a dying person and a material object that has significance for them. And because it is a physical manifestation it can also be seen by someone who has no particularly close emotional connection with the dying person. If these things really do occur, one can't help wondering how often they go unnoticed. Clocks and TVs are part of our everyday life. But if, say, an engine driver who had been in charge of the Caledonian Express for 30 years were to die in a hospice and the Express's power simultaneously failed for five minutes, nobody would think of asking, 'Is this old Fred saying goodbye to his engine?' Maybe there are many examples of this in our culture which we just don't see because we are not cognitively complex enough to be aware of them. Who knows whether, if we were to set out to look for them, we might find many more?

Though interesting, these episodes do not seem to carry the same sense of profound meaning as do the visions of the dying and the farewell visits which the bereaved receive from their dead relatives. However, Jung's concept of the archetype and syn-chronicity suggests that, as the universal archetype of the Grim Reaper is activated and death occurs, then in some profound sense, structures in the cosmos are changed and the repercussion is seen in everyday events and phenomena. The very word 'synchronicity' contains the idea of time – *chronos* – and so this linking in time manifested in the clocks' stopping can be regarded as part of the archetypal event of death.

Or should we take the view suggested by Glenys Howarth,[3] that all these experiences suggest that there is a continuing relation-ship between the bereaved and the deceased, and that the con-ceptual boundaries between the living and the dead are much more fluid than we suppose?

The events described in this chapter may indeed be coinci-dences, but that doesn't make them any the less interesting. Allan Kellehear[4] describes an occasion when he was struggling to find a comforting answer for a Japanese woman who had made a pact with her mother, to whom she was very close, that whichever of them died first would try to contact the other. Now the woman asked Allan why, two years after her mother's death, she had not yet heard from her. Did it mean that she had not survived, or was in difficulties, or had abandoned their pact? Allan sought advice from a friend who had worked in Japan for many years and was used to discussing such knotty problems with the Japanese. He told him that when he was asked such a question he would say, 'Are you absolutely sure that you haven't heard from them? Think carefully. Are you sure?' Very often, after a death, people will have dreams, or experience odd or inexplicable events, and feel with certainty that these indicate a connection with the person they loved. But often, although they may be desperate for such a sign, they may be afraid of over-interpreting what they see or feel and reject it, or are so absorbed in grief that they notice little of what goes on around them. But what is important is that if you have such experiences and they seem to you to have significance, you should trust your own instincts. Allan concludes:

You can make meaning out of anything. There is a fine line between self-delusion and personal meaning, for sure, but never let others decide for you. Only you know who loves you. And some love-letters are, and will always be, in secret code. Some messages will be for your eyes only. Even in death.

Odd animal behaviour

There is nothing new about the notion that animals can acquire information from some extra sense that, if we have ever had it, we have lost. Rupert Sheldrake's book, *Dogs That Know When Their Owners Are Coming Home*[5] analysed more than 2,500 case histories and concluded that three main areas of unexplained behaviour were exhibited by dogs and cats – telepathy, sense of direction (animals can find their way home across great distances) and premonition (they can often sense earthquakes and volcanic eruptions in advance). Most pet owners can probably quote some example of a cat or dog behaving like a mind-reader. Dogs often behave as if they know when their owner is setting off home, though the owner may be many miles away, and may wait by the door for them to arrive. Cats are notoriously able to sense when their owners are planning to take them to the vets (we have personal and incontrovertible evidence for this, based on a prospective study with one grey feline family member). Sheldrake contacted 65 veterinary offices in London and asked if they had any problem with cat owners keeping their appointments. Not only had 64 noticed such problems, but some were no longer making appointments for cat owners, explaining, 'Cat appointments don't work.' It isn't simply that the cats notice their owner approaching with a cat basket – the animals actually hide as soon as they sense that their owner is beginning to think 'I'd better start looking for Puss now if we're to make it by 11.15 . . .'

An awareness of death is certainly not restricted to our own species. Elephants, for example, have been shown to have an interest in and apparently to show compassion for other elephants who are sick, dying or dead, even if they are not of the same family. And the enormous interest generated by a recent paper by Dr David Dosa in the *New England Journal of Medicine*, 'A day in the life of Oscar the cat',[6] indicates the fascination that prescient pet behaviour holds for most of us. Oscar lives in a nursing home in Providence, Rhode Island, and has an uncanny ability to sense when a resident is about to die. When a patient is near death, Oscar nearly always appears and hops onto the bed. The staff have come to recognize and respect Oscar's instincts, and send for the relatives of any patient he has chosen to curl up alongside. But they have no explanation for it. He shows no interest in patients who are simply in poor shape, or who still have a few days to live. One theory is that a cat's acute sensitivity to smell might enable it to detect some subtle change in metabolism around the time of death, but no one has been able to suggest why it should show any interest.

Given this seeming extra-sensory ability of cats and dogs, it is not surprising that so many people, and so many friends, have told us of deathbed-related cat and dog incidents.

Ann Liddell described the odd behaviour of her Newfoundland dog on the night her mother died. 'At about 4.30 a.m. he started to bark – not his usual sharp warning bark, but howling. I knew instantly that my mother had died, and soon after we got the call from the hospital to confirm this.'

Michael Finch's mother was in a Macmillan unit, dying of cancer and in a coma. One night Michael left the hospital and returned home to let the dog out.

I will NEVER forget this as long as I live. At 10.45 p.m. on 12 November 1995 the dog began to howl like a wolf. It was spine chilling. I just knew that this was because Mum had died. For five minutes he howled uncontrollably and then took to his bed. The dog was a King Charles Cavalier, and in his then 12 years had never made such a deep, wild and rasping sound as that. When my father and sister returned about an hour later they confirmed my thoughts, that Mum had died at 10.45 p.m.

A friend of ours told us this odd and inexplicable dog story. Allan's parents were divorced when he was four, and after the divorce he and his Japanese mother went to Japan to stay with her family for some months. Most of the Japanese family were unhappy about permitting a 'mixed race' child to stay with them except for one maternal uncle who objected to this racism and took Allan and his mother in. After a few months they returned to his home country, and since then Allan has had very little contact with any of his Japanese relatives. In the 1990s Allan was reunited with this uncle and was able to thank him personally for his stand against negative elements of his family. Every year after that last meeting this uncle sent an annual Christmas letter to Allan.

One evening Allan and his wife Jan were sitting relaxing in their sitting-room when his dog, who was lying beside his wife's chair on the opposite side of the room to Allan, sat up and started to behave very oddly. She began to growl – something she has never done. She seemed to be growling at Allan, or at least something in Allan's direction. After a few moments she stopped growling but went on staring fixedly, not at Allan, but apparently at a point somewhere just to one side of Allan – as if there were a person sitting or standing next to where Allan was seated. But, of course, there was no one there at all. After a minute or two the dog settled down, but Allan and Jan remained puzzled. Next day, Allan's mother phoned to tell him that his uncle had died the previous evening, around the time the dog had begun to behave so strangely. Allan is a researcher and not a fanciful man, but the connection between the two events seemed too strong to attribute merely to chance.

Susan Burman described how, as her husband was dying, she was lying alongside him on the bed and their cat was curled up by his feet. As he took his last breath, the fur on the cat's back stuck out as if by static electricity.

We were told by a carer interviewed in our nursing-home study[7] of a very similar reaction by a resident's cat which normally slept on his bed. The cat happened to come into the room at the moment the resident died, and a nurse who was present reported, 'Its hackles went up. It shrieked and it just sped around the room a couple of times and then it shot out of the room as though it didn't want to be there. The cat sensed that the spirits had finally come for the resident.'

An even stranger story is that of the Cox's cat. It concerns two of our oldest friends, biochemists working in a university research department – a couple, you might think, not given to imagining things, or jumping to unwonted conclusions on flimsy evidence. For some years before she died, Brian's elderly aunt would visit them regularly. Each time she came she would spend most of her time sitting in one particular chair, and the cat (gratified, as cats usually are, to find a member of the household willing to sit still in one particular place for some considerable time) would spend most of its time sitting on her knee. The aunt had always insisted that when she died, Brian should ensure that she was buried beside her husband, otherwise, she said, she would come back and haunt him. Then, some months later, she died. Between the day she died and the day of her funeral the cat behaved strangely. On going into the sitting room, its hackles would rise and its fur stand on end. It avoided the aunt's chair and hid behind the sofa. After the funeral, when the aunt had indeed been buried beside her husband, the cat's behaviour returned to normal.

Far from reacting like Oscar the cat, who never lost his composure in the face of death, and indeed seemed to seek death out, most of the animals we have been told about seem to have been very disturbed by whatever it was they saw or felt. The dogs bark or howl, the cats' fur stands on end. Whether or not what they are experiencing is the presence of the dying, or an awareness of death, there is no question of them finding it a comforting experience. Humans do – but humans, after all, have a conceptual framework within which they can interpret it. For animals, it must simply be a new experience, beyond their understanding and so fearful.

The following story has an interesting twist, in that in this case it is the cat's owner who seems to be sharing a near-death experience with her in a dream, and then feels some sense of her presence after her death. Danny Penman's cat, Buffy, was old, blind and epileptic, and had been ill on and off for months.

She was the most wonderful little creature I've ever come across. She adopted me when I was in London and I loved her to bits. One night I was meditating, when something very strange happened. Halfway through, I felt myself doing that whole 'long dark tunnel' thing. It has never happened before. I was with Bella [Danny's partner] and we had Buffy between us. She started off limping like she does and became sleeker and faster and then became pale like a ghost. She began to fly away from us towards the light. We were both bathed in the most beautiful and intense light, and Buffy flew to meet it. For some really bizarre reason my arms flung themselves upwards, toppling me over onto the bed. Just outside the bedroom door in the 'real world' Buffy was becoming agitated and started to cry. Shortly after, she became desperately sick and we had to take her to the vet's. We had her put to sleep. She died in my arms. It was the hardest thing I've ever had to do but I couldn't watch her suffer any more.

That night I couldn't sleep and heard her tapping on the litter tray. Nothing else makes that sound. I heard herself cleaning her coat this morning (but that was less clear). It's all been a very strange and upsetting experience.

Before leaving the area of animal-related incidents, a word about birds. Birds are traditionally associated with death – usually as harbingers of doom – and several accounts sent to us concerned bird sightings. In two cases, shortly after the death a small bird flew into the house and perched, apparently unconcerned, on a piece of furniture before flying out again. Not all that unusual, though for the birds in question to appear unperturbed is certainly strange; it's more usual for a bird that has flown into a house to fly around, beating itself against the windows in a panic-stricken attempt to escape. But in each case the people involved felt that this was a visit intimately related to the death. Alison Hole, a nurse, wrote to us describing the moments after the death of one of her patients. The heaviness in the atmosphere of a room after a death, and the feeling that 'something' lingers on after a death and must be released has also been mentioned by several other correspondents.

. . . walking across the room was slow as the atmosphere was heavy and the floor was like walking through tar. Once I opened the window . . . the atmosphere in the room cleared and I noticed a white bird the other side of the window. While it is quite normal for birds to nest or rest on the hospital window ledges, this was around 4 a.m. in the winter, it was dark out and too early for the dawn, and this was not a seagull. I never saw another pale bird nor have I ever left a room without opening the window to allow the spirit to go free.

The three following stories describe bird behaviour that is way beyond what one would expect of a normal bird in normal circumstances. A crow, a jackdaw and a large brown owl are the central figures in these stories.

My father was gravely ill, and died in a small hospital in the village of Rustington from an enlarged heart disorder on 20 July 1999. My mother, sister and I moved in to stay in his room in the last week. During that time three big black crows continually walked around the grounds outside his window, moving away and then coming back, but pretty much always in view.

Ever since my father retired from business and moved out of London he enjoyed watching birds and reading about them, so we told him they were there, but unfortunately his bed was positioned against the window and he did not see them. A few days later when he became unconscious I asked the nurses to move him to a private room out of respect for his dignity. We stayed and slept in that room with my father for three further nights, singing to him through the night and holding his hand and speaking to him, although he was not conscious. During this time I spoke to my sister, telling her that some rough boys from a neighbouring school were scouting around looking for my son as they considered his old school as rivals to theirs. I told her that although I believed they would just give up and not find my son as he was now at college, I was concerned, feeling protective. The three crows had followed to this side and stayed outside in the grounds beneath his window, the whole hospital being on one floor. At 4 a.m. or thereabouts my father died, and later in the morning my sister and mother left. I stayed, reluctant to leave him to strangers, but also to keep vigil over his body, which I discovered I could keep warm by holding his arm and generating warmth to that area. I stayed for about four or five hours. I did not see the crows again at this point.

I live in Brighton, and my son who was then at A-level college had been called and knew the gravity of his grandfather's situation, and so waited at home in support and respect instead of going to his part-time job. When I arrived home some time in the afternoon, my son told me that something odd had happened – not inferring that it had any significance to his grandfather's death. He said that during the last two days a huge black crow had appeared in the back garden, sitting on the railing outside, and that our Abyssinian cat, who is a warrior breed attacking anything in his territory, came indoors and would not go outside, and he said that all the neighbourhood cats did the same. He said the crow just sat there for two days, and although he thought it was funny, it was quite unnerving as well. And then in the morning, hours after my father's death, the crow tried to come through the catflap.

I have never heard of a bird of this size behaving like that and actually forcing itself into an occupied place before. I suppose I felt as if my father had sent an emissary to my son to watch over him.

I think he had heard my conversation with my sister, as I have since found out that the unconscious have unimpaired hearing.

My father was a Russian Polish Jew and so fiercely protective and family orientated; to hear that his eldest grandson was in any danger would have made a huge impact on him as he always protected the whole family not only financially but also physically. I thought that it was as though the minute he died he came to my son in any way he could – as if my father had been so frustrated that he couldn't be there.

Sarah Quinnel:

My mum kept a jackdaw when she was a child and so it is a bird she would notice. We had never had them at our house until the day my granddad died, and one turned up, walked up the garden and into the kitchen – straight past the cat, which took no notice at all (my cat loved my granddad and spent all the time he visited sitting on his lap). It looked at my mum squawked and then left . . . it is all a bit odd and not something you can easily discuss with people as they think you are mad.

Olly Robinson's owl made its appearance some time after the death it was associated with, so it falls into the category of after-death communication rather than deathbed coincidence. But the extraordinary and totally out-of-character behaviour of the owl, together with the feelings it engendered in Oliver's mother, mean that the temptation to include it here was irresistible.

The first appearance of the owl was on one warm April morning, some months after the death of Oliver's grandmother. Oliver's mother here describes what happened.

There was a terrific commotion outside the kitchen, caused by our garden birds. When I went out to see what all the fuss was about, the birds were dive-bombing an owl which sat on one of the lower branches of the oak tree. It seemed strange that an owl was out in the middle of the day, and although the small birds were trying to frighten it away, it just sat quietly in the tree, mewing every now and then . . .

As the day warmed up I opened the French windows on the south side of the house. When I stepped out into the garden, there was a great flapping of wings and the owl flew down and landed right in front of me on the grass. It was a large tawny owl about 12 inches high. It looked up at me with big brown eyes and mewed. It seemed very tame. Thinking that it might have escaped from somewhere, I telephoned the police to see if anyone had lost a tame owl, but they had no record of it.

During the day, every time I went outside, the owl would come down and stand in front of me, mewing. It was almost as if it was trying to say something. The big brown eyes looked so human and reminded me of my mother, also brown-haired, who had died the previous summer, and it was rather a nice thought that perhaps there was some little message in the owl being there . . . When my husband and children came home that evening I told them about the owl but thought no more about it.

We always sleep with our top windows open, and that night, when we switched off the lights, there was a lot of scuffling and rustling at the window and the owl came down to sit on the window, a behaviour that my husband didn't like at all.

The next morning was a Saturday and we were all having a leisurely breakfast in the kitchen. It was already hot and I opened the kitchen windows. No sooner had I opened the large window over the sink, than there was a great flurry of wings and the owl flew right into the kitchen and up to the large chimney-breast over the Aga. It seemed best for the children and my husband to go out and close the doors while I opened the outside door, hoping to coax it outside, but it seemed to be quite at home in the kitchen. It flew down to the other end and onto the curtain rail and watched me. It had a tremendous wing-span and it was remarkable that nothing was knocked over or broken. Eventually it flew out of the window. The owl sat on the back porch, and when we went out to the car later that morning, it came straight down and perched on the pot I was carrying. As we drove out of the gate, it sat on the gate-post watching us.

My husband asked me not to feed it again, although I would have liked to have kept it around. It came down to our window again that night and to the porch the next day, but not down to my feet. After a few days it disappeared, but every now and then I heard the sound of it mewing nearby.

The ability to fly has always been regarded as a magical power, the stuff of dreams. Perhaps that is why birds have always been regarded as having an element of the supernatural and why, in so many myths and legends, they provide a link between the human world and the supernatural or divine, associated with both birth and death. In some cultures the human soul is believed to arrive on earth in bird form, and in many, birds are seen as carriers or symbols of the human soul, flying heavenwards after death, or as guardians who guide the soul to the afterlife. The ancient Egyptians believed that the soul, once freed from the body, took the form of a bird, and even built their tombs with access to the open air so that these birds could fly in and out, keeping watch on the body. In Jewish tradition the 'soul guide' is a dove; in Syria, figures of eagles on tombs represent the guides that lead souls to heaven.

Perhaps these delightful modern bird stories indicate the possible origin of these myths – or maybe they are a demonstration that these are more than simply legends.

Chapter 9

Visions of Light and Mist

Versuchung durch Hochmut:
Temptation through pride

In most religious and mystical traditions, light holds a special significance. People who meditate regularly say that they enter a band of consciousness composed of light, the primary qualities of which are of bliss, compassion and universal love. Light is a predominant feature of the near-death experience (in our own study it was experienced by over 70 per cent) and always its qualities are described positively – it is said to be warm, loving, peaceful, compassionate, and also compelling, so that people feel drawn towards it. Often light is seen at the end of a tunnel in the near-death experience, drawing nearer and growing brighter as the person passes through the darkness of the tunnel, but many people experience only the light, without the darkness.

I have seen a beautiful light and I was going towards it, I wanted to go into that light, it was so peaceful I really had to fight to come back.

151

She saw a light in the distance, she was being drawn towards it, but she said adamantly, 'I'm not ready yet.'

Diane Brown told us that the day before her husband Alan was diagnosed as having an abscess in his spinal cord, and septicaemia, he was in so much pain that several times he had begged God to let him die. What happened to him then has all the hallmarks of a classic near-death experience.

Suddenly, he began seeing the most fantastic colours, more beautiful than he had ever experienced before; he found himself floating and the colours changed to a blindingly bright white fluffy light (his words). All his pain was gone and then the clouds parted and hands were beckoning him. He went forward, he wanted to go forward with all of his might. He did not give a thought to me or our children, he just wanted to go towards the light. Then, in his words, 'Some bastard kicked me in the back and I was back in my bed.' Oh, he was so angry.

When one compares the experiences which are reported by the dying with the near-death experiences of people who – like Alan Brown – survive, there seem to be far more similarities than differences. It is logical to conclude that the two sets of experiences are related, that they form part of a continuum. This is seen very clearly from some of the accounts people have sent us, in which there is what one might call an approaching death prodrome for a few days or even weeks before the person finally dies. Light, for example, is often seen, not only at the time of death but in the days or even weeks before death. Mrs Judith Wilson, who used to work in an old people's home, commented: 'I have witnessed several people who spoke of a bright light a few days before death. They all said it was beautiful, and some said they could see people within the light. All of these people passed peacefully.'

Many others have noticed the same phenomenon.

. . . towards the end of his life, Mike . . . would often drift off to sleep and come back to us and say that he had seen a strong light, but that it was not time to go yet.

Approximately two weeks before my father's death he would tell me about various family members who had died, who he said had been to visit him, particularly my mother and my brother who had died years before. He would say there was a bright light, then he would see them and he could talk to them . . . I sat with the family for a while when he called me. I went to his room and he said, 'Look at that bright light' (apparently on the wall opposite his bed). He was staring at it and sitting up, 'Look at that lovely light, isn't it beautiful?' I could see nothing.

What is especially interesting, however, about light at the time of death is that occasionally people who are sitting with the dying *do* see the light, as though they are somehow sharing the same vision. This is a phenomenon often reported by carers or relatives as well as by the dying themselves. The light is usually described as bright and white and associated with strong feelings of love and compassion which at times permeate the whole room. It is often described as emanating from or surrounding the body, and it usually lasts over the time of the death process.

Suddenly there was the most brilliant light shining from my husband's chest, and as this light lifted upwards there was the most beautiful music and singing voices, my own chest seemed filled with infinite joy and my heart felt as if it was lifting to join this light and music. Suddenly there was a hand on my shoulder, and a nurse said, 'I'm sorry love. He has just gone.' I lost sight of the light and music, I felt so bereft at being left behind.

Light which surrounded her 'like a blanket' was a feature of Dilys Gannon's experience described on p. 64 (Chapter 4). The night her mother died in an accident, Diana Merchant had a nightmare in which she saw 'the most wonderful starburst or "solar ray", really white light, and I went back to a deep sleep'. She believed that in the 'unbelievably bright light' she had seen her mother's spirit 'ascending to heaven'. Joan Lovatt described what happened while she was holding the hand of her mother as she lay dying:

Suddenly I was aware that her father was stood at the foot of her bed. My mother was staring at him too and her face was lit up with joy. It was then I saw that her face appeared to be glowing with a gold light. The light began to leave through the top of her head and go towards the ceiling. Looking back to my mother's face I saw that she was no longer breathing.

Note that Joan says she was 'aware' of her grandfather standing at the foot of the bed – she does not say in so many words that she 'saw' him. It seems as though she was sharing the experience with her dying mother. Jackie Burton's description of what she experienced as her father died is also almost word for word what so many people have described in the near-death experience. She believes her eyes were closed, so that again it seems that these two people, the living and the dying, are sharing the same internal subjective experience:

Dad passed away in the early 1980s. At the moment of his last breath, I was at his side, holding his hand. I believe my eyes were closed. At this point I can only say that everything disappeared and was replaced by a bright white consuming light. Within this was total peace. No pain, no thought, no time. It could have lasted seconds or minutes. I have no awareness of its duration.

The following account also conveys the enormous emotional significance these moments have for the relatives who experience them.

My mother passed away 15 years ago and I experienced something quite indescribable a few hours before she passed. I saw beautiful circles of light around the room and felt something so peaceful that it is hard to forget. I kept rubbing my eyes, thinking I was imagining things, but they were still there. One could argue that I was extremely tired as I had had no sleep, but I felt so peaceful and it was as if the room was glowing in a shade of warm orange. My mother passed away a couple of hours later. I will never forget the experience.

Andrew Gordon remembers a dream he had the night his grand-mother died. Such a young child would have had no real concept of death, and certainly no preconceptions associating light with death, so it is interesting to see how closely his dream corresponds to the near-death model of the dying person approaching the light, as if he was indeed somehow sharing the experience with her.

I was only about six or seven at the time. I was sleeping and I dreamt my nan going up to a bright light. She was talking to me, but I cannot recall what she said; but I will always remember that moment, she was just floating up waving at me. I was very touched by this and I remember when I woke up the next day my mum telling me that my nan had died, but I never felt surprised. I will always remember that night – although my nan had died, it will always comfort me, seeing her smiley face being taken up to a safer place.

Dr Sue Brown's mother was taken ill with a brain haemorrhage late in October 1979 and taken into hospital in Liverpool. At the time, she was a postgraduate student doing a PhD at Swansea University, and it was several days before her aunt contacted her to tell her that her mother was in hospital and not too good. She drove up there immediately, desperately hoping she would get there in time, and feeling angry that she had not been told sooner. The next day when she went to the hospital:

My mother was awake and talking . . . and my aunt and uncle were there so I didn't have much chance for a personal conversation with her, but I do remember quite clearly that she said one very odd thing which I found unnerving – that my father had been to see her. He had been dead for five years, so I remember thinking that she must be confused due to her condition . . . Before we left at the end of visiting time, my mother asked if she could see me on my own the next day.

I should state that my relationship with my mother had not been good. I was nagged constantly and never seemed to do anything right, although I know that she was proud of my academic achievements . . . As an only child I had experienced a miserable childhood. Nevertheless, I had wanted to have some time with my mother, so had resolved to ask my aunt to give me some time alone with her the next day.

After returning from the hospital that night, I was drained and tired, but went to bed in my aunt's guest room quite late – after midnight I think, as naturally I was anxious and stressed. I slept, but at about 4 a.m. I awoke suddenly and felt instantly wide awake. The room was light (but there were no electric lights on – and this was November, so it was dark outside at the time) and I felt this warm feeling and was saying to myself (I suppose) that death was all right and nothing to be scared of. The room faded, and a few minutes later the telephone rang. It was the hospital, asking to speak to the next of kin. They said that they regret-ted to inform me that my mother had gone into a coma earlier and had died a few minutes ago. I remember distinctly saying, 'Yes – I know. Thank you.' I put the phone down, and after telling my aunt I went back to bed and slept.

I figured afterwards that my waking up after only a few hours sleep (when I was exhausted), apparently close to the moment of her death was a coincidence, or due to the anxiety and stress I was going through. But I have never been able to explain why the room seemed to be bathed in light – unless of course, I was having some sort of hallucination in the moments between deep sleep and being awake. The experience did help me. I am sure that it made me more able to cope with all the funeral arrangements and so on while staying with relatives I was not particularly close to. My main concern was that my mother would have been scared alone in the hospital, and this experience helped me think that the process was not too awful for her.

I am not religious, seeing myself as just a member of one of the species alive on earth. But I am open to possibilities about things we don't yet fully understand, and if some special communication is possible, and if something like that did happen, it seemed as if it might have happened because of unfinished business between me and my mother.

Sue comments that although she was much closer to her father than to her mother, nothing similar happened at the time of his sudden death in 1974. None of the experiences that have been described to us seem to provide any evidence that they are conjured up by the living, but many of them suggest strongly, as this one does, that they are somehow driven by the person who is dying. Sue's mother clearly felt she needed to talk to her on her own before she died, and Sue herself felt that there was unfinished business between them which her mother may have wanted to resolve. Sue's reaction – the feeling of warmth and calm, the fact that she went straight back to sleep afterwards, and the fact that she felt that the whole experience had helped her come to terms with her mother's death – suggests very much that this resolution between them was achieved. The importance of effecting reconciliation before death was stressed by many of the carers we talked to in our hospice and nursing home studies, and some also commented on the feelings of peace and love in the room of the dying when this kind of resolution had been accomplished.

In early October 1982, Neil Handley had a premonitory dream in which his father (who at the time was 76 and had no health problems) told him he 'had had enough and would be leaving at the end of the month'. Neil thought he had had an odd dream, but thought no more about it. Then on the last day of October:

In the middle of the night I woke up to hear Mum screaming that Dad had taken ill so I called the emergency doctor. Dad had suffered a major stroke and died the following evening. I was asleep at home when he died in the hospital and I felt an electric shock and saw a cord snapping which woke me up to find that my bedroom was lit up in what I can only describe as an electric blue light. Within a minute of waking and seeing this, the phone rang and a nurse told me my father had just died.

This experience of Neil's could be interpreted as an awakening from an anxiety dream about his father, in which he felt the electric shock and saw the cord snapping. It is also possible to argue that he then entered a drowsy, hypnopompic state in which he saw a hallucination of a blue light in the room, although he describes himself as being fully awake, which makes this unlikely. But the very precise timing of the telephone call makes it difficult to argue that his experiences were not connected with his father's death. It is far more reasonable to assume, as Neil did, that he was at that moment in some way linked with his dying father.

Mrs A. Bell is an only child who 'loved her father beyond words'. When he was dying of cancer 20 years ago:

We spent ten dreadful days with him in hospital in Southampton. The day he died we had all spent the day with him. My husband and I left at around 5 or 6 p.m., to go home to our young children in Surrey. My mother stayed with him. On our way home I felt this blue light come to me as if he were saying goodbye. It was a jolt, a feeling – I cannot describe it, I did not understand it at the time – but when we got home I was told that he had died at that moment. I will never forget it – he definitely came to me to wish me well and tell me he was on his way, Mum was with him but I was not, and that is why he came to me.

'Ali' gave us this wonderfully observed and detailed account of the death of her dearly loved great-aunt. The detail in this account must raise the question of whether, if we were taught about these phenomena, many more of us would be aware of their existence and thus more likely to observe them. It is a fundamental psychological principle that we tend only to see things we expect to see, and on which our attention is focused.

There was what I can only describe as a white light or form around the top of her head and face area. Her face looked so radiant in all that very bright light. I felt unable to move any further to be closer to her, I'm not sure if this was because I physically could not, or perhaps because I knew that this was such a special, significant and sacred moment, that it would be wrong of me to intrude. Something deep within me told me that this was the moment she was taking her 'leave' of this world. I knew that I was probably witnessing the 'moment', her spirit or soul, her inner being, leaving her body!

I have never been present at somebody's death before and was not sure or prepared for what to expect, but somehow when it happened, everything just fell into place . . . I don't know how long this vision lasted; in reality it was probably just seconds, but it was just so mind-blowing that I felt as though I had held my breath for the entire moment, not wanting to disrupt it in any way! Her hair seemed to be standing on end, as if the force or the pressure was lifting or blowing it all upwards, towards the top of her head. This light or form gradually disappeared from around her head and face area and what remained was what I can only describe as a 'total stillness' in the room. I calmly walked over to her side, kissed her and wished her a safe journey. I knew she was no longer here, the room felt so empty. Although it had been empty on many occasions prior to her death, there was definitely something 'different' now . . . as though the essence, the energy that had been there previously, had taken its leave too. I guess this is what death does!

Ali also echoed what many people have told us about the reactions of people to whom she tried to talk about what happened, and how painful and frustrating it is to have people deny the experience and doubt the evidence of your eyes, your ears and your intuition.

I have not been able to talk about what happened, or rather what I witnessed, on the night my great-aunt Odette passed away . . . I wanted to talk and talk about it, but not many people in my world are prepared or willing to listen . . . One particular response I received from a family member was, 'That's not right, that doesn't happen' . . . to completely deny my 'experience' I found very hard to accept.

What is clear from Ali's account is how few people know and understand the features of the dying experience, and how different it would be if these phenomena were more widely recognized.

The departing soul?

The first time I was introduced to the idea that shapes, forms or vapours are sometimes seen leaving the body at the time of death was at a conference in New Zealand, where I met a GP who told me the following story. He had been playing golf, when another player on the course had a heart attack. He went over to see if he could help, and as he approached he saw what he described as a white form which seemed to rise and separate from the body. He had seen many people die before, he told me, but this was the first time he had ever witnessed anything like this.

The perception of something leaving the body, or seen in its vicinity, around the time of death is a little discussed phenomenon, but it is often reported by professional carers and, most importantly, by relatives of the dying, though usually only when they are directly asked about it. The accounts are very varied, but central to the experience is a form or shape which is seen leaving the body, usually from the mouth, chest or through the head, though we have also had accounts of something leaving through the feet. (The idea of leaving the body through the head is often described in Buddhist literature, and people who have out-of-body experiences often say they seem to leave or re-enter the body through the top of their head – the crown chakra.) Many people who see it interpret it as being the 'soul' or 'spirit' taking its final leave of the body.

Clouds, smoke and mist

What is seen has been described to us variously as a 'smoke', a 'grey mist', 'a white mist', 'a very wispy white shape', which floated by and then disappeared. Sometimes it will hover above the body before rising to disappear through the ceiling, and it is often associated with love, light, compassion, purity and occasionally with heavenly music. Not everyone who is in the room sees the vision, its appearance is transient and its perception is sensitive to interruption – people coming into the room or talking often make it disappear.

Those who have this experience, particularly if it is associated with love and light, feel enormously comforted, a feeling which may go on for many days after the death – and more importantly, the experience remains a comfort over many years. Very often words are inadequate for what is actually seen, as Gill Fernley's account of what she saw at the time of her father's death demonstrates:

As he died, something which is very hard to describe because it was so unexpected and because I had seen nothing like it, left up through his body and out of his head. It resembled distinct delicate waves/lines of smoke (smoke is not the right word but I have not got a comparison) and then disappeared. I was the only one to see it. It left me with such a sense of peace and comfort. I don't think that we were particularly close, as my sister and I had been sent off to boarding school at an early age. I do not believe in God. But as to an afterlife, I now really do not know what to think.

One of the points which is so clearly made in this account – and indeed in almost every account we've been given – is that people don't expect these things to happen. They are almost invariably taken by surprise by them, and very few people have a ready explanation. Gill, like most people who have had this experience, had no expectations arising from religious belief, and it is also interesting that, like Sue Brown, whose experience is quoted on pp. 155–6, she felt she was not particularly close to her father.

The following two accounts are unusual in that the cloud-like formation was seen not leaving the body but at a distance from it, more suggestive of a deathbed coincidence.

My husband and I had gone to see his 83-year-old grandmother who was dying. When we left, we stood at the gate talking to my father-in-law and his sister. As we were chatting, I saw what looked like a grey cloud move from the back of the house (where her room was) and float up into the sky. I watched it for a couple of seconds and was on the point of saying to my father-in-law, 'Go in and look at Gran', but unfortunately I didn't and didn't mention what I had seen to anyone. When we got back home we had a phone call from my father-in-law to say they found that Gran had died when they got back into the house. It was a clear March night with no clouds, and none of the houses had smoke coming from the chimneys.

This next experience involves a father–daughter relationship which was not particularly close. Jean's sister, who wrote to us on her behalf, described what Jean saw one evening in 1966, the night their father died.

Our father was very ill in hospital following a heart attack for several days leading up to this event. Jean [his daughter] was at home knitting when she suddenly felt a presence in the room, so she stopped knitting and looked up to see what she described as a large ball of smoke. The ball looked like a cloud and was raised up off the floor by approximately two feet. This cloud came from across the room towards her and stopped in front of her. She turned around and looked at the clock, it was exactly 11 p.m. Jean turned back and as she did she felt that the cloud was waiting for her, as if the time was of importance, and then it carried on across the room and disappeared. Later that night a relative visited Jean to inform her that our father had died at 11 p.m., which was the time she had seen this cloud glide across the room.

Of all five children, our father was the harshest on Jean, who was very good to him during his lifetime; she has often wondered if he came to say goodbye. I wondered if it was remorse for the way he had treated her, and at the end he realized how wrong he had been and had visited her out of conscience and remorse.

Certainly this account suggests, as do many other deathbed coincidences, that if there is a 'driver' of the experiences, it is the person who is dying, and that the visits perhaps reflect the dying person's wish for reconciliation, or the resolution of tensions or conflicts with those they are leaving behind.

Although, as in all these end-of-life experiences, there is usually a strong emotional bond between the observer of these phenomena and the dying person, we've been told of several cases where this is not so. Like the New Zealand GP who introduced me to this phenomenon, the following account was sent to us by someone who had no personal link with the dying person.

While Gill was working as a nurse in a hospital environment, she says it was always understood that a patient known to be dying would be seen looking at and often talking to an unseen person in the room. While at the South Cleveland Hospital she had another strange experience that she could not fully understand:

At the time I worked night duty. We had a male patient in a side ward: his prognosis wasn't good, although death wasn't deemed imminent. He had two relatives who had decided to stay the night, in case his condition worsened. They retired to an overnight room reserved for relatives. Around 3 a.m., myself and the other nurse on duty were chatting at the nurse's station. The station was illuminated by a single anglepoise light. I saw a white mist at the end of the nurse station. It was there and it was gone. I immediately thought of a fire, perhaps from the kitchen a little way down the corridor. I walked to one end of the ward and my colleague went to the other end. She checked the side rooms and hurried to find me to say the man in question had died, seemingly only just.

We hurriedly phoned the Night Sister to urgently rouse the sleeping relatives. While waiting for them to appear, more relatives of the deceased arrived. They told us they had woken suddenly at home and just felt the urge to visit the hospital, feeling something was wrong.

In this case the 'mist' that was seen was a considerable way away from the body, and Gill says that she herself did not associate it with her patient's death until her colleague suggested that she might have seen his spirit. All we can be sure of is that she saw the 'white mist' and that its appearance seemed to be simultaneous with the patient's death.

Seeing a 'heat haze'
Sometimes what is seen is described as something reminiscent of a mirage, or the heat haze seen rising from a road on a hot day. Anne Lidell describes here what she saw immediately after the death of her closest friend: 'Gayle came in to tell us Annick had died and we sat around the bed quietly . . . what I saw then was totally unexpected. Above Annick's body the air was moving –

rather like a heat haze you see on the road but swirling slowly around.'

Other correspondents have given very similar accounts. This is Penny Bilcliffe's description of what she saw as her sister died:

I am in no way 'fey' but extremely down to earth, and despite having witnessed many deaths during the course of my work as a nurse (latterly in a hospice), I have never before witnessed any kind of apparition, and indeed have a fear of doing so. At the time, that was the very last thing on my mind. I was standing right next to her head, viewing from the side, and more or less as she stopped breathing (hard to be precise) I saw a fast-moving 'Will 'o the Wisp' appear to leave her body by the side of her mouth on the right. The shock and the beauty of it made me gasp. It appeared like a fluid or gaseous diamond, pristine, sparkly and pure, akin to the view from above of an eddy in the clearest pool you can imagine. Or like a clear heat haze. It was made up of two slightly thicker parts linked by a thinner piece in the middle, and it moved rapidly upwards and was gone.

Well, that is the bare bones of what I saw. I could talk more of the impact this has had on my life, the emotional aspects, and the comfort it has given me. Of course, it doesn't prove necessarily that there is an existence after physical death because I cannot know what happened to my sister after that. Maybe that was just part of the process of extinction.

The 'gentle breeze'

Several people have talked about a 'breeze' or a 'rush of air' at the time of death, and this is usually interpreted either as something entering the room, or as the 'essence' of the dead person making its final departure.

Mrs Cathy Holmes was sitting with her brother at her mother's bedside when she died:

I then felt a flapping of air around me and actually physically felt wind moving on my face and arms. It was as if a fan had suddenly been turned on, so I looked around me and up to the ceiling to see if this was the case. There was no fan to be seen. It was just after this experience that my mother died. After describing this to my own vicar, he told me that it was the angels coming to get my mother. My vicar has a great belief in the power of angels.

I know I physically felt something, even though there was nothing around me that could have given me the rush of air to my face. In fact, I remember moving my hand across my face a number of times as it felt as if something was moving there. I have an open mind about what my vicar said, although I also believe in angels. I know this experience has made me feel at peace with my mother's passing, as I feel it could have been as my vicar said, or it could have been my mother's spirit leaving her earthly body.

John Pennington had a similar experience when his father died in October 2006, aged 91, and this is one of the few cases when more than one of those present observed the phenomenon at the same time. In this case John, his sister and his son all felt the same breeze blow into the room.

My sister Margaret was sitting immediately next to the window and my son was on the other side. Dad suddenly closed his eyes and mouth for the last time and then they slowly opened again, as his face relaxed, and it never moved again. Just as that happened, Margaret cried out a little in surprise. That was because the curtains had suddenly blown up and inwards as a draught entered the room. My son also saw and felt it too and none of us could explain it. The window was open a little way and, although the day was not completely still outside, and there was a little wind about, the partially closed curtains had not moved at all throughout the morning.

My wife is convinced that someone, hopefully my mother, came for him at that moment. I am a natural sceptic and am aware that people are looking for comfort at such times, but I cannot explain it and it seems to be just too much of a coincidence really, so I believe something like that happened as well. It is hard not to think that.

David Watson says that although he has always been very scep-tical of claims of supernatural phenomena, he experienced something at the time of his father's death that he could not explain and has remained with him. His father suffered the first of a series of devastating strokes when David was 11, and died when David was 15 or 16 years old.

On the evening of his death, I was in my bedroom adjoining the room where my father was lying. We knew he was seriously ill and expected him to die in the short term – within days or possibly weeks. I became aware at some point of a very high-pitched sound – almost too high to actually hear really, more a sensation of pres-sure on the eardrum. It didn't pass and became more intense. For reasons I cannot explain, I felt compelled to go into my father's room where I found that the sound was even more intense. At the same time I became aware of what I would describe as a living 'presence' and the room seemed to be full of an overbearing pres-sure, such as one might experience before a violent thunderstorm. Just at that point I noticed that my father's breathing was becom-ing laboured, and a few moments later he passed away. The sen-sations also ceased at that point and the room became calm again. The whole episode lasted about five minutes, if not less.

The thing that has always struck me was that although I knew he was dying, the urge for me to go into his room at that specific point was overwhelming and coincided almost exactly with the moment of his death. I cannot fully articulate the feeling I had of a 'presence' in the room, just that it was very intense, but not scary.

The feeling that 'something' remains in the room for a while after someone has died has often been mentioned, and these same phenomena – the rush of air, or the feeling of pressure – are often felt some hours after a death. Often people feel com-pelled to open the window of the room after a death, as if to allow this departure:

After the undertakers had removed my husband's body, my sister-in-law and I were in the kitchen having a cup of tea. We both of us suddenly felt this rush of air that seemed to go among and between us for a few seconds. Then later, we went round the corner to his mother's house, as she had offered to cook us breakfast, and my sister-in-law suddenly said, 'I can feel that rush of air again. It's in here with us.' This was very odd and experienced by us all.

Accounts like this suggest that the whole process of dying may encompass more than just the moment of the final breath. Maria and Keith Lees' experience after the death of their son occurred a few hours after the actual time of death, and yet in its description of the 'shimmery haze' and the 'gentle blowing sensation' it is so similar to the previous accounts that it is hard not to accept that it was indeed a son's farewell visit to his parents. In September 2002 Maria and Keith's youngest son, David, died after crashing his motorbike. They arrived at the hospital he had been taken to, where he was on life support, in time to see him, talk to him and say their goodbyes, but he died that afternoon. That evening Maria and her husband were unable to face going to bed and, knowing they wouldn't sleep, they remained dozing in their sitting room, Maria in her usual chair and Keith lying on the sofa, which happened to be where David had spent a lot of his time. Then:

I was wakened from a very light doze by a gentle blowing sensation on my cheek. I turned my head to see if Keith was awake, and as I looked I saw a shimmery haze (similar to what you might see above a road on a hot summer day) hover above Keith's sleeping head, and then it gradually rose up to the ceiling and vanished. I had never before felt a draught in that room or experienced any type of draught similar to the one I felt that night in that room, despite trying to find a source. I believe with all my heart that David came to say goodbye and what I saw was his 'spirit', and what I felt was his last kiss. If it is true that we see our loved ones before we die, then I feel there is nothing to fear in death for us, and everything to look forward to.

The subjective experience of death

One interesting interpretation of these images – the 'smoke and mirage', the light – is that the people who see them are somehow seeing what the dying themselves are experiencing. In the West, dying is regarded as a purely physical event; no attempts have been made to investigate the subjective mental state of the dying. By contrast, the Tibetans, whose culture allows subjective exploration of mental states, and subjective exploration of the mental states of others, have a complex description of the slow process of the disintegration of consciousness in the dying process.

Supposing we compare these end-of-life experiences with the descriptions of the stages of dying as described by the Dalai Lama? Dying is, after all, a universal human experience, and so it makes sense not to limit the frame in which we view it to a purely Western or Christian one.

The Dalai Lama describes the several stages of dying, or dissolution, as follows. In the first level of dissolution the dying person becomes weak and powerless, has difficulty in opening the eyes, and there appears in one's mental state a bluish appearance, like a mirage. 'It is like an appearance of water when the light of the sun strikes the desert in the summer.'

With the second dissolution the dying person is no longer conscious of pleasure or pain or the feelings that accompany mental consciousness. The mental state of this stage 'is the dawning of an appearance called "like smoke" which is like blue puffs of smoke. It is similar to smoke billowing from a chimney in the midst of a mass of smoke.'

With the third dissolution one no longer remembers the names of one's parents, one's capacity to take food goes and the breath is no longer even but is piled breath on breath. The mental state of this dissolution is 'like fireflies. It is like burning red sparks seen within puffs of smoke rising from a chimney or like red sparks in the soot on the bottom of a pan used for parching grain.'

With the fourth dissolution movement is no longer possible, one is no longer able to use one's mind to understand the meaning of worldly activities, and this is the stage when the breath ceases to move in and out. The body is no longer able to experience sensation. The mental state of this level is 'like a burning butter-lamp. It is like the spluttering point of a butter-lamp's flame when it is about to go out.' There is a marked degeneration in the capacity to maintain consciousness.

With the fifth dissolution there is a further disintegration of consciousness; the mental state is the dawning of extreme clarity and vacuity as well as of light with a white aspect. 'Like a night sky pervaded by moonlight in the autumn when the sky is free of defilement.'

With the sixth dissolution there is further degeneration of the energy flows within the body and the mental state dawns with a red or orange appearance, empty, but much clearer than before, 'Shines like an autumn sky, free of defilement and pervaded by sunlight.'

With the seventh or penultimate dissolution, the process approaches completion. In the mental state is an 'empty black appearance, like an autumn sky free of defilement and pervaded by the thick darkness at the beginning of night'. Sometimes this is described as being intensely alive. This state is sometimes called 'the great empty' because it is devoid of mind. It is also thought to be associated (the first time in the death process) with a loss of consciousness.

After a short period of unconsciousness we awake with the eighth dissolution, into the clear light of death, and the 'all empty'. This is actual death, and the 'basic truth body' is formed. We are told that most ordinary humans remain in the clear light for three days. This is a very special time in Tibetan understanding as it is from this state that there is an opportunity to progress to full spiritual evolution, even to the point of ending the cycle of death and rebirth.

The Dalai Lama recommends that we learn these stages before our time comes to die so that they become internal and recognizable markers for us during the dying process. In his system the dawning of the clear light is an opportunity for progression of the soul; thus it is important for 'us' (the soul) to know when this state has arisen.

Certainly we can find some parallels with the Dalai Lama's

formulation. The light, the mirage-like haze, the mist and the smoke all fit into this framework very well. Several people also described something similar to the fireflies or red sparks of the Tibetan imagery. As Linda Lynch's brother lay dying of cancer, his wife and Linda both saw 'odd tiny sparks of bright light emanating from around my brother's body. Not many, just two or three very brief instances. I did not mention this to anyone else present. However, my brother's wife noticed the same thing and mentioned it, so I told her that I too had seen this.'

Other people have also given descriptions which could fit the Tibetan imagery: 'a yellow/orange "sparkly" light which entered my body for about half an hour. This was on the night of my husband's death.'

I could see tiny lights like little slits which kept coming and going, then, starting at the back of my head and slowly working to the front, I felt happiness and there was a bright light, getting brighter and brighter until it got so bright I could not see . . . Margaret had passed away in those moments.

In the Tibetan system, after the clear light described above, the person goes into the Bardo of death, where they meet figures. Could this be equivalent to the people encountered in the visions of the dying?

So are all the people who have told us of their experiences describing elements of a process – dying – common to everyone, though never studied or even acknowledged in the West? People can't 'prove' that they have these experiences, any more than you can prove that a beautiful sunset or a particular piece of music has the power to move you deeply. We don't know why some people have them and others do not. We certainly have no better explanation than the Dalai Lama's to offer for them. However, we are in a strong position as we can study these experiences. We can use our science to collect them, classify them, and find whether they fit a pattern. We can then see what meaning they have for us. It's the way science progresses. It's the way our understanding progresses. And in the West it's the way our culture progresses. Near-death experiences contain many of these same features, suggesting that possibly all these phenomena point in the same direction. What we can do is to acknowledge that for the people who experience them, they have a wider and deeper meaning over and beyond the phenomena themselves. To dismiss them as simply fantasy or imagination is to remain in the Dark Ages and to ignore a whole area of human experience which may, if we pay it enough attention, eventually tell us something very fundamental about life and death that we might otherwise never be able to learn.

Chapter 10

The Search for the Soul

Trost durch Demut:
Comfort through humility

The last act is bloody, however fine the rest of the play. They throw earth over your head and it is finished for ever. (Blaise Pascal, 1670)

There is something beyond the grave; death does not end all, and the pale ghost escapes from the vanquished pyre. (Sextus Propertius, c. 30 BC)

Is there any possibility that these spiritual experiences of the dying provide evidence that the 'pale ghost' does indeed escape the funeral pyre and survives the death of the physical body? And even if they do not, can we conclude that they lend any support to the much more dismal view of Pascal?

In nearly every religion and in every culture there is a belief in the survival of some aspect of human existence after death. In fact, it is likely that for as long as humans have been aware of the certainty of death they have contemplated the possibility of survival and wondered what happens next.

However, what people call 'soul' today has varied in meaning throughout history, and both the word and the concept have changed in their implications. Most hunter-gatherer groups have had a fairly hazy idea about the human soul. The Australian aboriginal people make no distinction between the sacred and the secular, or between humankind and the rest of the natural world. The aboriginal ancestors, or totems, were in the form of local animals from whom the people in a tribe or region were descended, and a man shared the same life with his animal or plant totem. Australian aboriginal people believe in multiple human souls, which fall into two broad categories: one is comparable to the Western ego – a self-created, autonomous agency that accompanies the body and constitutes the person's identity; and another that comes from 'The Dreaming' and/or from God. The latter emerges from ancestral totemic sites in the environment, and its power enters people to animate them at various stages of their lives. At death, the egoic soul at first remains near the deceased's body and property as a dangerous ghost, but eventually it ceases to exist. Ancestral souls, however, are eternal. They return to the environment and to the sites and ritual paraphernalia associated with specific totemic beings and/or with God.

Rituals associated with death are designed to ensure that the spirit has a safe passage on its return to the spirit world, and does not return to trouble the living. There is thus a pervasive belief in a persistence of life in a different form, and of death as merely a transition, while wellbeing in the afterlife is not influenced by the quality of the life they have lived.

The most common belief of the North American aboriginals, the Athapaskan tribes of Alaska and north-western Canada, ancestors of the Navajo and Apache Indians, is in a multi-component spirit; at death the good essence departs for the next world, while the evil one remains for a while near the body, and is liable to return to harm the living. Like most hunter-gatherer groups, they had relatively vague thoughts about the afterlife,[1] but these included the belief that the soul of the deceased was taken to the realm of the dead in a stone canoe. The canoe carrying the soul of a bad person would sink and they would be stranded in water up to their neck, never to reach the soul's final resting place.[2] Some groups also believed that reincarnation was possible – in animal form, as a different gender, or into a different lineage – especially if a person dies young.

The Navajo have a similar belief in a two-tier soul, one associated with breath or wind and the other with a shadow-like entity which lingers near the body for a time and may be a danger to the living. One wonders whether the idea of this 'shadow-like entity' might have arisen because then, as now, there were occasional reports of the cloudy, smoke-like phenomena discussed in the previous chapter. The Navajo have conflicting beliefs about an afterlife. One view is that there is an afterlife in which individuals keep their personal identity and that there is a deity of the underworld; another that there is no afterlife and that the soul is a part of the original life-force and the creative power of the cosmos: an individual's only immortality is through his descendants.[3] The Navajo's view of the underworld is a particularly gloomy one, a four-day journey to a place below the earth's surface, full of chaos and danger, inhabited by the souls of the dead, to which the deceased is led by his own dead relatives.[4] This dismal trip is a reflection of the Navajo's negative attitude to, and avoidance of, death and everything associated with it, but it also has an interesting echo of the deathbed visions we have been looking at. As a group, the Navajo hold different views about what becomes of a human soul after death. One view is that some elements of identity are maintained, and the other is that personality is 'washed clean' of the soul, which then returns to an undifferentiated pool.

The Greek notion of soul

Modern, Western notions of the soul have their roots in early Greek philosophy. The early Greek notion of soul was that it was specifically human. The Homeric poems use the word 'soul' in two distinguishable, probably related, ways – first, as something that a human being risks in battle and loses in death, and second, as the entity that leaves the body at death and travels to the underworld, to an afterlife as a shade or image of the dead person. And again one can speculate that the notion of a soul 'leaving the body' suggests, as does the word 'shade', that the idea might have originated in sightings of the insubstantial shapes and forms associated with the bodies of the dying and the dead.

But although the presence of a soul distinguished a live human from a dead one, it was not associated with any of the thoughts or actions of that life – it carried, in effect, no moral overtones. In the fifth and sixth centuries BC, under the influence of Plato and Aristotle, the concept of soul was broadened to include all living things, plants as well as animals – in fact, to distinguish living from non-living things. Thales of Miletus reportedly attributed soul to magnets, on the grounds that magnets are capable of moving iron and that since only living things can initiate movement, magnets must be alive and therefore must have souls.[5]

Gradually the soul acquired more attributes – by the end of the fifth century BC people were said to 'satisfy their souls' with rich food (and the concept of 'soul food' still exists). Intense emotions and, especially, courage, became attributed to the soul, so that eventually it came to be thought of as the source or bearer of moral qualities. The distinction between body and soul had begun.

The association of 'soul' with continued existence after death emerges around 500 BC with the speculations of Pythagoras, but it was Socrates who first suggested that the soul might be immortal, and also that these disembodied souls enjoyed lives of thought and intelligence. Plato's Socratean dialogues distinguish between things that are perceptible and subject to dissolution and destruction, and things that are not perceptible, but intelligible (grasped by thought), and imperishable. He concluded that the soul is most akin to intelligible being, and that the body is most like perceptible and perishable being. His most elaborate and final argument for the immortality of the soul concluded that since life belongs essentially to soul, the soul must be deathless – that is, immortal. Aristotle defined the soul as the 'essence' of a being, but argued against its having a separate existence. It was an activity of the body and so was not capable of existence or activity apart from the body. It could not, therefore, be immortal. However, he did believe that intellect, which he considered to be part of the soul, was immortal and separate from the body.

With the coming of Christianity, new ideas about the soul evolved. In Judaeo-Christian thinking the soul is a divine aspect of God which is in each one of us – the 'image of the Creator'. Death, and life after death have always been central to Christian belief. The body surrounds the soul and transmits to it knowledge of those thoughts and actions which are carried out here on earth. The soul is thus part of the individual's life on earth, but after death it separates from the body and progresses. According to Christian theology, only humans have immortal souls, while animals are purely physical, non-spiritual beings. This posed a problem when it came to evolution, which assumes a continuum between apes and man. It was solved, perhaps rather unsatisfactorily, by suggesting that at a certain undefined moment in the evolution of hominids, God intervened and injected a human soul or, in the case of fundamental Christian creationists, the problem was solved by denying the facts of evolution altogether. Traditional Christian teaching has it that the soul exists only in this life and has a one-shot chance of salvation before being consigned to either heaven, hell or (in the Catholic tradition) the 'holding centre' of purgatory for all eternity. So for Christians, the nature of one's final destination was a matter of very real concern.

After the Reformation less emphasis was laid on hell, but Walter[6] suggested that it was the hell-on-earth of the First World War that finally gave the kiss of death to the concept of hell, as no army chaplain would have dared to raise the possibility that the brave lad he was burying might end up there. And without the omnipresent threat of the horrors of hell, the struggle to attain the joys of heaven loses some of its urgency. Many churches now place less emphasis on life after death, more on the Church's work with the living and in society. A poll conducted in 1991 in 17 Christian countries by the International Social Survey Programme asked about a definite belief in the afterlife.[7] The USA topped the poll with 55 per cent confident in the existence of an afterlife. East Germany had the fewest believers (6.1 per cent), while the UK ranked 11th with 23.8 per cent. For most Western-ers, even if they do retain a personal belief in an afterlife, it is more likely to focus on reunion with others than union with God. Even now, in the twenty-first century, 'soul' is a term that one can only use very loosely indeed, as almost every religious group – one might almost say every individual – has its own concept of soul, and almost every concept is different.

Eastern concepts of soul

It is interesting to compare the Christian idea of the soul – a purely human attribute – with the corresponding Buddhist concept of mind. Evolution is not a problem for Buddhists, who believe that both humans and animals possess sentient minds (the equivalent of the 'soul') which survive death by dissolving into a deeper level of consciousness, called 'the very subtle mind', which has no beginning and no end. Because all living forms are sentient, and thus contain a soul, there is a moral imperative to all life. As reincarnation and development is part of the story, and as it is possible to be reborn as an animal, losing one's human form, the care that is automatically given to animals has a large self-serving component. Tibetan Buddhism suggests that at death the soul separates from the body and for a period of 47 days lives a discarnate existence before being born again. The quality of the incarnation in the next life will depend on the quality of the life previously lived. This philosophy carries with it the concept of an 'old soul' that has seen many incarnations, showing how difficult it is to escape the cycle of rebirth. However, the Tibetans suggest that there is one moment in the death process, which we shall discuss later, when this escape into uni-versal consciousness is possible, and one should not die without some knowledge of how to get free.[8]

The Qu'ran says very little about the soul, but Islamic belief is in many respects very close to Christian tradition. Muslims believe that this life is simply a test and that death is not the end but the beginning. The first sentence of this verse of the Holy

Qur'an is read whenever a Muslim hears of the death of another person, in Arabic: 'Ina Lilahee wa Ina Ilahee Rajeoon'. 'Every Soul shall taste death. And only on the day of Resurrection shall you be paid your wages in full. And whoever is removed from the Fire and admitted to Paradise, he indeed is successful. The Life of this World is only the enjoyment of deception (a deceiving thing).'[9] In Islamic tradition, just before death, the Angel of Death comes and questions the person, 'Who is your Lord, who is your prophet and did you perform the obligatory prayers?' If the person has led a good life his soul will be extracted peacefully, but for the wicked this will be a very difficult time. The soul remains in a Limbo-like place (called Al-Barzakh) and remains there until the day of resurrection, when God decides who will go to heaven and who will go to hell. Good souls are at peace during their time in Limbo and may even visit their living relatives as ghosts. Evil souls, however, will be punished and remain in a vile state until the day of reckoning.

Hinduism has many and varied beliefs about the purpose and fate of the soul. From their earliest history, Hindus believed that the soul survived the body and went to either a place of pleasure or one of torment. Eventually the idea of reincarnation emerged, in which the soul (after surviving death) was reborn into this world in a continuous cycle of reincarnations until it had achieved 'enlightenment'. In Vedantic philosophy, which represents mainstream Hindu thought, the soul is eternal and indestructible and can exist in any living form, whether human beings, animals, plants, or even in gods. All souls are alike, whatever life-form they inhabit. The rough equivalent of the soul is the Atman, and is that part of Brahman (God) which is within us.[10] The Atman is impersonal, universal, the underlying reality. The embodied soul is called the 'jiva'.

Various definitions of the soul exist in Jewish rabbinical literature. The Zohar, a classic work of Jewish mysticism, says that the soul has three elements. The Nephash is the part that is alive and vital in humans. It enters the body at the first breath, and is the part of the soul that can die. The Ruach, or middle soul or spirit, and the Neshamah or higher soul, are both created over time, depending on the actions and beliefs of the individual. It is the

Neshamah which distinguishes humans from all other life-forms, and allows one to have some awareness of the existence and presence of God. At death Neshamah returns to the source.

There are records of two cultures in particular which have shown a special interest in the process of dying. The Egyptian Book of the Dead and the coffin texts of ancient Egypt gave detailed instructions for the soul's journey to the next life. The Egyptian Book of the Dead refers to the 'Pyramid Texts' – funerary texts, many of which can be traced back to hieroglyphic inscriptions on the interior walls of some pyramids. These 'Pyramid Texts' originated between 2350 and 2175 BC and are not only the oldest written records in the entire history of humankind, but also refer to sources that are even older. The Book of the Dead reveals 'the unalterable belief of the Egyptians in resurrection and in the immortality of the soul'.[11]

In the Tibetan Buddhist tradition it is the monks who guide the souls of the dying through death to their next incarnation. The Tibetan Book of the Dead, first put into written form in the eighth century AD, integrates elements of much older, oral traditions, and provides a 'map of the territory', describing the journey of the disembodied individual from the moment of death through the after-death states – a journey remarkably similar to some aspects of the near-death experience.

The scientific pursuit of the soul

The essence of all these different views of 'soul' is that something – some aspect of our consciousness – can extend outside the confines of our body and perhaps survive it. Is there any evidence for the existence of this multifaceted and multicultural entity? What counts as evidence depends on how you define 'evidence'. On one side there are the mystical phenomena reported by serious practitioners in all spiritual traditions. These experiences cannot easily, if at all, be measured or tested by scientific methods, as traditional Western science is only now discovering ways of measuring subjective data. On the other side are the observable scientific phenomena – the backbone of empirical experimentation – that so far have given only hints of a consciousness that persists outside of the physical body (see Chapter 11).

An example of the difficulties which arise when mixing objective and subjective concepts is seen in the attempts to measure the soul. In 1921 the physician Duncan MacDougal devised an optimistic experiment designed to detect the existence – and indeed the weight – of the soul by measuring how a person's weight changes immediately after death. He monitored six deaths and reported that immediately after death people weighed something between 11 and 43 grams less than they had immediately before death. The average of 21 grams he assumed to be the material weight of the soul. Follow-up experiments failed to replicate this.

Other suggestions for physical detection of the soul have been less fanciful (though only just). Dr Gerard Nahum has proposed surrounding the body with an array of electromagnetic detectors to pick up any kind of radiated electromagnetic energy. He maintains that when a conscious entity dies, the soul embodied in it cannot just simply disappear, but must either be transformed into something else within our space–time, or transcend its existence here and move on somewhere else, with all its energy. The difficulty with this idea is that after death many energetic processes die down, with a molecular flux of charged particles, and these will of necessity radiate electromagnetic energy. It is not clear how soul energy could be distinguished from any other energetic sources. No one, so far as we know, has been willing to take this idea any further.

Out-of-body experiences and the soul

An intriguing hypothesis is that it is the out-of-body experience that is responsible for the concept of the soul. It has been suggested that out-of-body experiences are demonstrable evidence of the existence of the soul. But equally tenable is that the whole notion of a soul may have been generated by out-of-body experiences, which are relatively common and can occur spontaneously as well as being triggered by intense emotions such as fear. Philosopher Thomas Metzinger of the Johannes Gutenberg University of Mainz in Germany has suggested that early humans probably had these experiences and it would have been natural for them to have interpreted these as evidence that some aspect of themselves could separate from their physical body and have an entirely independent consciousness.

A journey to Elsewhere

So, do any common themes emerge from all these different views of the human soul? First is the notion that a human is not a one-dimensional creature, but has a spiritual as well as a corporeal aspect. Next is the concept that this spiritual bit is modified in this life and carries with it the deeds of its owner. Also central to the concept of a soul is the idea of continuity – that death is not simply a snuffing out, a ceasing to be, but that *something* happens. Finally, that the ultimate purpose of this non-physical aspect of humankind is to make a journey. The notion of a journey after death is an ancient one. The identity of the traveller and the nature of the destination vary, but as we have seen, the concept is an almost universal one. It's a journey the destination of which depends entirely on the framework within which it is viewed, and that framework is created from a combination of culture, religion and personal belief. All we can really say is that it is a journey to Elsewhere.

Intuitively, most people feel that the world has a meaning. A purely mechanistic and deterministic view of the world, seen only through the eyes of outdated and limited nineteenth-century mechanistic science, removes any possibility of personal tran-scendent values. We need a wider view to encompass the instinc-tive belief that we matter, that we are part of a greater whole, and that our actions carry a personal responsibility and have conse-quences for us or for the universe at some future time.

Although the idea of a soul makes little materialistic scientific sense, there is a strong move towards the re-spiritualization of the cosmos, and within the framework of these ideas the concept of the soul comes back again into its own (see Chapter 11). But much more important for us, it makes very good emotional sense to the people who have or who witness these experiences. The daughter of a woman whose mother was in hospital following a massive stroke was puzzled by the fact that she constantly mentioned being visited by her dead mother and sisters. She says:

I wasn't sure if the sightings were due to confusion caused by her illness but she seemed lucid. It all seemed very odd at the time and I mentioned it to the hospital chaplain when he came to visit Mum during her final days. He said that this type of thing was very common and he came across it all the time. He said that we should view the transition from life to death as a semi-permeable membrane in which the spirit could flit back and forth for a while before finally departing. His words made great sense to me at the time and I found them very comforting.

Belief in a spiritual or transcendental world seems to be part of being human. The ultimate human strategy for coming to terms with the fact that we do not live for ever and making the idea of death more tolerable is to conceive the notion of something which survives the body, or of a continuing existence following this transient earthly one. Whatever the culture, whatever the ethnic group, from prehistory to the present day can be found evidence of belief that something – whether we call it soul, or consciousness, or essence – survives the death of the body.

Perhaps the most feasible approach in the search for the soul is to look for experiential as well as material evidence; to see, for example, if there are any aspects of consciousness which seem to be able to function independently of the physical brain. Near-death experiences which are thought to occur during the total unconsciousness of cardiac arrest are one such possibility. These suggest that in this state of temporary brain death, consciousness may be possible. The nature and scientific understanding of consciousness and its relationship to the brain as discussed in Chapters 11 and 12 is crucial to our interpretation of this whole area.

In the last resort, without a soul we are merely mechanical entities, receptacles for the brief flame of life, responsible only to our biology and to our culture. Listening to people who are dying, or who have been with the dying and have reported these 'soul sightings', is probably the nearest any of us are going to get to a proof that we are more than just mechanical automatons.

Personal experience will not provide objective scientific proof, but it does suggest a way of understanding death. So most of us cling, like a child with its comfort blanket, to a belief in this 'pale ghost', and welcome any sightings, however fleeting, which reinforce this inner conviction.

Chapter 11

The Last Frontier:
The Unsolved Problem of
Consciousness

Versuchung durch zeitliche Güter:
Temptation through temporal goods

The first great lesson in the enquiry into these obscure fields of knowledge, [is] never to accept the disbelief of great men or their accusations of imposture or of imbecility as of any weight when opposed to the repeated observation of facts by other men, admittedly sane and honest. (A. R. Wallace)

One of the greatest stumbling blocks for neuroscience is the question of consciousness. We know the *mechanism* of the way stimuli from the outside the world pass through neural tissue to the brain, but we don't know how this gives rise to a subjective view of the world. In the West two major philosophical schools currently attempt to explain brain function and tackle the nature of consciousness. There are of course many associated positions, but to keep it simple we will stay with this major grouping.

Dennett's neurophilosophy characterizes one extreme. He argues that consciousness and subjective experience are just the functions of neural nets (groups of nerve cells connected together). Nothing is required to explain personal experience and wider states of consciousness except a detailed knowledge of neural nets. He derives this very incomplete and impoverished philosophy from his belief that only actions that you can see are the scientific basis of data, and that science must not take into account personal subjective experience – 'a peepshow into another's mind'.[1] Echoes of this view can be seen in the recent *Scientific American* article in which Christof Koch and Susan Greenfield, both leaders in the reductionist view of consciousness, give their views of the way different neuronal nets are excited with different experiences.[2] In the article, they say, quite correctly, that neuroscientists 'do not yet understand enough about the brain's inner workings to spell out exactly how consciousness arises from the electrical and chemical activity of neurones'. They add, 'Thus the big first step is to determine the best neuronal correlates of consciousness.' Unfortunately, the article is headed 'How Does Consciousness Happen?' and 'Consciousness Explained', and all the authors do is to look at the correlates of consciousness, which do not, and possibly never will, actually explain it.

The other extreme is characterized by the philosophy of Nagel, who argues that it is never possible to learn from an objective third-person point of view what it is like to have a first-person experience. Nagel argues that however much we understand about the neurophysiology of the functioning of a bat's brain, we will never know what is it like *to be* a bat.[3] This view suggests that the explanation of subjective experience requires a new principle which is beyond neural nets.

Searle[4] argues from an intermediate position. He regards subjective experience as being a property of neural nets, but he does not agree with Dennett that at present a full understanding of neural net functioning is sufficient to explain consciousness. He sees consciousness as only brain function; in the way that 'wetness' arises from a combination of oxygen and hydrogen to produce water, so consciousness emerges from neural nets. His viewpoint is centred on brains, not people, stating that the world we perceive is constructed for us by the brain. If you stub your toe, pain is felt not in the foot but in the brain. Sadness is a brain function. How are you today? My brain is very sad, thank you. Searle's view is that we need a Newton of neurophysiology to produce an entirely new principle – the emergent principle of consciousness. For a full review of the current hypotheses relating to brain and consciousness see *The Blackwell Companion to Consciousness.*[5] More important, if you have an interest in neuroscience, *Philosophical Foundations of Neuroscience* is a book which is a model of clarity and analyses the materialist approach to consciousness and points out many errors with the major hypotheses put forward by the leaders in the field.[6] The exciting point is that the question of consciousness is now firmly on the neuroscience agenda, and tentative theories are being put forward and discussed.

One of the most fundamental realizations of the late twentieth century was that science is culturally determined. It was Thomas Kuhn, in his influential book *The Structure of Scientific Revolutions,*[7] who introduced the term 'paradigm shift', and brought this concept to general attention. According to Kuhn, 'A paradigm is what members of a scientific community, and they alone, share.'[8] One barrier to scientific progress has been the failure of a core group of eminent scientists to shift their paradigm: their desire to hold on to their simple, mechanical, Newtonian science at all costs. It's a science that has been, and still is, outstandingly successful in examining and quantifying the objective world around us. But so far as the study of subjective, conscious experience is concerned, it is too limited. Western science can investigate only the physical aspects of any phenomenon – a 'view from nowhere' as it has been described. Yet a moment's thought, as Max Velman has pointed out,[9] shows that all phenomena are essentially psychological entities. It is the way that the evidence is obtained that makes the difference between 'objective' and 'subjective' qualities. Objective qualities are tested by asking individuals if their psychological concepts match; for example, do we all *see* the same pointer readings when we do the same experiment? Subjective qualities are also tested by discovering whether we all have the same psychological state in the same circumstances, but in this case there is no pointer reading; we have to rely on how the other person describes it.

'Scientific fundamentalism' – the belief that an understanding of the material properties of the world is sufficient to explain everything about it – is enormously restrictive for Western science when generating hypotheses about the nature of consciousness. This is particularly true in the biological and psychological sciences, where we are looking at brain function which, it is generally agreed, reflects conscious states. But this reluctance to move forward is nothing new. Science has always been like this, because scientists tend to have an unyielding adherence to the accepted position. As long ago as 1875, Alfred Russel Wallace, one of the leading evolutionary thinkers of the nineteenth century, and the century's leading expert on the geographical distribution of animal species, demonstrated the restrictions in this limited view.[10] Wallace was a polymath and also worked in the social sciences and labour reform. Having come across this restrictive attitude in his own work, he was well qualified to point out that new truths were never accepted without a challenge.

When Benjamin Franklin brought the subject of lightning conductors before the Royal Society, he was laughed at as a dreamer, and his paper was not admitted to the philosophical transactions. When Young put forward his wonderful proofs of the undulatory theory of light (one of the greatest discoveries in quantum mechanics), he was equally hooted at as absurd by the popular scientific writers of the day. *The Edinburgh Review* (1803) commented on the theory 'containing more fancies, more blunders, more unfounded hypotheses, more gratuitous fiction from the fertile yet fruitful brain . . . of Dr Young'. *The Edinburgh Review* called upon the public to put Thomas Gray into a straitjacket for maintaining the practicability of railways. Sir Humphrey Davy laughed at the idea of London ever being lighted with gas. When Stevenson proposed to use locomotives on the Liverpool–Manchester railway, learned men gave evidence that it was impossible that they could go even 12 miles per hour. The French

Academy of Sciences ridiculed the great astronomer Arago when he wanted even to discuss the subject of the electric telegraph.

This reluctance to accept scientific change has a long history. Even Copernicus mentioned that when in ancient Greece the Pythagorean school made its brilliant advances in mathematics and geometry, their habit was to impart their 'noble and arduously won discoveries' only to an inner circle of friends and intimates. Copernicus, in his preface to *De Revolutionibus*, predicted that as soon as certain people heard of his thesis they would 'cry out that, holding such views, I should at once be hissed off the stage'.[11]

Science, then, can no longer be regarded as the ultimate arbiter of the way the world works, because scientists are embedded in their local culture, and it is this that defines their understanding of science and what it means. There is not just one worldview, but many, and to explain them it may be that we need not just one science, but many. It will take a 'paradigm shift' to establish a different kind of science – a science that could study and take full account of subjective evidence, which would ask the kind of questions that need to be asked if we are ever to understand consciousness. This form of science is very much an Eastern perspective, and has been used with great effect to investigate the different psychological states which comprise consciousness. In Buddhist thinking, for example, the psychological effects of meditative states are defined and compared between groups to plot how consciousness changes with practice. There is a deep understanding of transcendent states and the pathways which lead to them.

However, in the West this tendency for rigid thinking from a limited intellectual base is beginning to give way. It is interesting to see how far it has already progressed in physics, always regarded as one of the purest sciences. A recent book by a group of the world's leading physicists examining the question of whether we live in a single universe or a multiverse[12] was recently discussed at an evening hosted at the Royal Society in London. The theory of multiverses is a theory only – the only evidence put forward for them is that they are possible mathematically. But the point is that although physicists are divided on the issue, the topic is not taboo among the modern physics community in the way, for example, that telepathy is not even up for discussion among conventional reductionist scientists. There is plenty of anecdotal subjective evidence for telepathy, and even some accumulating objective scientific evidence, some of which we will look at later in this chapter. There are theories to account for telepathy – for example that mind is a field – but they are theories only (although there is considerably more anecdotal evidence for them than can be mustered for multiverses). And yet the subject is taboo among many biological scientists, some of whom refuse even to discuss the topic on the grounds that it is all rubbish and so there is no need to do so. Evidence against an entrenched belief system does not apparently count as evidence and so can be ignored.

Wallace made another observation that those of us dealing in the evidential basis of new ideas need to remember. 'The first great lesson in the enquiry into these obscure fields of knowledge, (is) never to accept the disbelief of great men or their accusations of imposture or of imbecility as of any weight when opposed to the repeated observation of facts by other men, admittedly sane and honest.'

Wallace's lesson is very relevant to a study of end-of-life or near-death experiences. Any conclusions we draw are going to be based upon the observations of these 'sane and honest' men and women, and we must give them the weight they deserve.

Current views on consciousness

The current mainstream scientific view is that of Dennett – that psychological processes are generated entirely within the brain and limited to the brain and the organism. Our recent understanding of consciousness has been to a large extent built up by the use of imaging techniques (functional magnetic resonance imaging and positron emission tomography) which record blood flow within the brain during different mental states. The types of mental states examined have been very wide indeed, and include sleep and dreaming, guilt, planning and memory, the taking of internal and external actions, the appreciation of sensation, and the conception of ideas – to mention only a few. There is even some data on altered mystical states and those of special groups of people such as meditating monks, Carmelite nuns and people praying.

These data support the view that reductionist science will eventually be able to provide some explanation of some of the brain mechanisms underpinning consciousness, although it is doubtful if it will ever point directly to what consciousness (subjective experience) actually is. It will certainly not allow for the extension of consciousness beyond the brain; if consciousness is thought to be only the mechanical functioning of neuronal nets, it can never be non-local. A recent step away from the reductionist position was suggested in a recent paper given at the Royal Society.[13] The authors suggested that the reductionist mechanical science which assumed that causality within the brain was fully determined by the movement of small Newtonian particles, atoms, etc., is now over three-quarters of a century out of date. It has been superseded by the application of quantum mechanical theories of brain function. These follow the mathematics of Von Neumann who argued that both the physical world and the conscious world must be considered when looking at a quantum mechanical system. Their paper argues that the brain is a quantum mechanical system, not only because the neurotransmitter junctions are susceptible to quantum effects, but because the Von Neumann view of the world stretches right up from the level of the individual molecules of neurotransmitter to include the whole brain and the mental processes that occur within it. They showed very clearly that mental processes and the mental (social) context in which the brain is embedded are causal agents in their own right as postulated by Von Neumann's theory. The brain contains two domains, both causal: Von Neumann's Process 1 (the atoms and molecules which are catered for by Newtonian science) and Process 2 (those conscious processes, such as thoughts, feelings, beliefs, etc., which come to bear on the quantum mechanical system and are causative in their own right). Thus at one stroke consciousness takes its place in any theories which postulate how the brain works. But more exciting than that, the matrix of meaning in which the subject is embedded – culture, family relationships and so on – now extends brain function well beyond the brain.

Schwartz *et al.* show the causative effect of conscious processes very simply and elegantly. They point out that a placebo may consist only of chalk and is inactive when taken by mouth. However, if subjects with Parkinson's disease are told that it is a powerful anti-Parkinson agent and will improve their walking, then the subjects do indeed find that their Parkinson symptoms alleviate when they take the chalk pill and they move more easily. But, more importantly, the brain areas linked to the movement circuitry (the basal ganglia) become activated. This activation is nothing to do with the effects of chalk (the Newtonian molecular causative system) but with the conscious or mental set of the individual (non-local to the brain) which gives the chalk its anti-Parkinson power. In these circumstances the two domains as postulated by Von Neumann are both causal – the neurochemical in the improvement in walking (Process 1), and the alteration of consciousness in the suggestion that this was a powerful new drug (Process 2).

Another interesting contender which links consciousness with brain function, although this is not accepted in mainstream scientific circles, is a theory by Amit Goswami.[14] He argues that consciousness is a basic component of the universe and exists like energy. His main contribution is related to the nature of the observer, as he maintains that there is only one observer, and this is a universal, undivided consciousness. This view reflects the descriptions of the fundamental qualities of the universe as they are usually described by people who have had wide transcendent experiences and report that the universe is unitary and that consciousness underpins all phenomena.

The quantum mechanical theories of Chris Clarke and Mike Lockwood, and the quantum gravitational theories of Roger Penrose and Stuart Hameroff,[15] are also possibilities, though beyond the scope of this book to discuss. Quantum mechanical effects suggest that the universe is highly interconnected and that particles interact with each other at a distance (Rosen-Podolski Einstein paradox). The significance of this is that elementary particles can become entangled with each other and that in their entangled states they are linked with each other over huge distances. The argument runs that not only small atom or molecule size particles, but large conglomerates of particles, such as human beings, can also become entangled, and thus a linking together is possible. Thus the interconnectedness of minds through this non-local linking becomes a theoretical possibility. Dean Radin has written at length about this proposition, quoting the evidence from scientific studies which support it.[16]

Evidence for the inter-connectedness of mind

Over the last 50 years many experiments have been carried out which suggest that mind is not limited to the brain and that it is possible to demonstrate directly the effect of mind on other minds (telepathy) and of mind on matter (psychokinesis). For those interested in a more comprehensive review of this subject, *The Conscious Universe*[17] provides a wide range of references to the studies and examines some of the meta-analyses which have demonstrated these effects.

With the advances in neuroimaging it has become possible to study very complex mental states – a good example of the way in which the Newtonian principles of reductionist science can be used to investigate non-Newtonian principles, such as mind beyond the brain. Functional magnetic resonance imaging (fMRI), a method of imaging blood flow (function) and cerebral structure, which can show the different brain areas which are involved in complex experiences or thinking tasks, is one such method. The fMRI images are only able to show the brain correlates of the experience and are in no way the explanation of these states, but nevertheless they are helpful in gaining some understanding of the neural processes involved.

Consider the following study. A group of 16 Shamans in Hawaii were asked to choose a friend with whom they had a close emotional contact, and who they felt they would be able to heal at a distance. In the experiment the friend was put in an fMRI scanner and the Shaman healer was some distance away. An fMRI machine measures changes in blood oxygenation, and thus blood flow through each point in the brain. The Shamans, according to a fixed randomized schedule, spent time 'healing' or not healing. The subjects did not know at any one time whether they were being 'healed' or not. After the experiment was over the subject's brain function was studied, and the difference between the healing and non-healing sessions calculated. The whole group showed that very clear and highly significant changes in blood flow occurred in the healing sessions, and these changes tended to be in the emotional part of the brain (anterior cingulate, orbito-frontal cortex and so on). The experiment showed that 'healing energies' directed by one person towards another with whom they are emotionally linked ('entangled') can induce actual changes in the activity of the other person's brain structures. This is remarkable, and can only be explained by the assumption that in some way the minds and so the brains of the subjects are linked together, and supports the idea of mind being non-local.[18]

Telepathic meditation study

This study set out to determine whether consciousness (mind) was a field. A group of 1,500 meditators all meditated together at a prearranged time. Three meditators in three separate rooms over 1,000 miles away had their electrical brain waves (EEG) measured. Sometimes the meditators would meditate at the same time as the distant meditators, and sometimes at a different time. The electrical activity of the brain in these two conditions was compared and it was shown that a measure of brain function, the coherence, increased significantly when the distant meditators were meditating, adding support to the hypothesis that mind can act as a field.[19]

Telephone telepathy

Telepathy has also been investigated, this time with rather novel experimental paradigms and outside the laboratory. Rupert Sheldrake's study of telephone telepathy – the ability which many of us will recognize, of sometimes knowing who is calling you when the phone rings – recruited participants for his study by placing an advertisement in local newspapers and on a recruitment website which simply said, 'Do you know who is ringing before you pick up the phone? Good pay for fun and simple experiments as part of psychic research project'.

Participants in the first series were asked to choose four friends who they thought might be able to respond telepathically as potential callers. When the telephone rang they had to guess who was calling before the other person spoke. Because most people were unable to nominate four such people, in a second series the experimenters supplied two callers who were strangers to the participants, which also enabled the experimenters to compare the responses between familiar and unfamiliar callers.

By chance the success rate would have been 25 per cent. In a total of 571 trials, involving 63 participants, the overall success rate was 40 per cent, with 95 per cent confidence limits from 36 to 45 per cent. (i.e. success rate will be between 36 and 45 per cent most of the time). This effect was hugely significant statistically ($p = 4 \times 10^{-16}$). Similar positive effects were obtained whether the calls were made at randomly chosen times, or at fixed times known to the subject in advance. With 37 participants, the success rates with familiar and unfamiliar callers were strikingly different. With familiar callers, 53 per cent of the guesses were correct ($n = 190$; $p = 1 \times 10^{-16}$). With unfamiliar callers, only 25 per cent of the guesses were correct, exactly at the chance level. This difference between the responses with familiar and unfamiliar callers was highly significant ($p = 3 \times 10^{-7}$). They also investigated the effects of distance between the callers and participants. With overseas callers at least 1,000 miles away, the success rate was 65 per cent ($n = 43$; $p = 3 \times 10^{-8}$); with callers in Britain, the success rate was lower (35 per cent). In most cases, the overseas callers were people to whom the participants were closely bonded. It seemed that emotional closeness was more important than physical proximity in determining telepathic success.[20]

The study has been repeated by other experimenters who usually get positive results as well.

These experiments clearly demonstrate interconnectedness. From these and other similar ones, including several studies related to healing and prayer, a comprehensive account of which is given in Benor,[21] it is clear that there is an excellent case for considering mind as a field, not limited to a brain, and conscious experiences as capable of being transferred between people directly, probably as a function of the mind field.

However, it is important to remember that any theory which tries to explain non-local mind does not displace current neuro-science but leaves it as a valuable basis on which consciousness acts through and within the brain. If we can formulate theories which will allow the integration of conscious experience into brain states, then when the dying person says that he looks through into another reality, we would have a theory which would be able to correlate accurately their mental state with their description of an alternate reality. Without such a theory showing interconnectedness of mind, I do not believe we will find a satis-factory explanation of the deathbed coincidences so many 'sane and honest' people have described. More important, such a theory would allow the full range of subjective experience to become a legitimate part of our science of consciousness and allow a greater understanding of the spiritual nature of human kind.

Transcendental philosophy

If, as it appears both from scientific studies and anecdotal reports, emotionally close people are somehow linked by a field, it may be, as spiritual masters have suggested, that love is the structure that connects people together. The development of wider states of consciousness supports this view. A further reason for looking at transcendence is that the universal view seen from this state is in many respects similar to that reported by the dying.

The concept of individual development, first brought to a wider audience by Aldous Huxley's book *The Perennial Philoso-phy*,[22] received further popular impetus in the West in the 1960s, with the Beatles' espousal of the Maharishi Mahesh Yogi's Tran-scendental Meditation, and the subsequent explosion of numer-ous similar Eastern groups which enjoyed popularity in the West. But because Eastern philosophies are expressed and cloaked in

Eastern terminology, their concepts are not easily accessible to a Western mind. In the past 50 years a number of writers who I will call transcendental philosophers and who have each had the transcendent experience (enlightenment) described so clearly in Buddhist philosophy, have managed to explain the process of personal development that leads to the transcendent state in cultural terms we can understand. Besides giving an excellent description of the nature of the transcendent state, these writers use Western concepts to express the nature of ultimate reality and describe the pathway (and the hard work required) to achieve it.

These new ideas need to be investigated by science if we are to get a better understanding of the range of perceptual states that are possible for the human mind. Until recently it has not been possible to study the neurophysiology of natural spontaneous transcendence in laboratory conditions, as these states in untrained subjects are usually very short lasting, a matter of hours to one or two days. Moreover, it has always been assumed that people who had these experiences were exceptional and only to be found in caves in the Himalayas. But it now seems that a body of home-grown Western mystics is becoming available for study.

If you have no interest in the Eastern concept of 'enlighten-ment' you may want to skip the rest of this section. But for anyone who wants to go further, I have selected four of these modern transcendental philosophers from a much wider group going back to the late nineteenth century. One of the clearest accounts of the functioning of the ordinary ego mind and why its use will never lead to the gateway to the transcendent, a point which has been endlessly stressed in Zen Buddhism, is the work of Wei Wu Wei, who despite his nom de plume was actually an Irishman, Terence Gray (1895–1986). Wei Wu Wei is a taoist term that translates as 'action that is non-action'. His book, *Open Secret*[23] is an introduction to these new (to the West) ideas. He points out that the very act of cognition by the ordinary mind splits the world into subject and object. Before the cognition the world is a unity. After the cognition there are subjects and objects, neither of which have ever existed independently. Thus, although it is convenient to look out on a sunny day and see a beautiful hillside as different from yourself (the perceiver), this is already to misunderstand the nature of the reality you are looking at, for there is no 'you' (the subject) to look at anything. This does not mean that there isn't perception, because of course there is, but there is no true perceptual process that allows the split into subject and object. It is this subject/object split that is at the basis of the psychological processes that maintain our ego structure, the 'I' which we so dearly defend as being the real me but which according to Wei Wu Wei is a fiction. He deals equally abruptly with time, pointing out that from the point of view of true cognition there is only the present. As soon as the false ego cognizes, different brain processes are brought into play, and by the time the perception is formulated it is already in the past. So in that sense there is no present, only ephemeral memories of the past which decay with time. As to the future, as he points out, a moment's introspection leads to the recognition that the future is purely imaginary and thus we can dismiss it. So the picture of reality seen from the viewpoint of transcendence is that the world is a unity arising with true perception from the void. This is a different way of understanding the world and so calls for a different science.

An elegant description of the impossibility of achieving the transcendent view by using the subject/object split of the ego mind is given by Merrill-Wolff, an American philosopher who worked for years to achieve his own transcendent experience.[24] He was a mathematician and believed there to be a mathematical yoga of transcendence. The following is only allegory, but it gives the feel. Merrill Wolff points out that there are mathematical functions which demonstrate the impossibility of ever reaching a particular point using that path. As an example he gives the infinite function $1 + \frac{1}{2} + \frac{1}{4} + \frac{1}{8} + \frac{1}{16}$ etc., which will never when summed add up to 2. He uses this to show how the ordinary mind, because of its false and destructive cognition of reality by creating the subject/object split, as described above, will never be able to transcend to the universal. The false ego cannot access true reality, and thus another doorway must be found. This door involves long periods of mind-brightening by learning to stay only in the present. But he also has the most wonderful description of what it is like to be centred in universal consciousness and see the restricted and limited point source that is the egoic mind, which gives a picture of the severe limitation of our ordinary perception. One of his fundamental contributions is to point out that science is an intensely spiritual discipline, and one way of approaching the transcendent is through the endless enquiry into the phenomenology that underpins basic form. This is rather like the process of the creative state that Goethe described when he plunged into the nature of form in the plant world and came out with the recognition that 'all is leaf'.

For anyone who is interested enough to want to explore this new breed of philosopher further, I would also recommend Ekhardt Tolle for his illumination of the power of the present moment, and the transformation of perception that takes place as you sink deeper and deeper into the present. His book *The Power of Now*[25] is a good place in which to start. Finally Alain Forget, a Frenchman, describes four techniques which, if practised conscientiously and regularly, will clean perception and finally lead to the death of the egoic mind and to transcendence.[26] With all this new information the 'true' scientist can now learn how to hone his own mind so that he can experience the wonderful breadth and width of this creative universe, perceive its unity and experience the all-pervading power of love.

Dying and its relation to consciousness

The evidence from transcendent mystical experience suggests that consciousness is a unity and the ground stuff of our universe. However, discussing consciousness from a transcendent point of view seems to bear little relationship to what we experience here and now. So, more simply, one possible theory of consciousness is that it is universal and is a field through which we are all interconnected. Brain processes link onto consciousness in a way science has yet to define. We can now apply this theory to the process of dying. First, the deathbed visions which occur in the last few days of life, when the psychological pull is away from the external world to the interior world of the dying self. The visits by dead family members are very powerful, usually resulting in great pleasure, recognition and reunion. The dead 'say' they come for the specific purpose of collecting or helping the dying person through the death process. Sometimes they are in the room, while at other times they wait outside and only come closer towards the very end of life. They can be negotiated with and asked to hold off the dying process for a day or so. They say they are going to collect the dying, and the dying say they are going on a journey. When the dying do describe the terrain to which they are going then this is usually an area filled with light, love, joy and compassion. Occasionally this light and love 'leak' into the room just before death and surround the dying.

At the same time, there is a drive on the part of the dying to reach out and interconnect with people they love, sometimes across thousands of miles, usually to say goodbye and reassure them that all is well. Many different areas of the person's life seem to be interconnected at the time of death. Occasionally their animals behave strangely, their clocks may stop, bells may ring in their rooms, light may switch on or off. All these aspects of the dying process fit neatly into a theory of consciousness in which the universe is highly interconnected, and has love and light at its very core. They fit very poorly with the current neuro-science idea that consciousness is generated by the brain and remains local to that brain and disappears entirely when we die.

In my view, a satisfactory explanation of consciousness must include a detailed role for brain mechanisms, an explanation for the action of mind both inside and outside the brain, and an explanation of consciousness held in common, or the way we seem to be linked together. It should also give an explanation of wide mental states, including transcendent experiences in which the experiencer claims to see through into the structure of the universe.

In the West there are very few accounts of what the subjective view of dying is like – simply because the dead do not return to tell us and there has been no attempt to investigate this area as it is considered to be scientifically irrelevant. However, there is one important set of experiences which may help us to bridge that gap. These are the near-death experiences which occur during cardiac arrest. This is because cardiac arrest is the closest model we have to clinical death, and so if people claim to have experiences during this time when they are, to all intents and purposes, clinically dead, we should at least consider the possibility that what they describe is indeed the subjective experience of dying.

Chapter 12

Consciousness and the Near-Death Experience

Trost durch Abwendung vom Irdischen:
Comfort through prevention of the earthly

Truth is born into this world only with pangs and tribulations, and every fresh truth is received unwillingly. To expect the world to receive a new truth, or even an old truth, without challenging it, is to look for one of those miracles which do not occur. (From an interview with A. R. Wallace, published posthumously in 1913)

As outlined in Chapter 9, other cultures have descriptions of the mental states of the dying as the final steps of death progress and breathing stops. In the West this has not been attempted and, indeed, no ethical committee would be likely to countenance research which involved questioning a dying person about their mental state as they die. However, there is one group of people in a better position than most to tell us something about what it is like to die. These are the few people who have had a near-death experience during a cardiac arrest and have survived to tell the tale. During a cardiac arrest the person is clinically dead, and it is reasonable to suppose that the tale they tell is as near as we are likely to get to a description of what it is like to die. We will call this particular group '*temporary* death experiences' (TDEs) to distinguish them from other near-death experiences (NDEs) because we know that everyone who has a cardiac arrest is in exactly the same state of unconsciousness and undergoes the same resuscitation protocol. In other NDEs it is more difficult to be sure whether the person was actually unconscious at all or, if they were, of the level of unconsciousness. But first a very short review of the main features of NDEs, which in all essential respects are similar to those of TDEs.

Phenomena of the NDE

There is nothing particularly new about the notion that people can 'die' and live to tell the tale. There are written descriptions of similar experiences in myths and legends going back well over 2,000 years. The sixteenth-century Dutch painter Hieronymus Bosch painted what certainly looks like a near-death experience: a tunnel with angels and a light at one end.

Near-death experiences have been widely studied since Dr Raymond Moody brought them to public attention in his book *Life After Life*.[1] The first British study, published in 1985, was by Margot Grey, a psychologist who herself had had a near-death experience which had a profound effect on her.[2] Many other studies followed, including our own,[3] and it was what we learned while researching this book that aroused our interest in the whole process of dying, and especially in how these lucid, structured and clearly remembered near-death experiences could in some situations apparently arise while the person was not conscious at all.

Near-death experiences can occur in a variety of situations – not always when the person is genuinely near to death or simply unconscious, but sometimes spontaneously and also as a result of extreme stress, pain or fear, as well as during anaesthesia and serious, though not fatal, illness. No two near-death experiences are identical and there are some profound cultural differences. And yet within a culture there are uncanny similarities between them, common elements which crop up over and over again regardless of the person's age, sex, and even independent of their religious faith or lack of it. In a Western culture these are, first, overwhelming feelings of peace, joy or bliss and the complete absence of any feelings of pain the body may have been feeling. Often the person feels as though they leave their body and look down on it from some vantage point near the ceiling. They may enter darkness, usually a dark tunnel through which they travel towards a pinpoint of light which grows larger and brighter as they approach it. The light seems to act as a magnet, drawing the person in. At this point they may meet a 'Being of Light' – a religious figure if they themselves are religious, or simply a 'presence' which is felt to be God or God-like. At some point they may come to a barrier, which is sensed to be a point of no return, beyond which they cannot go. Dead friends or relatives are sometimes seen on the other side of the barrier, indicating to them that they must go back, that it isn't yet time for them to come; often some quintessential English garden or landscape is glimpsed beyond the barrier. A few people experience a 'life review'. Sometimes this is experienced as a kind of Day of Judgement in which the person's past actions are reviewed, but there is very seldom a feeling that you are being judged by some other being. Much more often is the conviction that you are your own judge, reviewing your own past actions, but with an awareness of their consequences and the pain you may have caused to others. Finally, there is a return to the body, rapidly 'snapping back' as though on the end of an elastic cord.

For most people the near-death experience is one of the most profound they will ever have, and is vividly remembered throughout their lives. Even if they have no particular religious faith, many, perhaps most, return believing that death is not the end. And virtually everyone reports that they have lost their fear of death, value their lives more and feel a renewed sense of purpose. However, these feelings are common to nearly everyone who has survived a close call with death, whether or not they have had a near-death experience, but those who have had an NDE seem to be more profoundly affected.[4]

Temporary Death Experience

Of particular interest to anyone interested in the problem of consciousness are the temporary death experiences which occur during cardiac arrest. The reason for this is that we know what happens to brain function during a cardiac arrest and so it is possible to infer the physiology which is active during the time of the experience.

What happens during a cardiac arrest

The signs of cardiac arrest are the same as clinical death. There is no cardiac output, no respiratory effort, and brain-stem reflexes are absent. Because the heart is no longer pumping blood to the brain, oxygen levels fall, blood pressure falls to zero, neural functioning is grossly disrupted and the patient becomes unconscious. Loss of consciousness is rapid – as it is in fainting. Simultaneous recording of heart rate and brain electrical activity shows that within 11 seconds of the heart stopping, the brainwaves go flat. You are, in fact, clinically dead. Remember the international definition of death – no respiration, no cardiac output and absent brain-stem reflexes (you can't cough or choke): this is the exact clinical state after a cardiac arrest.

Even if cardio-pulmonary resuscitation (CPR) begins straight away, blood pressure will not rise high enough to establish a competent adequate blood flow through the brain. Most people who survive a cardiac arrest have some residual brain damage, and a number of studies show that the longer CPR is continued, the more brain damage occurs. We are used to seeing successful resuscitations in hospital after cardiac arrest in TV dramas, but in reality, failure to resuscitate is the norm. In their 1999 study of cardiac arrest and brain damage, Nichol et al.[5] found that out of 1,748 cardiac arrest patients, only 126 survived, a rate of about 7 per cent. Most units range between 2 and 20 per cent successful resuscitation rates. Eighty-six of Nichol et al.'s survivors were interviewed, and most of the people who were resuscitated had some evidence of brain damage. When the heart does finally start, the blood pressure rises, and the circulation slowly returns to normal, but normal brain function doesn't return instantly. And the point to remember is that the mental state during recovery is confusional.

The flat EEG indicating no brain activity during cardiac arrest and the high incidence of brain damage afterwards both point to the conclusion that the unconsciousness in cardiac arrest is total. Some sceptical materialists claim that in this state there is still brain activity, but in fact, the data are against this from both animal and human studies. The brain is not functioning during the arrest, and does not begin to function again until the heart restarts. During this time every brain system that constructs our world for us is, in fact, down. The brain can't create images, so it should be impossible to have clearly structured and lucid narrative experiences, and because memory is not functioning, if experiences did occur they should not be remembered. So in theory it is impossible for anyone either to experience or to remember anything that occurred while they were in this state. And if an experience occurred during the gradual return to consciousness it would be confusional, and not the clear lucid story which is characteristic of the temporary death experiences.

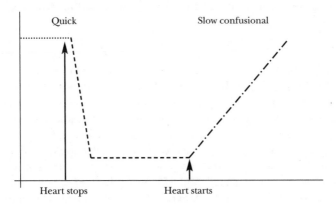

This figure shows how consciousness changes after the heart stops and restarts. Consciousness is lost in a matter of seconds when the heart stops, as in a faint, and may not be regained until hours to days after it restarts.

So, as far as science is concerned, the TDE cannot occur at any point during this whole process, and there are especial difficulties in accepting that it happens when those experiencing it say it happens – during unconsciousness. However, about 10 per cent of people report a TDE after a cardiac arrest, so let's examine these data further.

The problem is that it is very difficult to judge the exact timing of a TDE during a cardiac arrest. Most studies have been retrospective – that is, they have questioned people about their experience and looked at their medical records some time after the experience happened. One of the earliest of these was Sabom's 1982 study.[6] This included patients who had been in a variety of near-death circumstances, such as severe traumatic injury, comas from metabolic disorders or systemic illness, etc, as well as patients who had had cardiac arrests both in and out of hospital. Some patients claimed to have seen their own resuscitation procedures while they were unconscious, and Sabom correlated their accounts with the medical records and found that the evidence did indeed point towards the actual death experience having occurred during unconsciousness.

More recently, several prospective studies (studies carried out while the patient is under your care and you know exactly what has gone on medically and the time at which all medical interventions occurred) have been published. Dr Sam Parnia and I carried out the first prospective study to focus on people who had had cardiac arrests and been resuscitated in the coronary care unit at Southampton Hospital,[7] and it is described in Sam's book *What Happens When We Die*.[8] The reason for choosing a coronary care unit was not only that we know exactly what happens in the cardiac arrest, but also that all the patients in the study have the same medication and are given the same resuscitation procedures. Another advantage was that the patients could be questioned as soon as they were well enough. We wanted to know how many of them had a TDE, and whether, if they did, it was similar to the traditional near-death experience. We also wanted to see if we could solve the problem of exactly when the experiences occurred – was it before unconsciousness, during unconsciousness, during recovery, or after recovery?

Of the 63 cardiac arrest survivors Dr Parnia interviewed, 89 per cent had no memories during their arrest and about 10 per cent reported TDEs, which they said had occurred while they were unconscious. These TDEs were, as we expected, very similar to those NDEs already reported in the literature. We also found that the TDEs were not due to medication, electrolytes, blood gases, religious belief or any other cultural factors; all these factors were the same in the group who did not have actual death experiences. So something interesting was going on, and we are now trying to follow this up with a much larger study.

Science demands that any observations are repeatable, and other groups of workers have repeated this study and found similar results. A group in Holland has done a larger study of 344 cardiac arrest survivors which was published in the *Lancet*, a mainstream peer-reviewed scientific journal.[9] Forty-one survivors (about 12 per cent) reported TDEs. The occurrence of TDEs was not influenced by the duration of either unconsciousness or cardiac arrest, or by medication. But they did find that more TDEs were reported in the group of survivors who did in fact die shortly after their experience, so it looks as though the closer you are to death, the more likely you are to get a TDE.

Other recent prospective cardiac arrest TDE studies have reported similar findings. In Schwaninger *et al.*'s US study[10] a higher rate of 23 per cent was found. Greyson[11] found 10 per cent. Dr Penny Sartori's study in an intensive therapy unit found about 25 per cent.[12] What is clear is that death experiences do occur in association with cardiac arrest, and their contents are similar to those reported in the NDE literature.[13]

These studies are interesting to the layperson as well as to the scientist, because none have so far been able to provide any definitive scientific answers to the most fundamental problem of the temporary death experience: when does it truly occur? In our study the patients themselves felt that the experiences occurred during unconsciousness – important because, as discussed above, we have no idea how clear consciousness can be experienced during a period of clinical death with a flat EEG. This question is absolutely crucial because it is central to one of the biggest problems facing neuroscience: is consciousness entirely a product of brain function and is it confined to the brain? We hope that TDE research might be one way of filling the 'consciousness gap' in neuroscience. From the point of view of science, TDEs cannot occur during unconsciousness, and yet there is some tantalizing evidence that that is just when they do seem to occur.

The out-of-body experience (OBE)

Many – about one-third – of TDEs are preceded by an out-of-body experience in which the experiencer says they leave the body and rise to the ceiling and can see the resuscitation taking place. Anecdotal evidence points to the OBE and therefore the TDE occurring during unconsciousness. There is also anecdotal evidence that the OBE may include accurate perceptions of what happened during the resuscitation. Sabom[14] found that some of his research participants described their own resuscitation procedures accurately, suggesting that their TDE had occurred when the brain was 'down'. The case of Pamela Reynolds, described in the BBC's documentary film *The Day I Died*, is also suggestive of that. Kenneth Ring[15] has described cases of NDEs in blind people who claim to have what he calls 'mind sight' and are able to 'see' the resuscitation room when out of their bodies. So, is the out-of-body experience which occurs during TDEs truly veridical – that is, does it consist of verifiably accurate perceptions that would have been impossible to perceive except from a vantage point outside that person's physical body? If this is so, then it should be possible for the first time to be sure exactly when in the resuscitation process the TDE is occurring.

One very persuasive piece of evidence that this may indeed be so has been produced by Dr Penny Sartori, who studied a group of cardiac arrest survivors in a coronary care unit. Several of the subjects in her study said they had left their bodies and witnessed the resuscitation process. She compared their accounts of their own resuscitation with those of another group of patients who had had no TDE during their resuscitation but had been asked to describe what they thought had happened. It is usually argued that everyone sees so much resuscitation on TV that everybody knows the procedure. In fact Dr Sartori was able to show convincingly that the patients who claimed to have seen their resuscitation described it much more accurately than those who could only guess what had happened, and who made significant errors.[16]

Dr Sam Parnia hopes to conduct a similar study in about 40 hospitals. Assuming that each hospital has 200 cardiac arrests in a year, with 50 survivors, 10 per cent of whom will have had TDEs, this will give five OBEs per hospital, so 20 hospitals should yield a target group of 100 TDEs. Of these, at least one-third should have out-of-body experiences. As well as monitoring the individual's account of their resuscitation he also has hidden cards in cardiac care units above the beds so that they are out of the sight of people standing in the room, but could be seen by someone who was having a veridical out-of-body experience and would provide evidence that the TDE occurred while they were unconscious. We don't know whether this will work – the evidence we have suggests that people who have out-of-body experiences are usually so intent on looking at themselves lying unconscious below them that they may pay no attention to even the most intriguing cards placed tantalizingly within their view. However, it is the only way to get objective scientific proof, which would be impossible to refute, that they did indeed leave their body during their cardiac arrest. Otherwise we are again forced back on anecdotal evidence.

It is surely illogical to think of end-of-life visions and temporary death experiences as isolated, entirely unrelated events. It makes more sense to regard them as part of a continuum, or as different views of the same event – the dying process. It is easy to spot the similarities between them. Both give a glimpse of a transcendent realm suffused with love and light, and both seem to eliminate any fear of death. The presence of dead relatives who seem to be there for a purpose is common to both experiences – to take you on your journey, in the case of an end-of-life experience, or to send you back, with the message that it was not your time to go, in a TDE.

There are obvious differences too. First, the feeling of being out of one's body has not been reported in any of the end-of-life visions we have been told about, though it probably occurs in

THE ART OF DYING

about one-third of TDEs. Neither has anyone described a tunnel experience as part of an end-of-life vision. Instead, although the dying person sometimes describes being able to move into and out of another transcendent realm, only a movement towards rather than a real journey seems to be involved, just a feeling of going to and fro with great ease. Perhaps it is the mental set of the dying which makes the tunnel experience less likely to occur. The dying often spend some time on the edge of consciousness, and at some level at least may know that death is approaching; they are embedded in a psychological matrix of ongoing, a journey to elsewhere, in which the process of leaving may be prolonged. In the TDE the movement into the experience – through a tunnel if there is one – and the return, usually described as a 'snapping back into the body' are very precise and abrupt events. There is a clear beginning and a clear end. But the end-of-life experience is a one-way journey only, guided and supported by those they have loved.

The accounts we have can only give us a partial view of the mental processes of the dying, taking us up to the moment of death. The accounts given by those who return from a TDE have a higher definition and paradoxically seem to give a much clearer insight into the mental state of the dying as they start the journey. But despite these differences, the amazing similarity of the transcendent realm strongly supports the idea that there is one transcendent reality which, although accessed differently, is where the dying go.

Chapter 13

Dying a Good Death

Die Todesstunde: das glückliche:
The death hour: the happy end

It is not faith, but the texture of a life lived that allows one to give oneself into the arms of death. (Marie de Hennezel)

The Plague, or Black Death, was one of the most devastating pandemics in human history. It probably started in Asia and by the late 1340s it had killed an estimated 75 million people worldwide, with an estimated 20 million deaths in Europe alone – between one-third and two-thirds of the population. One of the results of this decimation was a lack of priests to administer comfort and the last rites to the dying. And a consequence of this was the publication of two related texts, the *Ars Moriendi*, in about 1415 and 1450. *Ars Moriendi* ('The Art of Dying') was a blueprint, illustrated by a number of woodcuts, setting out the protocols and procedures of a good death and on how to 'die well', according to Christian precepts of the late Middle Ages. It was very popular, was translated into most Western European languages, and was the first in a Western literary tradition of guides to death and dying. It included advice to friends and family on the general rules of behaviour at the deathbed and reassurance that death was nothing to be afraid of.

We need a new *Ars Moriendi* now for the twenty-first century. Medical advances have given us the power to prolong life, but have not taught us anything about how to die. Our fear of death and love of life mean that we seldom prepare either for death itself or the process of dying. So although all of us will die, hardly anyone is prepared, or is preparing, to 'die right'.

The view of most of the esoteric literature, and that taken by the Christian Church, is that we should be ready for death at any moment, for we don't know when that moment is. The saint has no possessions (literally no attachments); each day he rolls up his sleeping blanket and tidies away his cooking utensils, sets every-thing in order and is mentally prepared for his own death that day. Most people's personal view, however, is that when the time comes, they will be prepared to face it, although in fact, when the time comes we have no option but to face it. But it's odd that while we make quite serious preparations for marriage, parent-hood and retirement, we are reluctant to prepare for death, or even to think about it seriously, when we are still in good health. We may fail to make a will or keep it up to date if family circum-stances change, to clear out an attic containing a lifetime of memorabilia, or to try to repair strained or torn relationships so that at least our survivors don't have the additional burden of anger or guilt to cope with. We know we should do it; our reluc-tance to take practical steps is at least partly because we're reluc-tant to face up to the possibility of our own personal extinction.

Death in modern times

The twentieth century was the first in which death had not been for most people in the West a common, everyday, domestic occur-rence. In the past, not only did people die younger, they usually died at home with their families around them. Death was part of everyone's experience, and perhaps less fearsome for that. Because bereavement was so common, there was little hesitation in talking about it, and this in itself is a natural source of comfort. Many, perhaps most, children had to come to terms with the deaths of siblings – in 1863 child mortality in England was nearly 7 per cent (compared to 0.7 per cent in 2002). The family doctor was intimately involved with death and would sit with the family by the bedside because he could do little else. With no antibiotics and few pain-killing drugs, his role was as much to support the family as to comfort the patient. There were no quick fixes, just the natural history of the illness with death as its all-too-familiar end.

And now, in the twenty-first century, although we go to greater lengths than ever before to prevent and avoid death, or at least to postpone it, we are at the same time much more casual about it. On the one hand the medical profession will go to extraordinary lengths to prolong life so that often the final days are spent in the intensive care unit. Here, in this sterile atmosphere with the wheezing of the respirator, the busy ritual of the ward routine, the beeping of the heart monitor and with tubes in almost every orifice, the patient passes his or her final hours. Silence only comes when mechanized life support ends and the cardiac monitor is finally flat. Melvin Morse[1] has suggested that we need to make the deathbed more crowded with people, less crowded with machines, and this is something we'd do well to keep in mind – if the choice is open to us. High-tech around the deathbed is sometimes more concerned with the feel-good factor of the relatives and the medical profession, who need to know they have done everything they can, than with the peace and comfort of the dying.

Last year my father died of stomach cancer. He was in hospital for seven weeks and was in intensive care when his niece visited him. She reported to me the strange thing that he said to her. He said that her father and the rest of the family were outside waiting for him, but they (indicating the doctors and nurses nearby) would not let them in yet. At that time he was wired up to monitors, drips, drains etc. and the hospital staff were working very hard to keep him alive. About five weeks later I had a call from the ward to come immediately. I rushed there expecting the worst, and the

215

nurse said that she had sent for me as my father had said that he was talking to my mother. The nurse said, 'You know when they see the dead that their time to go is near.'

And then, as soon as life finally ceases, the body is whisked away in almost indecent haste to the refrigerated shelves of the mortuary or, if the death was at home, to the undertaker's parlour, to be made, strangely, as lifelike as possible for the family to view. The old idea of a wake where family and friends could gather round the coffin, say their final goodbyes and come to terms with the reality of their loss in their own way and in their own time, has long gone, perhaps because we no longer have the time (or feel we do not have the time) to do this. Death has become a much more private affair. And this is a loss – how much of a loss we probably don't realize or acknowledge. Graham Norton, in an interview with Barbara Ellen in the *Observer* (18 November 2007) described how, disenchanted with Ireland, the 'torture chamber of his youth', he was helped to make his peace with it after seeing the way the local community handled his father's death. 'You think you won't like that kind of thing, but when you lose your dad it's lovely everyone coming around and bringing cake or a bottle of whiskey and telling you nice things about him. You think: Oh, that's why they do this – it's a really good idea.'

The best place in which to die

In an ideal world, most people would probably prefer to die at home, well cared for and in their own familiar environment. Usually their families would prefer this too, provided they can be given sufficient support. Dying at home is rather like childbirth at home – you can create your own conditions and retain at least a small measure of independence and control. In one's own home, friends and family can come and go as they please and there is none of the sense of isolation that may be inevitable in hospital.

But this is not always a realistic option. This is partly due to changes in society. Not everyone has their own accommodation, or relatives able to provide suitable help. Single-parent families dependent on one income, and families with both partners working mean that in many cases there is no one freely available to care for an elderly parent at home. There is no doubt that unless there is a lot of family support, nursing a terminally ill patient at home can be a huge emotional and physical load, and patients may be reluctant to impose this on their families. If an illness is at all protracted, it is hard for one carer to cope alone. As more and more of the elderly now live alone or go into nursing homes, the opportunity for dying at home becomes more and more remote. The reality is that most of us still die in hospital and there is a steadily increasing trend towards hospital death. In Scandinavia 90 per cent of deaths take place in hospital. In England and Wales in 1975, 58 per cent of deaths took place in hospital; by 2001 this figure had risen to 67 per cent; only 19 per cent of people die at home.

However, a recent Department of Health paper, *Building on the Best: Choice, Responsiveness and Equity in the NHS*[2] accepts that if people genuinely want to die at home, then they and their families should have access to the services needed to make this possible. Relatives of cancer patients need not feel they are coping alone; specially trained Macmillan nurses will visit the homes of people dying of cancer, giving support to the family and bringing the experiences of the hospices into the home. Pain is one of the fears that most of us have about dying. But with modern techniques such as motorized syringes which can inject a slow and continuous dose of pain-killers under the skin; and more importantly, with modern drugs, control of even severe pain need not be a problem for the person who wants to die at home.

What are the alternatives? Hospitals, however good the staff are at providing the necessary medical and nursing support, cannot always answer the emotional and social needs of the dying patient and his or her family. Many junior doctors and nursing staff feel that their training did not equip them to care for the dying, and in any case, on an acute ward staff are often too busy to sit and talk with a dying patient. It isn't always practical for relatives to be with them all the time; quite often the person dies alone. Hospices, because they are set up especially to care for the dying, and also to help their families, are probably the best solution. But few patients other than those with cancer die in hospices – and even of cancer patients only 16 per cent die in hospices, while 57 per cent die in hospitals and 22 per cent at home.

Elizabeth Kubler Ross[3] and Cicely Saunders,[4] who pioneered the attitude and the recognition that the dying need support, care and comfort, and are not medical failures to be rejected, and showed that hospice care was a real alternative and not just a second-best for people for whom dying at home is impractical or impossible. Hospices are experts in pain control, but it isn't only their expertise in giving the right amount of medication which benefits the patient. Many hospices have been designed to provide the quiet and supportive atmosphere which the dying require, and in which experience has shown that people don't seem to feel pain to such an extent and require less analgesia. Staff are specially trained in the care of the dying and nurses are able to sit with patients throughout the death process so that no one need die alone. Hospices have chaplains from several denominations who visit and comfort the dying and their relatives. There is also a support team within the hospices who care for the bereaved, and most hospices have groups which families can attend for support during the grieving process. However, it is coming to be recognized that although hospices are excellent in pain control and care and support of the relatives of the dying, spiritual care of the dying is an area which is not well catered for and staff are not always trained to understand, or to help patients understand, end-of-life experiences, and rarely discuss these experiences even among themselves.

A good death

What exactly do we mean by a 'good death?' A 'good death' should simply mean that the person has died as he or she wanted to die. For some this might mean at home surrounded by their family, for others it might mean a hospice with professional carers. Some people wait to die until they are alone, others seem able to hold on to life until someone they particularly want to say farewell to has arrived at their bedside. For most people a 'good death' probably means dying with an untroubled mind, with conflicts and misunderstandings resolved. For everyone it probably means that death should be as quick and as painless as possible. Dying in one's sleep is the ideal death as far as most people are concerned.

The spiritual approach to terminal care

We are now very good at making sure that when people die they are as comfortable and pain-free as possible. What we are not so good at is catering for and teaching others to care for the spiritual needs of the dying. Many health-care workers who are involved with end-of-life issues also feel that if they are to help their patients 'die well' they need a better understanding of the dying process, and further education or training to deal with existential issues. As one such worker said: 'We take them apart emotionally by exploring things with them, but we don't have the skills to put it all back together again all the time. There's a danger you could be left with a broken patient. With the best will in the world, if we are not careful, we can make things far worse.' Others voiced concerns about the difficulty of 'teaching' spirituality, or of prescribing ways of doing things because there was no 'prescription for death'. 'Some people try to get patients to die in a way they believe is the way to die. But people will die in the way they are going to do it. We're not going to change that.'[5]

People who have strong religious beliefs or who have had some transcendental personal experience such as the deathbed visions described in Chapter 3 often find their own reassurance in the face of death. Others may be helped by discussion of these end-of-life phenomena even if they have no personal experience of them.

However, twenty-first-century Britain is largely a secular society, holding a mass of vague, mixed and often contradictory beliefs. Over 170 distinct religions were counted in the 2001 Census. Between 1979 and 2005, half of all Christians stopped going to church on a Sunday and although 71 per cent of the population still describe themselves – on paper at any rate – as

'Christian', 66 per cent of the population have no actual connection to any religion or church, only 50 per cent have a vague lingering belief in a God of some sort, and only 6 per cent go to church on a Sunday. A Mori poll in 2003 found a similar discrepancy between theory and practice – 18 per cent said they were a practising member of an organized religion, while 25 per cent described themselves only as *members* of a world religion, presumably for traditional or social reasons.

About 60 per cent say they are theists, though which god is unspecified. But only 52 per cent believe in heaven and far fewer – 32 per cent – in hell, so it is clear that many are neither Muslims nor Christians. About 12 per cent described themselves as atheist and 14 per cent as agnostic. And 68 per cent believe in souls – rather more than declare a belief in God.

However, there are many people – about 24 per cent according to the Mori poll – who would describe themselves as 'spiritual', but who do not subscribe to any formal religious belief. Two wider definitions of 'spiritual' which might resonate more easily with what the non-religious feel are, first, the Dalai Lama's definition of it as 'compassionate actions, thoughts and feelings', and second (and this is the definition which seems most appropriate in the context of this book) as something which gives profound direction, meaning and purpose to an individual's life. By this definition everyone has spiritual needs, and this was at the heart of the teaching of Dame Cicely Saunders who founded the modern hospice movement.

Within the nursing and medical professions – and in society at large – 'spiritual' and 'religious' are usually taken as synonymous, but from the above it is quite clear that this is not so. The NHS Patient's Charter, for example, believes it has met its patients' spiritual needs by ensuring that they have access to a minister of religion. The aim of the hospice is to treat each patient as an individual, 'to live fully until he dies as himself'[6] and to help each patient die in the way he or she wants. 'We are not at all concerned that a patient or family should come to think as we do, but that they should find strength in their own inner values.'[7]

Reconciliation

One of the most impenetrable barriers to a 'good death' is unfinished business, and one of the most important facilitators – one might almost say it is a necessity – is reconciliation. If we are to die in peace, we need to forgive others, seek their forgiveness, and forgive ourselves for any wrongs or misunderstandings. If you are caring for the dying, the most valuable thing you can do for them is to make sure they have the opportunity, however late in the day, to try to mend broken or troubled relationships. If there is unfinished business, rifts in the family or problems with relationships unresolved, it is important that everyone has the opportunity to try to heal them, to say, 'I'm sorry', or 'I forgive you', or 'I love you'. This is not only so that the dying person can let go in peace, but so that the people left behind can have a peaceful and guilt-free parting. How important this is can be seen from the following account by Les Wilson of something that happened to him 40 years ago, when he was just 21 years old.

My father and I had never got on, and so I left home six months after leaving school at the age of 16. I managed to find work and get myself stabilized in the south of England where I worked in the transport industry. I never visited home in the following five years, nor did I think about the family I had left behind in Yorkshire.

However, one morning at 7.30 a.m. I was on my way to work as I had done for quite a few years when suddenly I turned right where I always turn left for my workplace, and started heading for London and the north. I could not reason with this, other than I found a sudden urge to visit my home in Yorkshire. I just felt a sudden need to do this.

When I arrived at my parents' front door, Mum came rushing out in tears and threw her arms around me saying, 'Thank God you're here . . . we hadn't a clue where to get in touch, but your dad is dying of cancer and you're the only one left to see him.'

I went upstairs and made my peace with my dad, who said that now he had seen all his family he was ready to go, and, next morning, when my elder brother called to see him, he was dead in his bed. I could not explain this phenomenon and it has troubled me ever since.

Many of the carers who were interviewed in our study said that the death process itself may somehow create the conditions that make the resolution of personal conflicts easier. They say that in the two or three days before death the room becomes extremely peaceful and dominated by feelings of love, and it is within this setting that families find it is easier for conflicts to be resolved and for reconciliation to be achieved. This isn't always possible, but it is always worth making the attempt. The nursing home staff interviewed in our survey who had managed to effect reconciliation between estranged family members felt a sense of completion, as if the resident could rest. And the following account shows how profoundly such reconciliations can help the grieving process of family members.

Peter Beresford, his wife Suzy and their children, had always had a difficult relationship with his mother, and because she would always refuse to talk through any differences or disagreements, their problems were always left unresolved. As he says, it is the most troubled and complicated relationships that are the most difficult to resolve after death, and he and his family were given the chance to escape all that through the kindness of a hospice nurse who had been with her on the night she died and who wrote to him describing the conversation she had had with her that night. His mother had been anxious to talk about her past, and about things she wished she had done differently. He described the effect this had had in an article in the *Guardian*:[8]

What was so wonderful about the nurse's letter was that here truly was a voice from the grave, a kind of deathbed confession, where you knew that the messenger had no ulterior motive, had no interest other than to try and help as an unbiased outsider. Just as we felt we were not judged, so we knew that neither was my mother, so what had rarely ever happened before, for once did. We heard an authentic warm voice from my mother . . . Of course . . . some of her comments can still be read as self-serving. But in what she said, there was appreciation, there was recognition, there was apology, above all there was warmth to Suzy . . . Over the years I have been able to develop an honest picture of my mother and mourn that. And that is greatly due to the nurse's simple, diligent and generous action.

Choosing a time to go

Some hospice carers have told us that residents seem instinctively to know they are nearing the end of life. 'It's almost like something has told them "You're nearly there, just calm down because something is going to happen",' said one interviewee. 'I think the people who are dying know right at the end that something is happening,' said another nurse.

Towards the end, from being very agitated they may calm down and just lie there peacefully. Sometimes they will get a sudden burst of energy, so that they are able to talk to their family for the last time. 'You get times when people suddenly seem to perk up just before they die. They seem to get better – enough sometimes to say goodbye to relatives . . . It's really strange, it's like an extra energy that they've got just prior to them going right off. They become coherent . . . and then they seem to just go.'[9]

It certainly seems to be quite common for people to have some intimation of their own death, almost as though it is a decision they have made themselves. They may tell those close to them, quite matter-of-factly, that it's time for them to go, that they won't be there when their friend next comes to visit them. The following account describes Sylvia's experience with her friend, Gwen, who was dying of cancer. Although Gwen was in great pain and often got very depressed, she was afraid to die and never wanted to talk about death. For the last two weeks of Gwen's life, Sylvia and her husband visited her daily in her hospice.

Although she was over 70, Gwen was still very vain about her hair, which was jet black. She would agonize if she saw a single silver strand, and the visit of the hairdresser every Tuesday was the highlight of her week. On the evening of Monday, 6 July 1992, we talked to her. She was in some pain, but quite alert. I asked her if she was going to see the hairdresser in the morning. When she

223

said 'No', I thought perhaps she was in too much pain, but she explained that she had seen 'some people' who had promised to take her out on Tuesday. She did not know where they were going, but they had promised to come for her.

The nurse assured us that no one had been to visit, and Gwen was not going anywhere. She explained that Gwen was on quite powerful medication and it was not unusual to be confused. But she did not seem at all confused to us.

The next morning I rang the hospice, but the doctor advised me that Gwen needed to rest and would only fight the drugs if she had visitors. Her family were coming later in the day. The following morning I rang again, already knowing what I was going to hear. Sure enough, Gwen had died peacefully on Tuesday evening, 7 July 1992.

It's clear that Gwen had the expectation that she was going to be collected and go 'somewhere'. What is interesting is that this was not seen by her as in any way strange – even though she seemed not to know who 'these people' were. This we have seen repeatedly in other accounts – even when the dying don't seem to know who is going to pick them up, the strangers hold no threat and the dying are happy to go with them.

A nurse told us the following incident which happened when she was on night duty at a Manchester hospital. An elderly couple had been involved in a car accident. The man had been badly injured, but the woman suffered mainly from shock and bruising.

I went for my break at midnight and on my return I was told the gentleman had died from his injuries but his wife was not to be told yet. I went to her bedside and asked if she would like a cup of tea. She excitedly told me that her husband had just been to see her and told her he would come back at 4 a.m. and they would go home together. I thought that she was still affected by shock. Her blood pressure suddenly began to fall about 3.30 a.m. and the Staff Nurse sent for the doctor.

She was still watching the door intently, waiting for her husband. The doctor saw she was deteriorating fast and did all he could to save her. She was smiling and watching for someone before she passed quickly into spirit. Death was noted at 4 a.m.

It is intriguing that the time of death can sometimes be known so accurately by the dying, even though at the time they tell their story there is no clear evidence that they are sufficiently ill to die. How could she know that she would actually 'go' at 4 a.m. when her blood pressure had not even begun to fall?

We have been told numerous stories about the lucid interval that occurs just before people die. They may come out of coma, move limbs that – as in the following case – have been paralysed, sit up in bed when they have not sat upright for months; they may even, after a long, severe, dementing illness, suddenly recognize the family and talk lucidly to the people who have come to take them, when in the days before they had no speech and no recognition. Clearly the time before death is a very special time. The woman who gave us the following story was by her father's side for the 48 hours before he died of lymphatic cancer. At the time, the nurses had told her that the 'people' her father said he could see were just memories coming back to him. That there might be another interpretation she found helpful and comforting.

At around 3 a.m. the night before he died, three people entered his room whom I could not see. He became very animated and even moved his arm that he had not been able to move for over a year. I asked him who was in the room and he replied, 'Thomas (a good friend who had passed on), Elizabeth (an auntie that he was very close to) and Phyllis (my mother, who had also passed on). These people stayed with him for three hours and he laughed and was very happy.

At around 6 a.m. he waved them goodbye (and blew kisses) and his eyes followed them out of the door. I asked him if he would have a sleep then and he said 'Yes'. Immediately, his face lit up and he watched them enter the room again. They stayed a further one hour then left. He passed away at 2.15 p.m.

Even when the end is near and inevitable, many hospice and hospital staff have told us the same thing – that terminally ill people seem to have some control over their departure, to make that final switch off at will. They spoke about how – against all odds – some residents cling on to life until a special relative arrives at the bedside. Veronica Stanton visited her grandmother in hospital on the day she died. Her sister had just returned from the US and went directly to the hospital where her grandmother said, 'I asked them to wait so I could see you to say goodbye.' The family were never able to discover who 'they' were, as she died that day without explaining.

Occasionally delaying tactics are employed. Chris Alcock's father, for example (Chapter 3, p. 27) was heard persuading his angel visitors to wait a while until his son had arrived to say goodbye to him. Geoffrey Watson describes a similar experience when his mother-in-law was dying:

My mother-in-law was ill in hospital, frail in body but robust in mind. On this day, Midsummer's Eve, the four-bed ward was empty except for Hilda, my mother-in-law, who was propped up in bed, talking lucidly to my wife and me. Suddenly, and quite crossly, she said, 'And they can go away, I'm not ready for them yet,' looking at and addressing the empty space of the ward wall at the end of her bed. I have to say I was discomfited as I thought a member of staff had come in unannounced, but there was no one, or nothing that I or my wife could see. Hilda died shortly before Midsummer's Day. All of her sisters and husband had died within the previous two years and we have often wondered if Hilda could see them. It was somewhat unnerving.

Often when someone we love dies and we are not there at their bedside to hold their hand and say a final goodbye we feel as if we have failed both them and ourselves. But hospice staff who have seen many deaths say that although many people in their care seem able to postpone their time of departure until they have had a chance to say a final goodbye to the people they love, others choose a moment when they are alone to take their final leave. So it's worth remembering that this may have been their choice, as this account suggests.

My daughter Eleanor was in hospital dying from breast cancer which had spread to her brain. We sat with her as she fell into a coma and her doctor said she would pass away soon. She was in a coma for three days but then around 4 a.m. she just woke up as normal and said to another daughter, 'My spirit sat on the edge of the bed and I thought , "Shall I go now?", but I thought, "No, not now".' Eleanor lived another four weeks and slept and talked on alternate days. She talked as if she had seen a glimpse of another place, it was such a precious time that we would have missed if she had died earlier, it would have been so raw and unfinished. Eleanor was so calm and peaceful, completely unafraid.

She fell into a coma again and the Macmillan nurse said she would probably go when we were not there. We could not understand, as we were by her bed day and night. At the end the nurses came and said they just wanted to freshen her up. We went into the day room and had barely sat down when we were called back as Eleanor had passed away while we were out of the room. Macmillan nurses see this often, as if the dying person wants to start the journey alone, when their dearest ones are out of the room.

And yet we must remember that death is at no one's beck and call. Many people long for death, would welcome it, and yet are forced to linger on for months or even years, however old, or tired, or ill they may be. It may well be possible to juggle the actual time of departure by a few hours or days, but probably no more than that. The following account is unusual in that a more extended stay seems to have been granted

On 10 June 1997, my father and I were told that my mother had only hours or days to live. She was in the special heart unit, very ill. She rallied enough to be transferred to another ward.

About two weeks before she died, my mother greeted us on our daily visit with such radiance and happiness that we were astonished. When she told us her story, my father laughed it off, but, although I was sceptical, I questioned her further. This was her story.

Elsie (aged 75) was in a single room at the end of a short corridor, leading to the nurses' station and main ward. It was the early hours (about 4 a.m.) and she was unable to sleep after her oxygen tubes had awoken her as she turned in bed. Suddenly the corridor filled with the brightest white light, and a lady, clothed in white,

227

walked towards her. The lady was the most beautiful woman Elsie had ever seen. Although the light was bright, Elsie could see the lady very clearly. The lady came close and smiled, telling Elsie to go with her. She took Elsie into a wonderful garden and the lady explained that, because Elsie had been ill for so long and had been so brave, she was going to be allowed a little more time to spend with her family. They went back to Elsie's room and the lady walked away.

My mother's whole being changed. She had her hair washed, cut and styled in her room for the first time, ate better and became more cheerful. During those last two weeks, most of her family had visited Elsie and she had particularly enjoyed the hours with her great-granddaughter. Knowing she would not see her for long did tinge her last days with some sadness. She knew she was going to die but wanted to go home. With some urgency we organized that and, on the afternoon of 3 July, Elsie finally went home.

At 8.55 a.m. the morning after she went home, Elsie died in rather traumatic circumstances, but I had the very distinct feeling that God had taken over her life. Elsie was not a very religious person, but she believed that the lady had been God's angel, blessing her with a few more days with her loved ones. It made such a difference to her in those last two weeks.

Letting go

Often it is the family who cannot face the thought of death, not the person who is about to die. One ward sister remembered a patient, a young man who had been ill for a long time. 'One day when his mum left his bedside, he looked at me and said, "Is it OK if I go now?" I sat with him while he died.'

Quite often the dying person seems to need 'permission' to go, as Linda Steward's account of her grandmother's death illustrates very well:

In 1953, my paternal grandmother was terminally ill with heart disease. Rather than stay in her own home, she and my grandfather decided to come to stay with me and my parents. My mother was good at looking after her (with the help of a district nurse), and made her as comfortable as she could. She would touch her and stroke her a lot, hold her hand, keep her comfortable and talk to her, even though towards the end of the time my grandmother was not always conscious.

One day, my mother heard Grandma talking. I should explain that Grandma's brother was called Gladstone – 'Gladdy' for short. Grandma was saying, very clearly, 'I want to come, Gladdy, but they won't let me.' My mother told the district nurse, who was middle-aged and very experienced. The nurse said to her, 'In that case, my dear, we must do as little as possible to hold her back. We must only keep her clean and comfortable and not try to keep her with us, because she wants to go.' This is what my mother did, and my grandmother died soon afterwards, very comfortably.

Should you talk about death to the dying? Take your cue from them, but try to make it easy for them to do so if they want to – and certainly don't go to great lengths to avoid the issue. Tony Walter[10] describes how a good nurse will use what he has called 'the therapeutic gaze' – the ability to get a patient to reveal how he or she feels when taking their nursing history rather than simply eliciting facts about their symptoms and situation. The technique is to ask open-ended questions (i.e. a question that can't be answered with a simple yes or no, putting an end to any discussion) so that the person is encouraged to talk about the illness and its impact on their life. This can, if they want it to, lead quite naturally on to their knowledge of whether or not they are dying and their sadness about this.

The carers interviewed in our palliative care study[11] had found that quite often it was difficult for patients to talk to their families about dying, because the family found it so hard to accept the fact of their death and could not bear to talk about it. The carers were the only people they could talk to.

Marie de Hennezel is a psychologist who was on the staff of the first palliative care unit in a Parisian Hospital and has written both wisely and sensitively about the emotional and spiritual needs of the dying and what one can do to help meet these.

The worst kind of solitude when you're dying is not being able to say to the people you love that you're going to die. To feel your death approaching and not to be able to talk about it or to be able to share with others what this leave-taking inspires in you often results directly in mental breakdown, a kind of delirium, or some manifestation of pain that at least gives you something you are allowed to talk about.

She goes on to point out that usually the dying person *knows*. What they need is some help in being able to articulate that knowledge. But everyone else's distress makes it hard for them to talk – the dying are in essence being forced into a position of having to protect their survivors. Once they are able to say 'I am going to die' they become, in Marie de Hennezel's words, 'not the victim of death but rather the protagonist in their own dying'.[12]

So it is sometimes the relatives who have to make a conscious effort to let go, to acknowledge that death is imminent, even sometimes giving the dying themselves the permission they seem to need to go. Kathleen Rosseau described how she felt she needed to let her father know he was 'allowed' to die, even before he had contracted his final illness:

My father was a strong person both physically and mentally. About three years after my mother's death, one day out of the blue he said to me, 'Kathleen, I am so tired. I cannot go on any longer.' I realized he had kept going, trying to help me – we had been so close to my mother and the grief was painful. I told him that I was OK now and he must not keep going for me any more. Two weeks later he caught a chest infection from which he never recovered. The evening before he died I had been in and out of his room when he sat up and said, 'Kathleen, leave me alone for a while. Go and have a lie down. I just need to be on my own.' I went back into his room two or three hours later and he was gone.

Being with the dying

We have become so used to believing that we have to shield each other from the idea of death, that it takes a cultural shift to realize that death is perhaps something we have to help each other through rather than shield each other from. We realize the value of the 'birth companion' during childbirth. Perhaps we should now consider that the 'death companion' may have an equally important part to play and that the interaction between the carer and the person who is dying may have a profound effect on them both. As Geraldine English, who helped to look after her father as he was dying, commented, 'I consider myself privileged to have been able to spend the last weeks of my father's life with him, I almost felt that we (me, my mother and ex-husband) were acting like "midwives".'

When you are with someone who is dying, the main requirement is that you be there, not that you do anything. In practical terms, make sure his or her surroundings are both peaceful and cheerful, and try not to take over completely, making all the decisions, removing from the other person every vestige of control over what happens.

It is always worth remembering that we may have a very limited or inaccurate picture of what the dying person can experience. Even when someone is apparently unconscious, as usually happens in the terminal stages of an illness, he or she may be able to hear more than we imagine they can, may be able to feel our touch even though they do not respond. Holding their hand, talking to them, may give more comfort than we realize. We can't ever know this for certain, but we can at the very least draw comfort ourselves from knowing that we tried to round off their life with a loving farewell.

Above all, remember that at a time like this people are treading so delicately, being so careful not to say the wrong thing, that it is easy for many of the right things to go unsaid. And later, when you realize there isn't going to be another chance to say them, this can be yet another source of grief.

End-of-life experiences suggest that the dying process is taken care of, that the dying are often more aware at the end than was previously thought and that the support of family at this time is of enormous value. The phenomena themselves are fascinating, however we try to explain them, but not everyone will experience them. Everything we have learned so far about death and dying points to something that is ultimately far more important because it affects every one of us. And that is that the real barriers to a good death are those of unfinished business such as family conflicts, and unresolved personal issues such as guilt or hate, and the most effective tool in helping those we love experience a peaceful and a 'good' death is to help, if we can, in the process of reconciliation.

Marie de Hennezel[13] describes a conversation she had with Francois Mitterand shortly before he died. They talked first about the question of time, the will to live and how much time he had left. She pointed out to him that the will to live can often win out over medical opinion, that you can be clear-headed about the approach of death, and yet stay absolutely alive until the end. 'You mustn't start dying until death comes.' They also discussed the question of whether believers face death with greater serenity than non-believers, and she told him of a woman who met her death with absolute serenity, who had told her, 'I am not a believer, but I am curious to know what happens next.' And Marie de Hennezel adds, 'It is not faith, but the texture of a life lived that allows one to give oneself *into the arms of death.*'

Chapter 14

The Journey to Elsewhere: Coming to Terms with Death

One does not discover new lands without consenting to lose sight of the shore for a very long time. (Andre Gide, 1869–1951)

Unfortunately, it is in the nature of death that there are no survivors. No one can tell us what it is really like. All we can know for sure is that it is inevitable and that it means the end of our existence; we – our bodies – will not 'be' any more.

We may fear death, but it fascinates us too. *Bartlett's Familiar Quotations* has nearly 11 columns of entries on death and dying, compared to six on the soul and only a single column on immortality. Death is often still referred to as a taboo subject, but the evidence suggests that it is now more of a hot topic than a forbidden one. In 1987 Simpson's English language bibliography found over 3,000 books on death and dying in print. Tony Walter[1] has drawn attention to the revival of interest in death. He cites the success of the hospice movement and the growth of bereavement counselling, the deluge of articles, books and television programmes about death in both Britain and the USA, the success of death-related charities such as Cancer Research, and the fact that as long as 30 years ago there were over 1,000 college courses in the USA on death and dying. Interviews with the bereaved are a regular feature of the media, and in Britain several journalists have written personal and deeply moving accounts of their own terminal illnesses.

We, who are not dying, find the approach of death both a threat and an embarrassment. We fear most the *manner* of our death, the pain, the moments before extinction when we realize there is no escaping the inevitable. We fear death because we cling to permanency, and death marks the end, involves losing or

233

leaving everything and everyone we love. It is unknown and irreversible. It is the annihilation of our personal sense of 'I' – our own ego which we have cherished and pumped up all our life, is seen to disintegrate, and then nothing. It would be easier if we were not so wedded to a linear way of thinking about human life with an absolute end, rather than a cyclical one with concepts of death and rebirth being just part of the same cycle.

It is probably because of our own fear that we so often fail to help the dying prepare for death. We have few special rituals to prepare for death, or to mark it. Ann Liddell, who works with old people, wrote to us stressing the need for this preparation, which is often not being met by either the medical profession or the family. 'Having lived in Java, where all stages of life are prepared for in very beautiful and special ways – even the first time a baby's feet touch the ground is marked by a special celebration and ritual – I am always in a state of shock when I return here . . . our treatment of our old is totally inexplicable to them.'

Children and bereavement

Not only is it hard for us to help prepare the dying for death, many people fail to prepare themselves or their children for bereavement. Nothing can make the death of a parent easy for a child, but if death is known to be inevitable, failure to prepare a child, under the guise of 'protecting' them, will almost certainly make it worse. The following letter illustrates this very well.

My father died when I was 11 years old. My mother was told that he was dying – this was kept from me – I had no idea just how ill he was. The doctors told her that he was unlikely to make it through the night, so she packed me off to my godparents. Oblivious to what was going on, I had a great evening and was sent to bed at my usual bedtime. In the middle of the night I woke up. I was grief stricken. I lay quietly, sobbing my heart out. I knew my father had gone. I cried myself back to sleep. In the morning my godmother came to my bedside to gently wake me. She knelt beside me and told me that my father had died in the early hours of the morning. I have always believed that my father came to me that night to say goodbye.

I was a young girl and had no notion of the gravity of the situation. I had every reason to believe that he was coming home after his operation. This was 30 years ago, and I have always wondered about what happened that night. It was an extremely powerful experience – nothing had happened like it before, or since.

There is one obvious explanation for this experience – that the writer had somehow picked up on the emotions of the adults around her and realized that her father was seriously ill, so we asked her whether she thought this was possible. We also asked whether she felt that the visit had helped her to grieve, because it so evidently lacked the 'comfort factor' described by most people who have had these farewell visits. She replied:

I can't rule this out. Their emotions must have been very strong, but I can say quite categorically that no part of my being knew he was dying. If I did pick anything up, it would have been very much subconsciously.

The adults around me – including my dad – must have gone to great lengths to 'shield' me from the truth of the situation. My dad died the week before Christmas, and when out Christmas shopping with my mum I bought his Christmas present. I had no idea that my dad was terminally ill. I thought he was going to be home for Christmas – and had no reason to think otherwise.

Did the farewell visit make grieving more bearable? Definitely not. I didn't say goodbye to him. In the darkness of the night I encountered his departure alone and without warning. It was a shock, it came from nowhere. As an adult, what I think is that that experience halted my grieving process. I didn't grieve as others around me did. For many years I believed my dad was with me. Grieving for my father's death began when I was in my early twenties, and by that time no one could figure out why I was crying so much. My grieving was happening out of context and I couldn't really explain it to anyone. I don't think that grieving out of context is a good thing – it probably makes it less bearable for everyone concerned.

The most difficult thing for me was not having anyone I could talk to or cry with, which resulted in suppressed emotions and a long and confusing grieving process that has taken me years to come to terms with, and I still can't talk to my family about this.

So perhaps the real lesson to be drawn from this is that when there is a terminal illness in the family, children are better able to come to terms with it if they are gradually prepared for an eventual end and not entirely shielded from reality – and, most importantly, that they are allowed to say a final goodbye. Keeping them in the dark achieves nothing, except some temporary emotional respite for the adults who may not feel able to cope with a child's grief as well as their own. Make it easy for them to ask the questions they want to ask, and answer them as honestly as you can.

When a child has to be told that someone they love has died, a parent or someone they know and trust should break the news. It is best to do this soon, and to do it simply, without using euphemisms or circumlocutions, giving the child the comfort of being held. Tears are normal, and as the letter above emphasizes, giving the child someone to grieve with and talk to is supremely important. If the child feels comfortable about seeing the body, they should be allowed to. It confirms the finality of death and allows them to say a final goodbye. Devising some simple ritual in which they can take part is often helpful too. The child may want to write a farewell letter or choose some favourite toy or possession to put in the coffin. All this will help them to express the emotions they are feeling, and to accept the reality of what has happened, both of which are necessary parts of coming to terms with their bereavement.

Rounding off a life

Many dying people feel isolated, because many of us still find it hard to know the right thing to say either to the dying or to bereaved friends. As friends or family of the dying, we tend to share Dylan Thomas's view that death is something to be fought every step of the way, that we should 'rage, rage against the dying of the light'. But the dying themselves may be more philosophical about it. When Elizabeth Kubler Ross[2] defined the five stages that the dying passed through before finally coming to terms with the fact of their own death – denial, anger, bargaining, depression, and finally acceptance – the patients she was working with were those with terminal cancer. Many of these were probably young people forced to face the prospect of a premature death. She was careful to point out that not everyone goes through every stage – and indeed that it isn't always easy for anyone who isn't highly trained even to recognize the stages. What might look like denial, for example, might well be simply that the patient is trying to protect the people he or she loves from the reality of their condition.

But most people in the West now die in old age. And most old people don't feel the need to 'rage against the dying of the light'. They are much more likely to face death with equanimity – perhaps even, if old age is proving burdensome, to welcome it. There seems to be an almost instinctive need to prepare yourself for death as you grow older – to look back on your life and assess it. The need to talk about old times, to search out old friends who have played an important part in your life at some stage but with whom you have lost touch – all these can be thought of as rounding off, preparatory behaviours.

You are certainly less likely to fear death if you come from a culture where death is freely discussed and seen as a stepping-stone to further experience. There is also less fear if your personal belief system has taught you how to cope with loss, and if you have learned some spiritual practice such as meditation which reinforces the possibility of the transcendent over the ephemeral nature of this world. Ten per cent of the population have had deep and powerful transcendent experiences (defined in questionnaire studies as 'seeing through into the fundamental structure of nature') which confirm for them that this life is only a small part of what can be experienced and that the transcendent is the fundamental nature of experience.

However, many people manage to face death with serenity and without belief – like Marie de Hennezel's[3] patient (p. 232) who told her, 'I am not a believer but I am curious to know what happens next.' And she suggests that when facing death this 'confidence in the unfolding of things' is more important than a belief which may not be rooted in the experience of a deep inner trust.

If we are prepared to accept the evidence of the experiences that have contributed to this book, it does seem as though fear of death might be a groundless fear. A common element in near-death and end-of-life experiences is the conviction that existence continues after bodily death and that reality lies in the non-physical being. So it is perhaps no wonder that one of the almost universal consequences of all these experiences is a loss of the fear of death.

More interestingly though, Bruce Greyson[4] has shown that this same loss of the fear of death is true for anybody who has had a close brush with death and survived. Van Lommel[5] studied a group of patients who had had cardiac arrests and come very close to death and found that although only 10 per cent had NDEs, all showed a reduced fear of death. The same seems to be true of those people who experience deathbed visions. Whatever it is they experience seems to lead to tranquillity in the face of death. For their relatives too, witnessing or being told of these experiences profoundly affects their own attitudes towards death.

But perhaps the most important consequence for anyone who has faced death is that it affects the way they live their life *now*. It makes them value life without clinging to it, appreciate each day as though it was their last. This is how Elizabeth Rogers describes the effect her near-death experience had on her:

I now feel that every day is a new gift to me. Material things are not nearly as important as they used to be, and I now look forward with peace and joy to the day of my death. Before that (her near-death experience) I was not afraid of death really, but I didn't like the thought of it. But now I am looking forward to dying, to death. It has absolutely no fears for me. Recently someone asked me what I would say if I was told I had to die now. My answer was, 'I'd say, this is a lovely "now" . . .'

By accepting and living in the *now* our attitude towards both life and death can be transformed. No one has expressed this truth more movingly or with greater clarity than the playwright Dennis Potter, in his final interview with Melvyn Bragg in March 1994, a few weeks after he learned that he had terminal cancer, and a few weeks before he died.

However predictable tomorrow is . . . there's the element of the unpredictable, of the 'You don't know'. The only thing you know for sure is the present tense, and that nowness becomes so vivid to me that, almost in a perverse sort of way, I'm almost serene. You know, I can celebrate life.

Below my window in Ross . . . the blossom is out in full now . . . and looking at it, instead of saying, 'Oh, that's nice blossom', I see it as the whitest, frothiest, blossomest blossom that there ever could be . . . Things are both more trivial than they ever were, and more important than they ever were, and the difference between the trivial and the important doesn't seem to matter. But the nowness of everything is absolutely wondrous . . . The fact is, if you see the present tense, boy, do you see it! And boy, can you celebrate it.

The power of 'now', the present moment, has been widely written about in the works of Eckhardt Tolle, one of the new breed of transcendental philosophers referred to in Chapter 12. 'To have your attention in the now is not a denial of what is needed in your life, it is recognizing what is primary . . . Now is your friend, not your enemy. Acknowledge it. Honour it.'

If we have never had a transcendental experience we can only theorize about what a transcendental existence might be like, or indeed whether it is more than a theoretical possibility. But perhaps we can learn more by listening to the people who have first-hand knowledge of the experiences the rest of us can only talk about. So perhaps the first step is simply to accept, as Alfred Russel Wallace would have us do, that these things do happen to sane and sensible people even if we cannot for the moment find a satisfactory framework to fit them into. There are, after all, two approaches to a jigsaw puzzle. One can start with the outside edges, building a structural framework – sky at the top, green fields at the bottom – within which to fit the rest of the picture. This is the usual adult approach. But watch a small child with a puzzle. He or she is much more likely simply to try to fit random pieces together, without attempting to get an overview of the whole picture. At the moment we are more or less in the position of the child. We don't yet have the concepts to build up a satisfactory contextual framework – after all, we don't even yet know what consciousness is – and the best we can do is to look at the pieces we do have and see how far we can fit them together to make a coherent whole.

So let us recap the journey and see how near to completion we can get our jigsaw. We have to start by acknowledging that our science has no proper understanding of subjective experience. But if we do not use a traditional scientific framework, but accept at face value the subjective experiences and observations of 'sane and sensible people', these data suggest that consciousness is not limited to the brain but is spread out and links together in a very real way those who have close and loving relationships. Next we can see that the view of the universe which we normally perceive in our everyday state of consciousness may be a very limited one. In the words of the artist Thetis Blacker, who recently died and had a transcendent experience in her early twenties, 'It's only one small speck, one small part, one tiny atom of what we can experience.' This transcendent universe appears to those who see it to be full of love and light, and, strangely, just one thing that we are all part of and are not separate from.

The next piece of our jigsaw puzzle concerns what happens in the death experiences reported during cardiac arrests. This is the closest we can get to the mental state of those who, clinically speaking, have started the journey of death. Their experiences suggest that as death approaches we enter into a highly charged spiritual arena, an area of intense personal meaning, which reflects the insight of the transcendent reality of love, peace and light as described by those who have had transcendent or mystical experiences. Sometimes spiritual presences appear to those who are able to see them, and have been reported to be composed of light.

The deathbed visions and coincidences described in this book fit quite neatly into this corner of the jigsaw. Some of the dying transcend into an area of light and love similar to that reported by people who have had cardiac 'death' experiences. Within this area and sometimes manifesting independently of it in the room, people appear, usually dead relatives whose sole purpose seems to be to accompany the dead person on a journey from this reality to elsewhere. Their presence is so evidently real and vivid for the dying person that, even though they may have been unconscious or barely lucid, they may, just prior to death, have a brief final moment of lucidity in which they sit up to extend a hand to welcome the unseen presence that may look after them and lead them forward to elsewhere.

As we move towards the final moments, a new spiritual domain is entered by the dying which has consequences for those around and those to whom the dying person is intimately and closely linked. That others in the room, who are close both physically and emotionally to the dying person, sometimes experience both the light and the accompanying feelings of peace that the dying themselves experience does suggest a linkage of consciousness that could only be achieved if consciousness did, in these particular circumstances at least, extend beyond the brain. The 'visits' of the dying at their moment of death to someone they are emotionally close to, seemingly to say a final goodbye or reassure them that 'everything is all right' only seem explicable in terms of an extension of consciousness. And if, as is often the case, the people who receive these visits may not even know that their visitor is ill or dying, and occasionally may not even have given them a thought for years, this suggests very strongly that the 'visit' is driven by the dying person – and as a logical corollary, that some aspect of that person's consciousness may therefore have survived bodily death. Not only does the dying consciousness reach out to friends and family, and may leave a trail as it passes from the body: cats and dogs also seem to sense the dying consciousness, and it also at times achieves a materiality – the clocks that stop, the bells that ring – that raises questions about the very structure of the universe as we now understand it.

All the experiences we have been told of point to death being part of a structured and supportive process. They also suggest that a greater understanding of what happens when we die would lead to a removal of our fear of death and open up the possibility of a new beginning, the start of a new journey – it is perhaps worth remembering the 'journeying language' which the dying so often seem to use when they make their final farewells. This is where the evidence from the dying leads us, although at present there is nothing to show us where the journey may lead.

To complete our jigsaw we will need to expand our current scientific framework, and hope that this may provide an explanation. But it's also important to realize that these experiences have their own validity, that in their powerful emotional and spiritual impact they have meaning for us, and only those who have had the experiences are entitled to judge their personal meaning. These experiences leave a strong and marked impression on those who grieve and are a source of comfort over the years that follow. They also find, as Ali found, whose experience is quoted on pp. 158–9, that it helps them to come to terms with what they no longer see as an absolute loss.

This whole experience – if indeed, this is the right word to use – has given so much more meaning to my life now. Whether or not I did really see or feel what I believe I did, it has left a very positive view and comforting understanding of the whole process of death and dying, particularly the moment of death. I know now that there is nothing to fear, it is such a peaceful and graceful moment, and it has proved to me, beyond a doubt, that the spirit or soul does exist, outside of the body; I saw it!

The evidence points to the fact that we are more than brain function, more than just a speck in creation, and that something, whether we regard it as soul or consciousness, will continue in some form or another, making its journey to 'Elsewhere'. It suggests that when we enter the light we are coming home, that we do indeed touch the inner reaches of a universe that is composed of universal love.[6] This is the territory of the dying. Until then, perhaps the best we can do is to continue living, prepare for death, and take as guidelines what we have learned about the process of dying. And also keep in mind this Zen story which, as always in Zen, redirects our attention to living in the now because, for the living, death is someone else's feast.

A nobleman asked Master Hakuin:

'What happens to the enlightened man at death?'
'Why ask me?'
'Because you are a Zen master.'
'Yes, but not a dead one.'

Notes

Chapter 1

1. Kellehear, A. (2007) *A Social History of Dying*, Cambridge University Press.
2. Gurney, E., Myers, F. W. and Podmore, F. ([1886]2005) *Phantasms of the Living*, Adamant Media Corporation.
3. Barrett, Sir William (1926) *Deathbed Visions*, Rider and Co.
4. Osis, K. and Haraldsson, E. ([1977] 1986) *At the Hour of Death*, Hastings House.
5. Parnia, S., Waller, D., Yeates, R. and Fenwick, P. (2001) 'A qualitative and quantitative study of the incidence, features and aetiology of near-death experiences in cardiac arrest survivors', *Resuscitation* **48**, 149–56.
6. van Lommel, P., van Wees, R., Meyers, V. and Elfferich, I. (2001) 'Near-death experience in survivors of cardiac arrest: a prospective study in the Netherlands, *Lancet* **358**, 2042; Swaninger, J., Eisenberg, P. R., Schechtman, K. B. and Weiss, A. N. (2002) 'A prosective analysis of near-death experiences in cardiac arrest patients', *Journal of Near-Death Studies* **20**(4), 215–32; Greyson, B. (2003) 'Incidence and correlates of near-death experiences on a cardiac care unit', *General Hospital Psychiatry* **25**, 269–76; Sartori, P. (in press) *A Five-Year Clinical Study of Near-Death Experiences in a Welsh Intensive Therapy Unit*, Edwin Mellen Press
7. Osis, K. (1961) *Deathbed Observations by Physicians and Nurses*, Parapschology Foundation Inc.; Osis and Haraldsson, *At the Hour of Death*.

Chapter 2

1. Dewi Rees, W. (1971) 'The hallucinations of widowhood', *British Medical Journal* **4**, 37–41; McCready, W. C. and Greeley, A. M. (1976) *The Ultimate Values of the American Population*, Sage; Osis, K. and Haraldsson, E. (1977) 'Deathbed observations by physicians and nurses: a cross-cultural survey', *The Journal for the American Society for Psychical Research* **71**(3).
2. Weisman, A. D. (1972) *On Dying and Denying: A Psychiatric Study of Terminality*, Human Sciences Press; Callanan, M. and Kelley, P. (1992) *Final Gifts: Understanding the Special Awareness, Needs and Communications of the Dying*, Hodder & Stoughton; Heyse-Morse, L. H. (1996) 'On spiritual pain of dying', *Mortality* **1**(3), 297–315; Patterson, E. M. (1997) *The Experience of Dying*, Prentice-Hall; Brayne S., Lovelace, H. and Fenwick, P. (2006) 'An understanding of the occurrence of deathbed phenomena and its effects on Palliative Care Physicians', *American Journal of Hospice and Palliative Medicine* **23**(1), 17–24.
3. Seravalli, E. (1988) 'The dying patient, the physician and the fear of death', *New England Journal of Medicine*, 29 December, 1728–30.
4. Patterson, *The Experience of Dying*.

Chapter 3

1. Osis, K. and Haraldsson, E. ([1977] 1986) *At the Hour of Death*, Hastings House.
2. Osis, K. and Haraldsson, E. (1977) 'Deathbed observations by physicians and nurses: a cross-cultural survey', *The Journal for the American Society for Psychical Research* **71**(3).
3. Osis and Haraldsson, 'Deathbed observations'.
4. Brayne S., Lovelace, H. and Fenwick, P. (2006) 'An understanding of the occurrence of deathbed phenomena and its effects on Palliative Care Physicians', *American Journal of Hospice and Palliative Medicine* **23**(1), 17–24.

Chapter 5

1. Kircher T. T. and Thienel, R. (2005) 'Functional brain imaging of symptoms and cognition in schizophrenia', *Progress in Brain Research* **150**, 299–308.
2. Houran, J. and Lange, R. (1997) 'Hallucinations that comfort: contextual mediation of deathbed visions', *Perceptual and Motor Skills* **84**, 1490–1504.
3. Barrett, Sir William (1926) *Deathbed Visions*, Rider and Co.
4. Brayne S., Lovelace, H. and Fenwick, P. (2006) 'An understanding of the occurrence of deathbed phenomena and its effects on Palliative Care Physicians', *American Journal of Hospice and Palliative Care* **23**(1), 17–24.
5. Brayne S., Lovelace, H. and Fenwick, P. (2008) 'Perceptions of nursing home carers on the spiritual experiences of residents at the end of life', *European Journal of Palliative Care* (in press).
6. Houran and Lange, 'Hallucinations that comfort'.
7. Lerma, J. (2007) *Into the Light*, Career Press Inc.
8. Osis, K. and Haraldsson, E. ([1977] 1986) *At the Hour of Death*, Hastings House.
9. Betty, L. Stafford (2006) 'Are they hallucinations or are they real? The spirituality of deathbed and near-death visions', *Omega* **53**(1–2), 37–49.
10. Fontana, D. (2005), *Is There an Afterlife?*, O Books.

Chapter 6

1. Sheldrake, R. and Smart, P. (2003) 'Experimental tests for telephone telepathy', *Journal of the Society for Psychical Research* **67** (July), 184–99.
2. Fenwick, P. and Fenwick, E. (1995) *The Truth in the Light*, Headline; Levine, S. (1982) *Who Dies?*, Doubleday; Moody, R. A. (1975) *Life After Life*, Mockingbird Books.
3. Kelly, R. E. (1992) 'Present at the moment of death: implications for counseling of emergency service personnel', *The Forum Newsletter: Newsletter of the American Association of Death Education and Counseling* **17**(4), 1 and 17–19.
4. Kelly, R. E. (2002) 'Post mortem contact by fatal injury victims with emergency service workers at the scenes of their death, *Journal of Near-Death Studies* **21**(1), Fall 2002, Human Sciences Press, Inc., 25.
5. Parnia, S., Waller, D., Yeates, R. and Fenwick, P. A. (2001) 'Qualitative and quantitative study of the incidence, features and aetiology of near-death experiences in cardiac arrest survivors', *Resuscitation* **48**, 149–56; van Lommel, P., van Wees, R., Meyers, V. and Elfferich, I. (2001) 'Near-death experience in survivors of cardiac arrest: a prospective study in the Netherlands, *Lancet* **358**, 2042; Schwaninger, J., Eisenberg, P. R., Schechtman, K. B.

and Weiss, A. N. (2002) 'A prospective analysis of near-death experiences in cardiac arrest patients, *Journal of Near-Death Studies* **20**(4), 215–32; Greyson, B. (2003) 'Incidence and correlates of near-death experiences on a cardiac care unit', *General Hospital Psychiatry* **25**, 269–76.
6. http://www.biomindsuperpowers.com/Pages?CIA-InitiatedRV.html..
7. Utts, J. and Josephson, B. (1996) *The Journal of Scientific Exploration* **10**(1) (http://www-stat.ucdavis.edu/users/utts/).
8. Tarnas, R. (1991) *The Passion of the Western Mind*, Ballantine Books.
9. Tarnas, R. (2007) *Cosmos and the Psyche: Intimations of a New World View*, Plume.

Chapter 7
1. Greeley, A. M. (1975) *Sociology of the Paranormal: A Reconnaissance*, Sage.
2. Haraldsson, E. *et al.* (1976) 'National survey of psychical experiences and attitudes towards the paranormal in Iceland', in W. G. Roll, R. L. Morris and J. D. Morris (eds), *Research in Parapsychology*, The Scarecrow Press.
3. Guggenheim, B. and Gugenheim, J. (1996) *Hello from Heaven*, Bantam Books.
4. Dewi Rees, W. (1971) 'The hallucinations of widowhood', *British Medical Journal* **4**, 37–41.
5. Fontana, D. (2005) *Is There an Afterlife?*, O Books.

Chapter 8
1. Radin, D. (1997) *The Conscious Universe*, Harper.
2. Playfair, G. (1980) *This House is Haunted: An Investigation of the Enfield Poltergeist*, Souvenir Press; Fontana, D. (1991) 'A responsive poltergeist: a case from South Wales', *Journal of the Society for Psychical Research* **58**, 341–50; Fontana, D. (1992) 'The responsive South Wales poltergeist: a follow-up report, *Journal of the Society for Psychical Research* **58**, 827, 225–31.
3. Howarth, G. (2000) 'Dismantling the boundaries between life and death', *Morality* **5**(2), 127–38.
4. Kellehear, A. (2000) *Eternity and Me: The Everlasting Things in Life and Death*, Hill of Content.
5. Sheldrake, R. (1999) *Dogs That Know When Their Owners Are Coming Home*, Arrow Books.
6. Dosa, D. M. (2007) 'A day in the life of Oscar the cat', *New England Journal of Medicine*, **357**(4), 328–9.
7. Brayne, S., Lovelace, H. and Fenwick, P. (2008) 'End-of-life experiences and the dying process in a Gloucestershire nursing home as reported by nurses and care assistants', *American Journal of Hospice and Palliative Medicine* (in press).

Chapter 10
1. Vanstone, James W. (1974) *Athapaskan Adaptations: Hunters and Fishermen of the Sub-Arctic Forests*, Aldine Publishing Company.
2. Birket-Smith, Kaj (1930) *Contributions to Chipewyan Ethnology: Report of the Fifth Thule Expedition 1921–24*, Vol. VI, No. 3, Gyldendal.
3. Levy, Jerrold E. (1998) *In the Beginning: The Navajo Genesis*, University of California Press.
4. Kluckhohn, C. and Leighton, D. (1946) *The Navajo*, Oxford University Press.

5. Aristotle, *De Anima* 1.2, 405a, 19–21.
6. Walter, T. (1994) *The Revival of Death*, Routledge.
7. http://www.religioustolerance.org/rel_comp.htm.
8. Dalai Lama (1997) *Sleeping, Dreaming and Dying: An Exploration of Consciousness*, Wisdom Publications.
9. Qu'ran Surah, Chapter 3: Al-Imran, verse 185.
10. Sanford, J. A. (1991) *Soul Journey*, Crossroad, p. 64.
11. Grof, S. and Halifax, J. (1977) *The Human Encounter with Death*, Clarke, Irwin and Co.

Chapter 11

1. Dennett, D. C. (1991) *Consciousness Explained*, Penguin.
2. Koch, C. and Greenfield, S. (2007) 'How does consciousness happen?', *Scientific American*, October, 50–7.
3. Nagel, T. (1974) 'What is it like to be a bat?', *Philosophical Review* **83**, 435–50.
4. Searle, J. (1992) 'The problem of consciousness', in P. Nagel (ed.), *CIBA Foundation Symposium No. 174, Experimental and Theoretical Studies of Consciousness*, pp. 61–80, John Wiley.
5. Velman, M. and Schneider, S. (eds) (2007) *The Blackwell Companion to Consciousness*, Blackwell.
6. Bennett, M. R. and Hacker, P. M. S. (2003) *Philosophical Foundations of Neuroscience*, Blackwell.
7. Kuhn, T. (1962) *The Structure of Scientific Revolutions*, University of Chicago Press.
8. Kuhn, T. (1967) *The Essential Tension: Selected Studies in Scientific Tradition and Change*, University of Chicago Press.
9. Velman, M. (ed.) (2000) *Investigating Phenomenal Consciousness*, John Benjamins Publishing Company.
10. Wallace, A. R. ([1874] 1975) *On Miracles and Modern Spiritualism*, Arno Press.
11. Tarnas, R. (2006) *Cosmos and the Psyche*, Viking Press.
12. Carr, B. (ed.) (2006) *Universe or Multiverse*, Cambridge University Press.
13. Schwartz, J. M., Stapp, H. P. and Beauregard, M. (2005) 'Quantum physics in neuroscience and psychology: a neurophysical model of mind–brain interaction', *Philosphical Transactions of the Royal Society of London: B, Biological Sciences* 29, 360 (1458), 1309–27.
14. Goswami, A., Reed, R. E. and Goswami, M. (1995) *Self-aware Universe: How Consciousness Creates the Material World*, Tarcher.
15. Clarke, C. (1996) *Reality Through the Looking Glass: Science and Awareness in the Post-Modern World*, Floris Books; Lockwood, M. (1989) *Mind, Brain, and the Quantum*, Oxford University Press; Penrose, R. (2001) 'Consciousness, the brain, and spacetime geometry: an addendum. Some new developments on the Orch OR model for consciousness', *Annals of the New York Academy of Science* **929**, 105–10; Hameroff, S., Nip, A., Porter, M. and Tuszynski, J. (2002) 'Conduction pathways in microtubules, biological quantum computation, and consciousness', *Biosystems* **64**, 1–3, 149–68.
16. Radin, D. (2006) *Entangled Minds: Extrasensory Experiences in a Quantum Reality*, Pocket Books, Simon & Schuster Inc.
17. Radin, D. (1997) *The Conscious Universe: The Scientific Truth of Psychic Phenomena*, HarperCollins.

18. Achterberg, J., Cooke, K., Richards, T., Standish, L. J., Kozak, L. and Lake, J. (2005) 'Evidence for correlations between distant intentionality and brain function in a functional magnetic resonance imaging analysis', *Journal of Alternative and Complementary Medicine* **11**(6), 965–71.

19. Orme-Johnson, D., Dillbeck, M. C., Wallace, R. K. and Landreth, G. S. III (1982) 'Inter-subject EEG coherence. Is consciousness a field?', *International Journal of Neuroscience* **16**(3–4), 203–9.

20. Sheldrake, R. and Smart, P. (2003), 'Experimental tests for telephone telepathy', *Journal of the Society for Psychical Research* **67** (July), 184–99.

21. Benor, D. J. (2002) *Spiritual Healing*, Vision Publications.

22. Huxley, A. (2004) *The Perennial Philosophy*, HarperPerennial.

23. Wei Wu Wei (2004) *Open Secret*, Sentient Publications.

24. Merrill-Wolff, F. (1994) *Experience and Philosophy: A Personal Record of Transformation and a Discussion of Transcendental Consciousness*, State University of New York Press.

25. Tolle, E. (2001) *The Power of Now*, Group West.

26. Forget, A. (2006) *How to Get Out of this World Alive*, http://bethechange.org.uk.

Chapter 12

1. Moody, R. (1973) *Life After Life*, Bantam Books.

2. Grey, M. (1985) *Return from Death*, Arkana.

3. Fenwick, P. and Fenwick, E. (1996) *Truth in the Light: An Investigation of over 300 Near-Death Experiences*, Headline.

4. Fenwick and Fenwick, *Truth in the Light*; Ring, K. (1984) *Heading Toward Omega: In Search of the Meaning of the Near-Death Experience*, William Morrow; Sutherland, C. (1992) *Transformed by the Light: Life After Near-Death Experiences*, Bantam Books; Nichol, G., Stiell, I. G., Hebert, P., Wells, G. A., Vandemheen, K. and Laupacis, A. (1999) 'What is the quality of life for survivors of cardiac arrest? A prospective study', *Academic Emergency Medicine* 6, 95–102.

5. Nichol *et al.*, 'What is the quality'.

6. Sabom, M. (1982) *Recollections of Death: A Medical Investigation*, Simon & Schuster.

7. Parnia, S., Waller, D., Yeates, R. and Fenwick, P. (2001) 'A qualitative and quantitative study of of the incidence, features and aetiology of near-death experiences in cardiac arrest survivors', *Resuscitation* **48**, 149–56.

8. Parnia, S. (2005) *What Happens When We Die*, Hay House.

9. van Lommel, P., van Wees, R., Meyers, V. and Elfferich, I. (2001) 'Near-death experience in survivors of cardiac arrest: a prospective study in the Netherlands', *Lancet* **358**, 2042.

10. Schwaninger, J., Eisenberg, P. R., Schechtman, K. B. and Weiss, A. N. (2002) 'A prospective analysis of near-death experiences in cardiac arrest patients, *Journal of Near-Death Studies* **20**(4), 215–32.

11. Greyson, B. (2003) 'Incidence and correlates of near-death experiences on a cardiac care unit', *General Hospital Psychiatry* **25**, 269–76.

12. Sartori, P. (in press) *A Five-Year Clinical Study of Near-Death Experiences in a Welsh Intensive Therapy Unit*, Edwin Mellen Press.

13. Sartori, *A Five-Year Clinical Study*; Sartori, P., Badham, P. and Fenwick, P. (2006) 'A prospectively studied near-death experience with corroborated

out-of-body perceptions and unexplained healing', *Journal of Near-Death Studies*, **25**(2), 69–84.

14. Sabom, M. (1982) *Recollections of Death: A Medical Investigation*, Simon & Schuster.
15. Ring, K. and Cooper, S. (1997) 'Near-death and out-of-body experiences in the blind', *Journal of Near-Death Studies*.
16. Sartori, *A Five-Year Clinical Study*; Sartori *et al.*, 'A prospectively studied near-death experience'.

Chapter 13
1. Morse, M. and Perry, P. (2001) *Transformed by the Light*, HarperOne.
2. Department of Health (2003) *Building on the Best: Choice, Responsiveness and Equity in the NHS*.
3. Kubler Ross, E. (1969) *On Death and Dying*, Macmillan.
4. Saunders, C. (1970) 'The moment of truth: care of the dying person', in L. Person (ed.), *Death and Dying*, The Press of Case Western University.
5. Brayne, S., Lovelace, H. and Fenwick, P. (2008) 'End-of-life experiences and the dying process in a Gloucestershire nursing home as reported by nurses and care assistants', *European Journal of Palliative Care* (in press).
6. Saunders, C. (1965) 'The last stages of life', *American Journal of Nursing* **65** (March), 1–3.
7. Saunders, C. (1992) in T. Walter (1994) *The Revival of Death*, Routledge, p. 29.
8. *Guardian* (18 August 2007), Family Section, 2.
9. Brayne *et al.*, 'Perceptions of nursing home carers'.
10. Walter, T. (1994) *The Revival of Death*, Routledge.
11. Brayne, S., Farnham, C. and Fenwick, P. (2006) 'An understanding of the occurrence of deathbed phenomena and its effect on palliative care clinicians', *American Journal of Hospice and Palliative Care*, January/February.
12. de Hennezel, M. (1997) *Intimate Death*, Little, Brown & Co.
13. de Hennezel, *Intimate Death*.

Chapter 14
1. Walter, T. (1994) *The Revival of Death*, Routledge.
2. Kubler Ross, E. (1970) *On Death and Dying*, Tavistock.
3. de Hennezel, M. (1997) *Intimate Death*, Little, Brown & Co.
4. Greyson, B. (2003) 'Incidence and correlates of near-death experiences on a cardiac care unit', *General Hospital Psychiatry* **25**, 269–76.
5. van Lommel, P., van Wees, R., Meyers, V. and Elfferich, I. (2001) 'Near-death experience in survivors of cardiac arrest: a prospective study in the Netherlands, *Lancet* **358**, 2042.
6. Tolle, E. (2003) *Stillness Speaks*, New World Library.

Index